FOOTPRINTS IN THE SNOW

LAURA CHURCHILL DUKE

AUTHOR OF *TWO CROWS SORROW*

Footprints in the Snow
© 2024 Laura Churchill Duke

Cover art: Emily Ellis, from an image by Haley Lewis
Cover layout: Rebekah Wetmore
Editor: Andrew Wetmore

ISBN: 978-1-998149-50-6
First edition September, 2024

Moose House Publications
2475 Perotte Road
Annapolis County, NS B0S 1A0
moosehousepress.com
info@moosehousepress.com

Moose House Publications recognizes the support of the Province of Nova Scotia. We are pleased to work in partnership with the Department of Communities, Culture and Heritage to develop and promote our cultural resources for all Nova Scotians.

We live and work in Mi'kma'ki, the ancestral and unceded territory of the Mi'kmaw people. This territory is covered by the "Treaties of Peace and Friendship" which Mi'kmaw and Wolastoqiyik (Maliseet) people first signed with the British Crown in 1725. The treaties did not deal with surrender of lands and resources but in fact recognized Mi'kmaq and Wolastoqiyik (Maliseet) title and established the rules for what was to be an ongoing relationship between nations. We are all Treaty people.

Also by Laura Churchill Duke

Two Crows Sorrow

Rooted in Deception

...both available from
Moose House Publications

Nova Scotia

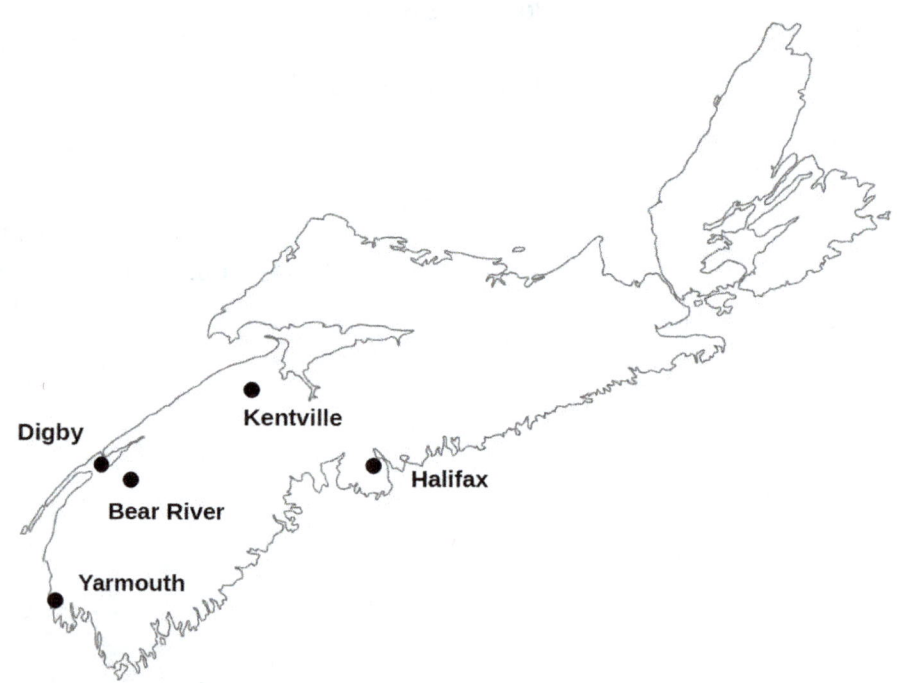

Figure 1: Key places in the story

For David, Daniel and Thomas
for always making life an adventure

This is a work of fiction, drawing on very real events. The author has made use of characters who appear in the historical record, and has created or dramatized conversations, interactions, and events. Any resemblance of any character to any real person, with the obvious exception of the historical personages, is coincidental.

Footprints in the Snow

Images

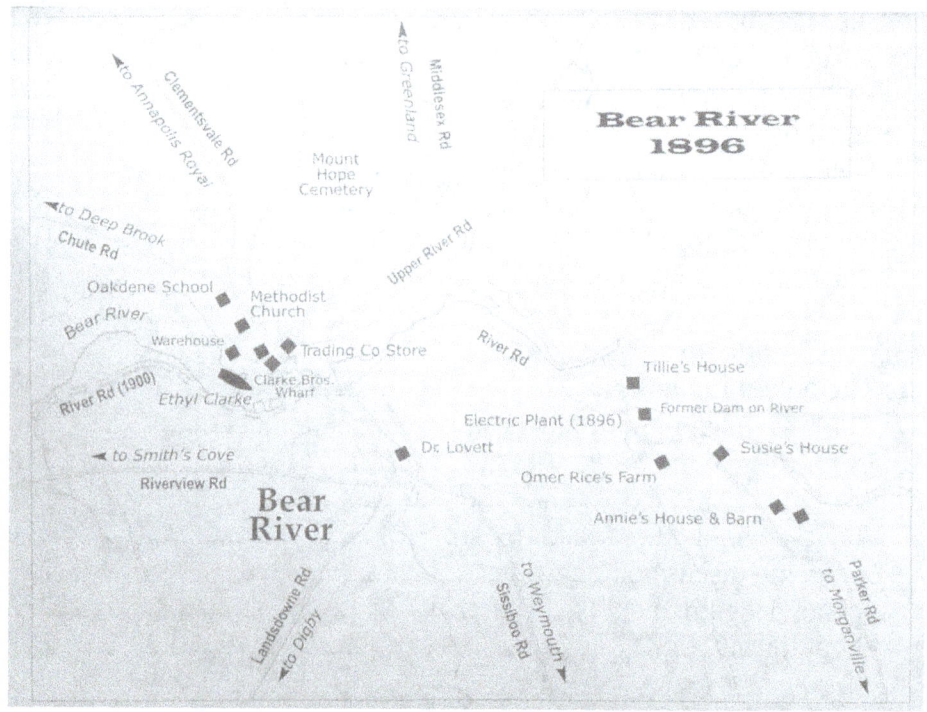

Figure 2: A map of Bear River published in 1896, courtesy of the Admiral Digby Museum and Rupert Haley.

1: A difference in appearance means a defect of character

January 28, 1896

Courier Special.

DIGBY, TUESDAY AFTERNOON, Jan. 28, '96.

MURDER AT BEAR RIVER

Annie Kempton, 16 Year Old Daughter of Isaac Kempton, the Victim of an Outrageous Assault.

Bear River Startled This Morning. -The Details are Sickening -The Worst That Digby County has Ever Seen- and There Have Been Few More Revolting Crimes in all Canada.

quilt around her, her hair blood-clotted, her limbs all bruised and showing fearful usage, her skull broken in, a gash across her face, her throat cut from ear to ear, and both jugular veins severed. Blood was spattered all around; a pool was by her head and there were even drops on the window panes.

The stick of stove-wood that had dealt the blow diagonally across her face lay by her side, blood-stained; two silver case-knives were also near her head and blood on them; a butcher's knife was on a table in the room, but not stained; a cup and spoon, however, also on the table, had blood on their edges.

When and why the foul deed was done is a mystery. It was evidently committed very early, at one or two o'clock, the body being cold and stiff when found this morning. The girl was presumably dragged from the bed

Figure 3: The news breaks

The reporter

"Next stop, Bear River!"

Benjamin Shaw was jolted awake by a figure looming over him, tapping pointedly at the train ticket above his head.

"It's your stop, sir."

The conductor straightened his hat, which had become lopsided from having peered down into the sleeping man's face. He then continued down the carriage, carrying on with his announcements.

Benjamin used the sleeve of his coat to clear enough of a circle on the foggy carriage window to peer through, and what he saw took his breath away.

To his right was a vista of open water with a few small islands close to shore and another land mass behind it. Only a gap in the land, which he could see in the distance, prevented this from becoming yet another lake. Just beyond the gap, Benjamin caught a glimpse of a paddlewheel steamer making its way towards the open ocean.

But what really caught his attention was the extensive lattice-work bridge before him. He had only read about this engineering feat, but now he wondered how it would be able to support the train in its journey across the mouth of the river.

He could now understand why the train company had left building this structure to the end. Formerly, its absence was known as the "missing link"—until the bridge was built, there was no continuous route for the railway from Yarmouth through to the Annapolis Valley, and beyond to Halifax.

I'll soon be the missing reporter, he thought, *if the train doesn't make it across the bridge.*

Should that be the case, it certainly wouldn't be the worst tragedy that had occurred in the area that week.

Benjamin patted his knees and motivated himself to stand, gathering the few belongings he had managed to pull together at the last moment before boarding the train in Halifax, several hours earlier.

Having made it successfully across the expansive bridge, the train came to a stop. Benjamin looked through the window of the train door for the station and, beyond that, the town, but all he could see was a small building that looked more like a warehouse, and trees.

Benjamin once again rubbed the sleep from his eyes, rereading the sign on the end of the building: Bear River. Yes, he was indeed in the right place, so he cautiously climbed down the steps and onto the platform.

The station master was not there to greet passengers, but instead was unloading the baggage car himself. Benjamin strolled over, picked up his leather case with a nod of thanks to the station master and made his way through the tiny station, still scanning the horizon for any sign of a town.

A cold wind blew off the Annapolis Basin, causing Benjamin to set down his case, adjust his collar and tighten his scarf.

"You must be the reporter."

Benjamin looked down at himself clutching his leather satchel and case, shivering in the cold winter wind, wondering how conspicuous he was. He looked back up at the man who stood before him.

"Nice to meet you," said a man, roughly the same as his own 40 years, sticking out his hand.

Benjamin took it, thankful for the extra warmth.

"Benjamin Shaw. And I am indeed the reporter just arrived from Halifax."

What Benjamin didn't say was that he was, in fact, the life blood of his newspaper and had worked hard to earn that description. For the past 25 years, he had worked his way up through the ranks of the newspaper business, creating not only a name for himself, but helping to build a strong reputation for the *Halifax Herald*.

When he started out, there were five competing daily papers in Halifax, plus another five weekly papers. To quell the competition, Benjamin had devoted himself to the *Herald*'s promotion and circulation.

He knew what others said about him. They said he had a vigorous policy of reporting that frequently flirted with the sensational, while others called him a live wire. He didn't think that was quite true, but any press was good press.

He was hoping to soon be promoted to editor-in-chief, and to perhaps own the paper himself one day.

He had earned every one of the grey hairs that were starting to create a salt and pepper look. With his sophisticated style, people usually treated him with the utmost respect.

"The Bear River Hotel advised me of your arrival and asked me meet you here and take you back to the village."

"Can't I walk?" Benjamin scanned the horizon again for any signs of civilization.

The man guffawed. "It's about a five-mile journey from here, but fill your boots."

"We really are in the middle of nowhere," Benjamin muttered.

"Follow me. I have my team hitched over there, and I'll take you right where you want to go."

Benjamin climbed up into the sleigh and snuggled under the blanket the driver tossed to him. The soft fur felt comforting on his skin, and he unconsciously burrowed his hands into it.

The driver noticed. "You like it? I shot that bear meself."

Instinctively, Benjamin dropped the blanket and raised his hands in the air like he had just handled something on fire.

This made the gruff driver laugh harder. "City boy."

"Is that how Bear River got its name? Because of all the bears?"

The driver laughed again. "No, but everyone seems to think so. The answer lies almost three centuries ago. You see, back in 1615, a vessel was bringing supplies to the French colonies at the head of the river here. There was a big storm, forcing them to take refuge on one of those small islands out in the basin. After the storm, the captain, Simon Imbert, noticed this river and began exploring it. So, the French called it Imbert after him. When the British came along, they pronounced it in the English way, which turned from Imbert River to eventually Bear River."

"Makes sense."

"But, if you ask any of the school children around here, they'll tell you it's because we've got more bears than school masters!"

Benjamin laughed, but then he realized it was probably true.

The driver guided the team onto the snow-covered road, which followed the curve of the river further inland.

"It's a beautiful place," said Benjamin, surprised at how much he meant it.

"Wait till you see the village. People call us the Switzerland of Nova Scotia. Probably on account of the river valley and everything built in amongst the steep hills. I can stand on my front porch and look at the foundation of my neighbour to one side, and the chimney of the house below me. It's like the Rhine, or that's what they say. Not sure who 'they' is, and not something I'm likely ever to see for myself. Why travel there when you have the same view for free right here? I'm not much one for travelling. I like the comfort of my own bed, my own food, and my own people."

Benjamin nodded along, happy not to have to carry the weight of the conversation.

"You know, there is not a single spot where you can get a complete view of the whole town, as some parts of it will always be hidden in the valleys or by the winding river. There are eight different roads that come into town, all ending at the main bridge. Someone told me that when the roads were originally built, one man would stand on one hill and another man on an opposite hill, shouting back and forth while the workmen laid out the road between them. No joke."

Benjamin couldn't tell if the man was egging him on or not. So, he responded with, "Look at all the trees!"

"It's trees as far as the eye can see! Makes for good logging, but most people do their logging further back in. But you know what kind of tree grows well here? It's the wrong time of year now, but cherry trees! Knew you would never guess. Last couple of years we've even started our own cherry festival to celebrate them. It's a sight to be seen. You'll need to come back when the weather is nicer, and they blossom. Never much fun in the winter. Everything looks the same, but there is some comfort in that, too."

"What else can you tell me about the village?" Benjamin thought he might as well take advantage of the time to get some background information for his story.

"Well, how many other villages do you know that are half in one county and half in another?"

Benjamin looked at him quizzically.

"That's right. The river runs right through the middle of the village. Everything on the east side is in Annapolis County and the west is Digby County."

"That's confusing."

"Not if you live here."

"Is it still a French village then?"

"Nah," said the driver. "The French live in other parts. We are all English, except for the Reserve on the outskirts of town. They mostly keep to themselves and have their own ways."

The driver directed the team round a bend, holding tight onto the reins, slowly navigating the snowy, icy road.

"You're here like the rest of them, are you? Here for a glimpse of the scene?"

Benjamin just nodded.

"Figured."

Now that they reached the main part of the village, the man steered the sleigh up a hill towards an imposing white building that Benjamin figured could only be the Bear River Hotel. It was the only building that didn't look like the rest.

"There has been a non-stop stream of people coming here from back and beyond. All wanting to look for themselves. Such a tragedy. Poor Annie Kempton. She was such a sweet child. Almost 15 years old, so maybe not quite a child, as young woman." He hung his head and let his voice trail off.

"You knew her, did you?"

"It's a small village. Everyone knows everyone here, plus my children know her." He paused and corrected himself, "*Knew* her, from school. She had such a joy for life."

"Tell me about her."

"I just know the story I heard my daughter and her friends talking about last summer. You know how girls talk."

Annie

"What's going on back there?"

The two girls looked up from the back corner of the shop, laughed even louder and buried their heads together to finish their whispered conversation.

"Silly schoolgirls," muttered William Rice from behind the counter.

"What colours do you think we should get?" asked Annie, thumbing through the pile of coloured tissue paper.

Grace took a sheet of yellow paper and held it up towards the window to get a better look. "Maybe a few of these."

"They are going to look so pretty in the hall tonight!" sighed Annie. "It's going to be the best night ever!"

"Are you going tonight?"

Annie shrieked, startled by the voice coming from the opposite side of the aisle. This sent the girls into gales of laughter once again.

"Hardy! You scared the living daylights out of me!" said Annie, moving a few items from the top shelf to get a better look at their classmate staring at them.

Hardy Benson was a typical fifteen-year-old boy, still growing into his own body. He was tall and gangly, but strong and handsome. His father and grandfather were reputable and hardworking shipbuilders in the community, and on weekends and during the summer, Hardy himself was starting to learn the trade. When he wasn't working on ships, he was working on getting Annie's attention.

"Of course, we are going!" said Grace. "Everyone in town is going!"

"We're making paper flowers to decorate the hall for the party tonight," Annie explained, holding up several sheafs of coloured paper.

"It's going to be so magical!" added Grace.

"They are going to look lovely if you are making them," Hardy said, speaking only to Annie, but trying to avoid making full eye contact.

Annie blushed and said nothing until Grace elbowed her. "We like making flowers," she stammered, unsure of what else to say.

"Are you going tonight with Mr. and Mrs. Kempton?" Hardy asked, shifting uncomfortably in his boots.

"No, Ma's down in the Boston States with my sister, and Pa was hoping to make it back from the woods in time for the big event. I'll probably go down with either Grace's sister, Etta, or Tilly Comeau. One of them will be staying with me at the house tonight."

Annie blushed again, realizing how much she had shared.

"Well, maybe you will save me a dance tonight before the fireworks," said Hardy.

"That would be fine," Annie said, looking down, also avoiding eye contact.

"See you tonight, Annie," said Hardy as he turned and left the shop, the bell above the door signalling his departure.

"Goodbye to you too, Hardy Benson," Grace said.

She elbowed Annie again. "Cat got your tongue? He seems awfully sweet on you!"

Annie groaned. "'We like making flowers'? I can't believe I said that. I sounded so stupid!" she said.

"He definitely seems to fancy you, Annie."

"I'm not sure why. I know what the other girls at school whisper about me. I have this coarse black hair, and I hear them calling me fatty behind my back!"

"That's simply not true," Grace assured her. "You are the most beautiful and wonderful young woman I know, and that's why you're my best friend."

Annie smiled and hugged her.

"Let's just get the paper, so we can get home to make the flowers and get back to the hall to decorate before the social," Grace said.

The girls linked arms and set forward to put their plan in motion.

~

"Wasn't that the most marvellous evening?" Annie closed her eyes, flung her arms open wide and spun around with her chin to the sky.

Hardy Benson laughed, watching her joy.

"I don't think I have seen anything so grand, nor will I in my entire life," she said. "It was a blaze of power! They were like colourful rockets, imitating the comets of the sky."

"Like jets of flame arising from the ground!"

"Yes!" Annie said, clapping her hands with delight. "Sounds like we are writing a poem for English class. I just cannot wait to describe it to Ma. She'll be so disappointed to have missed it."

"I bet you dollars to doughnuts that she's seen them before, in Uncle Sam's domain. They seem to have fireworks for every celebration and occasion down there. But having them right here in Bear River? Now, that is something to write about!"

"It was just so nice of Mr. Parker and Mr. Miller to bring them back with them from their last trip! And then for Mr. Miller's father to set them up and fire them off from his house! How they reflected in the river! I never want this night to end!"

As the two continued walking along the road towards the Kemptons' home, Hardy inched his way closer to Annie. When they rounded the corner, he stretched out his arm to put it around Annie's shoulder. From a few feet behind them, he heard a loud cough.

Tilly Comeau, who was chaperoning Annie, reminded the young pair of her presence, and shook her head when Hardy turned back towards the noise. He immediately dropped his arm back to his side.

"The whole evening was a delight," said Annie, not seeming to have noticed the interaction. "The party at the hall before the fireworks was wonderful! Everyone seemed to lend their talent at the piano, violin, tambourine and even the harmonica. The dancing!"

"The decorations!"

"I shan't sleep a wink tonight!"

"I don't think I shall either. I will be thinking of how nice of a time I had with you, Miss Annie."

By this point, they had reached the Kemptons' gate and Tilly had caught up to the youngsters. "Good evening, Mr. Benson," she said, making it perfectly clear that the evening was over.

"Thank you for accompanying us home. It was most kind," said Annie, regaining her formality now that Tilly was with them.

Hardy smiled broadly, nodded in farewell, and headed back down the hill, with visions of the blue, crimson, and green lights dancing in the sky, and Annie's face through it all.

The reporter

"She sounds charming. Thank you for sharing that story with me, for it paints a vivid picture of her in my mind's eye," said Benjamin, smiling at the driver.

For once the man was at a loss for words, and just nodded. He lurched forward up the hill and stopped the sleigh in front of the hotel.

"Tilly Comeau and her daughter Hattie work here, you know," he said, looking at Benjamin like he ought to know what he was talking about. When he saw the quizzical look on Benjamin's face, he continued. "Tilly is great and all. She's a hard worker. Four children, though, and she's not married. Peter Wheeler boards with them." He let his words hang in the air between them.

Peter Wheeler was the one who had made the discovery. Benjamin remembered that much from the telegram that had arrived at the office of the *Halifax Herald*. He had read enough to know that he needed to get himself to Bear River to cover the story.

"You're here just in time. The inquest is going to start at two o'clock, up at the house."

"I think I'd like to go up there now. See if I can interview a few people before the inquest. If I run in to drop my luggage, would you be willing to wait and take me over?"

Benjamin dashed inside to leave his luggage in the foyer before coming back out to find warmth again under the bearskin blanket.

The driver turned the team around, and descended the hill, turned right, and continued further away from downtown.

"That there is what we call the electric light station," he said pointing to a wooden building on the edge of the river. "It's got enough power to run the lights here in town, not to mention in the town of Digby! We've got some of the best waterpower in the country."

Benjamin smiled and nodded. For a community to have electric lights, it must be fairly affluent. Judging by the power station, though, he couldn't tell, as it looked like every other outbuilding in the village.

"And we turn here to head up to the Kemptons' place," continued the man, heading up yet another stark hill. "But, if we went up that next road, which follows along up the hill on the other side of the river, it leads right to that Reserve I was telling you about."

Just before getting to a small wooden bridge, the driver raised another finger to continue his guided tour. "That there is Tilly's house. Remember? She's the unwed mother Peter Wheeler was boarding with, or maybe more than just boarding with, if you get what I mean. He was the first on the scene."

"Speaking of the first on the scene, I don't think we are the first ones here today!"

Benjamin saw a throng of people walking up and down the hill. He wasn't sure how the driver was going to guide the sleigh amongst them.

"I'm not sure I can take you all the way up the hill, for all the people. Might have to let you out here at Omer Rice's farm."

"Not a problem," said Benjamin shouldering his work satchel and trying to store up as much heat as he could from the bearskin.

"You going to be all right walking through the snow here, city boy?"

"I'll manage."

"You'll need to get yourself a pair of these larrigans," said the man pulling up his pantleg to reveal a pair of stitched-leather, moccasin-style boots. "Everyone around here wears them, especially if you are out in the woods and snow much."

"I'll keep that in mind," said Benjamin jumping down from the sleigh once the driver had turned it around in the neighbour's farmyard.

"Just continue up ahead. Follow the crowds. You can't miss it. It's the next house up there on the left."

"Thank you. You have been most kind. I will probably call upon your services again."

With that, Benjamin followed the path through the snow up the hill to what the telegram that had arrived at the office had described as one of the most gruesome scenes in Canada's history. He was going to get to the bottom of this story, and it would be the one to make his career.

Annie

"It's going to be the best day ever!" Annie Kempton opened her arms wide and spun around and around.

"Annie, get yourself together! We're going to be late!" her mother scolded. "Fetch your bonnet, too. We're going to be out in the hot sun all day."

"Yes, Mother! I'm just so excited! It's always my favourite day of the year."

"How can every day be your favourite day of the year?"

"Oh, Ma! But it is! We get to spend the whole day on the open schooner, fresh air, friends, adventure—what could be jollier than that?"

Annie ran through the house to find her bonnet.

"Decorum! You are still a young lady, and you will need to act as such on this excursion!"

As they headed out the door, Annie realized she was empty-handed. "I've forgotten the picnic basket!"

"Oh, Annie. Your head is in the clouds. I've already told you three times what is happening today."

"Tell me again. This time I'll pay attention!"

The two began walking down the road and were soon joined by Mr. and Mrs. Rice, their closest neighbours down the hill.

"Good morning! I assume you are also going to the wharf to board the schooner for today's sailing excursion."

"A beautiful day for it!" said Omer Rice, tipping his hat to the ladies.

"You still haven't answered my question about why no picnic basket this year," insisted Annie.

Susan Rice chuckled.

"Don't encourage her!" said Mrs. Kempton. "She's been high as a kite all day and forgets her manners."

"It's not every day that you get to take a sailing schooner out into the Bay of Fundy for a day's adventure!" said Mrs. Rice. "Point Prim Lighthouse, and then a special dinner at the Bay of Fundy House Hotel! I don't think I slept at all last night either," she said, winking at Annie.

"I've heard the sunsets from the hotel are spectacular," said Mrs. Kempton.

"I don't think we will be staying that late, I'm afraid. Home in time for dinner," said Omer Rice.

At the foot of the hill, they added Tilly Comeau, her children Hattie, Herbert, and Walter, and Peter Wheeler to the party.

"Let me take that," Peter said, reaching for Mrs. Kempton's bag.

"Are you as excited as I am about today, Peter?" asked Annie.

He laughed, pleased to see her so joyful. "To be honest, it's not much of a novelty of me, going to sea. I've been sailing since I was twelve years old! Just about your age."

He then sensed her disappointment in his answer, so quickly added, "But it's always thrilling to be on the open water. And it's a perfect day for sailing, weather wise."

Annie smiled and ran ahead to walk with the children, leaving the adults to saunter along.

When they reached the wharf, it was crowded with families. Young children were running circles around their parents. The excitement was high. Lined along the road were teams of carts and oxen that would take those who did not wish to sail. Instead, they would meet the ship at the coastline just beyond Digby harbour, to join the day's adventure.

Annie caught a glimpse of her best friend, Grace. She waved goodbye to her mother and ran to join her other friends, her bonnet bobbing in the breeze behind her, its ribbons tight under her chin.

The reporter

When Benjamin had caught his breath at the top of the hill, he studied the farmhouse. He tried to get the lay of the land. It was an awkward property, long and thin like a rectangle along the side of the road.

The farm was perched on the edge of the hill, with the farmhouse being the closest building to the road. Behind the house there was a pig pen and behind that was a steep cliff falling off to the river more than a hundred feet below. To the right of the house, on the uphill side of the property, was a barn, and beyond that there was another, older-looking barn. Below the house, there was a hollow, in which lay a cultivated plot set lower than the road.

In its entirety, it was quite the property and farm. It confirmed what he had heard: that Isaac Kempton was one of the wealthiest men in the area.

He willed his cold frame to walk up the five steps that led to the front door of the two-story home before him. Inside, he could hear a cacophony of voices.

As Benjamin reached the top of the steps, the door flew open, and several people burst out of the house. A woman buried her face in a handkerchief, while a man put his arm around her, guiding her safely across the snowy path.

Benjamin caught his eye and saw pain there, before he took a deep breath and entered.

He walked through the parlour to the dining room, where over fifty people were standing. There was little space to walk around. But, from his vantage point, it looked like any other rural home he had been in.

There was a fireplace and mantelpiece along one side of the room. Resting on the mantelpiece was a lamp, without oil, and beside it a box of matches. Hanging above that was a needlepoint reminding everyone to 'Do Right and Fear Not.' Benjamin guessed it was stitched by one of the daughters, or even by Mrs. Kempton herself.

In the corner of the room was a rocking chair, piled on top of which were a corset and a fur cape. It made Benjamin think of his sister, who would casually toss off her outer layers and corset on any nearby surface as soon as she got home, in preparation for getting comfortable for the evening.

He walked towards the window which faced east, down the hill. There were no close neighbours who could have seen through this window. The house was so remote that no one would have heard anything and come to help.

He walked over to the south-facing window. In the distance, across the narrow valley, he could see a few houses; but, again, this house was definitely not accessible from there, especially at a moment's notice and with the river to cross. Benjamin reckoned it would take at least twenty minutes of hard effort to make the trip down, across, and up the valley to the house in which he stood.

He examined the window more closely. It wouldn't have been easy to escape out of it quickly, without breaking it at least. Outside the main window was a storm window attached to the exterior frame, warding off the winter cold.

He tapped the glass, testing how easy it would have been to move it. That's when a folded piece of paper fluttered down between the two panes. Benjamin looked over his shoulder to make sure no one was watching. Everyone seemed to be deeply involved in conversations, and the buzz from their voices covered his actions.

He slid the interior window up just enough, a couple of inches at most, to reach his long fingers in and pinch the folded paper, then quickly and quietly he slid the window back into position.

With his back to the crowd, Benjamin unfolded what he discovered to be a letter. It was dated last week and was addressed to Annie. He flipped the page over, to discover the author: Mother. He quickly scanned the letter, realizing it spoke mostly of the banalities of life, encouraging Annie to keep well and not work too hard.

Benjamin re-folded the paper and slipped it into his coat pocket. *You never know when something like this might be useful*, he mused.

He turned his attention back to the conversation in the room. He gathered that Mr. Kempton had arrived in Bear River twenty-five years earlier from down Lunenburg way, closer to the South Shore. He and Mrs. Kempton had five children, one son and four daughters. Most were in the States, and all but Annie had fledged.

Mr. Kempton had worked hard to get a start in the world as a lumberman and farmer, and had amassed quite a sum of money. But then, after the crash of the Long Depression of earlier decades, like many others Mr. Kempton was left with few worldly possessions and the family fell on hard times.

Mrs. Kempton was often in the Boston States, trying to earn extra money for the household. Her daughter there was looking for a housekeeper, so she went.

Finding the room too crowded to see much more, Benjamin retreated and headed to the kitchen, where he squeezed through a gap in the crowd towards the kitchen table.

On the table was a butcher's knife and two silver-plated knives with rounded handles.

Benjamin picked up the two smaller knives and held them to the window to get a better look. He ran his fingers across the blades. One was dull; probably too dull to cut anything, but the other nearly sliced open his thumb.

He next picked up the larger knife, which was more like a sheath-knife or a hunting knife. He wondered if the family used it for cutting bread. The wooden handle allowed for a firm grip and the point was sharp, as he discovered as he pressed it into the palm of his hand.

"Omer found that in the living room under the mat. It was all but covered."

At the sound of the woman's voice over his shoulder, Benjamin nearly dropped the knife.

"Sorry, I didn't mean to startle you," she said, stepping back.

"I'm so sorry for your loss," said Benjamin, bowing his head slightly. "Mrs. Kempton, I presume."

"Thank you, sir, but, alas, I'm afraid Mrs. Kempton is not at home. She's down in the Boston States with her daughter. A telegram has been sent. Not the way you want to hear the news. Not that there is any good way with news like this."

"And Mr. Kempton? Is he about today?"

"No, he's out in the woods lumbering down near Lint Lake. Near the clothespin factory? He's also been sent for, and we hope he will arrive presently."

"Apologies, madam," said Benjamin although she was at least a decade or more younger than himself. "I did not catch your name."

"Mrs. Rice. Mrs. Susan Rice. I'm the nearest neighbour down the lane. You probably passed our place on your way up. I was one of the first ones here this morning."

Benjamin nodded, remembering how his driver had turned the sleigh at a neighbouring farm.

"And you are?"

"Apologies again. I'm Benjamin Shaw with the *Halifax Herald*. I'm here to cover the story."

"Well! News does travel fast, then. It's all so tragic, isn't it? We get caught up in the scene and the details, and we forget that a living being was on the other end of it."

Benjamin quickly placed the knife back on the table, suddenly feeling sick to his stomach. He flushed from his neck to his face.

Noticing, she reached out and lightly touched his arm.

"Please, do tell me about her," Benjamin said. "Who was Annie Kempton?"

Susan Rice smiled through what Benjamin now realized were tear streaks on her cheeks. She sighed. "Annie was the most remarkable young woman. She would have been fifteen only next month, you know. She had a joy for life. She was also an independent young lady. When you are the youngest child and your siblings are grown and moved away, and your parents not often at home, you have to become capable, and you have to grow up quickly."

Benjamin smiled at the portrait offered by Mrs. Rice, wondering how his sister would react in a similar situation, living over a mile from town, distant from neighbours, and with the burden of daily farm chores. Never mind his sister, he wasn't sure if he could survive, either.

Then, he thought, neither did Annie.

He cleared his throat. "I would love for you to share your story with me. You don't mind if I take notes, do you?"

Before Susan Rice could answer, Benjamin reached into his satchel and took out his notebook and pencil.

"I guess the story will be out soon enough," she said with a sigh, taking a step back to lean against the countertop, not caring who else was listening in.

Susan

"Don't dawdle! You're going to be late for school!" Susan Rice scolded her three boys as they procrastinated. "You don't want to get the strap again for being tardy!"

She stood at the front door with schoolbooks in hands and handed them to the appropriate child as they left for the mile-long walk to the Academy.

With the older children gone and the two younger ones down for their morning nap, Susan took advantage of the empty room, grabbing the corn broom from the corner to sweep out the kitchen.

Suddenly there was a loud knock, and the door flew open. Susan jumped, startled by the noise and the intrusion. She instinctively pulled the broom to her chest as if attempting to hide behind it.

Before her stood a pale Peter Wheeler, clutching a kettle.

"Peter! Whatever is wrong?"

"Mrs. Rice!" he cried. "Annie Kempton is lying dead on the floor with her throat cut."

Susan stood gaping at him. She could hear his words, but they were not making any sense. "What are you saying?"

"It's Annie!" he repeated. "She's lying dead on the floor with her throat cut!"

"Peter!" Susan started again, but Peter had already turned and gone out the door.

Just as the front door closed, the back door opened, and her husband Omer appeared. "Who was that, dear?"

Susan just stood there, shocked and unable to find the words. "Annie."

"What about Annie?"

"Peter Wheeler says she is up to the house, lying on the floor with her throat cut!"

"What in tarnation? I need to go help!"

"I'm going with you," said Susan, grabbing her wrap from the hook by the door, and tying her bonnet beneath her chin. "Alice will be here momentarily and can look after the babies."

"No, I can't let you. It might not be fit for your eyes to see."

"You will not stop me, Omer."

Together, they trekked up the hill. Susan followed in her husband's footprints in the snow. The snow was about 15 inches deep in some places, and only one set of tracks was visible, which she presumed were Peter's.

When they reached the front door, Omer put up his hand. "You wait here. I don't want you getting unnecessarily upset. Wait in the barn if you need to get out of the cold."

He cautiously opened the front door, and called out, "Annie!"

Susan stood outside, stamping her feet and wrapping her cloak tightly around her to try to keep warm. It took everything in her power not to go inside behind her husband.

"Good morning, Mrs. Rice!"

For the second time that morning, Susan was startled by someone calling her name. She turned to find Louis Jeremy standing behind her.

"Louis!" she cried. "Oh, it's dreadful! Peter Wheeler appeared this morning at our house to say that Annie Kempton was dead!"

"I just received word myself. Apparently, after calling upon you, Peter went back to Tilly's house to let her know what had happened and she came up to get me. I came straight away. Shall we go in?"

"My husband said I should not, but I cannot stand another moment not knowing. So, please lead the way."

Susan walked cautiously through the kitchen and into the dining room, where she heard her husband pacing. She grabbed the doorframe and willed her eyes to open. When she did, she nearly fainted. Louis caught her elbow and carefully guided her to a nearby chair.

When she regained her composure, she scanned the room, which was in total disarray. A table and chair were turned over, a cup and saucer were spilled on the floor. On the chair beside her, her eyes locked onto two bloody knives.

Omer saw her fixating on the knives. "They were on the floor next to her," he said, motioning with his head, "and I picked them up and put them on the chair."

That's when Susan gasped. She still had not taken in Annie's poor life-less body lying on the floor on her left side, head tucked down, in front of the fireplace. A coat covered her from the neck down.

Susan started to rise to go to the child, but Omer stopped her. "It's no use. She's gone."

"That looks to be Mr. Kempton's coat," Louis said. "Peter must have covered her with it when he found her."

"How did she die?" Susan's words came out almost in a whisper.

"We'll have to wait till the doctor gets here for an examination, but I'm seeing a lot of blood around her neck and shoulders. It's thick, like she's been here for awhile, and it is starting to clot," Omer explained. "Her hair is matted with blood. I'm not sure if her head is cut, or if it was lying in this pool of blood."

"Heaven help us! Who did this?" cried Susan. "The poor child!"

"What needs to happen now?" Louis asked.

"We need to send a message to Mr. Kempton back in the woods, we need to telegraph Mrs. Kempton in Boston, we need to call for Dr. Lovett to come, and we probably need to see to the animals out in the barn." For each task he listed, Omer counted off on another finger.

"If you do the milking, Omer, I'll prepare it afterwards. Those cows must be so uncomfortably full if Annie hadn't milked them since last night."

The reporter

"What happened next?" asked Benjamin, looking up from his notepad.

"When Omer brought in the buckets of milk, I strained them into this brown dish," Susan said, pointing to the bowl at the back of the table. "It seemed to be an awful lot of milk, but I'm also not sure what is normal for these cows. We just have the one and I have never milked these cows before."

Benjamin looked at Susan with sympathetic eyes, having a hard time understanding how much had happened in the past few hours.

While he was trying to get his thoughts in order, someone else cut into the conversation in the dining room, so he excused himself from Mrs. Rice. There was now a clearing in the crowd, so this time he could have an unobstructed look at the brutal crime scene.

The carpet was rumpled up, and the table and chairs were overturned as if there had been a severe struggle, or a tornado had gone through.

On the stand beside the fireplace stood a teacup with a spoon. Beside that was a half-eaten jar of preserves. When Benjamin peered to investigate the mug, he saw grounds at the bottom, as if the drinker had finished the contents; however, he quickly stepped back, startled by seeing blood marks on the spoon.

He took a closer look at the empty lamp on the mantelpiece. From where Benjamin stood this time, he could see spots of blood on both the match box and the chimney lamp, as if someone had grasped it with bloody fingers.

Beside the fireplace were a pair of women's rubber overshoes. No detective himself, Benjamin could only guess that someone who was bleeding or holding something bloody stood there, held the lamp chimney, and then let four or five drops of blood fall on the shoes below. Benjamin could see that the blood had run down the outside of the shoes.

Many were still kneeling around what he presumed was the body. He was glad he couldn't see it yet, as he wasn't sure he was quite ready.

As he elbowed his way through to the opposite side, heading towards the back bedroom, he caught sight once again of the splotches of blood along the window casings. He had been so preoccupied with finding the letter that he never paused to consider what it meant. *Was someone trying to raise the window to get out? Was the girl trying to escape? Was the murderer looking for a getaway route?*

He didn't have time to consider it further, as the sea of people pushed him forward towards what must have been the girl's bedroom.

The bed was not made, and the sheets were pulled back completely over the foot board. *Could the struggle have started here? Was the poor girl torn from her bed, or did she immediately jump from her bed upon hearing an intruder?*

Benjamin reached out as if to touch the blankets, to see what warmth remained, feeling the panic that must have come with their disarrangement.

Finally, he made full circle and found himself back in the kitchen next to Mrs. Rice. The poor woman was repeatedly telling her story to every new guest. When he could find a break in her narrative, he fired off more questions.

"What happened after the cow was milked? Was the doctor called for? Was he the next to arrive?"

Susan pressed her fingers to her temples as if trying to recall the order of events. It had been a stressful morning. "No, that would have been Mr. Parker who next arrived."

"Who?"

"Bernard Parker. He also lives in the village."

"My, word does spread quickly in a village this size!"

With the sound of his name, a man in his mid-thirties stuck his head around the corner. "Someone call?"

"Speak of the devil and he shall appear!" Susan laughed at the naughty use of this expression, before quickly covering her mouth.

Bernard Parker entered the kitchen and stuck out his hand to shake Benjamin's. The reporter could not only feel the man's strength but could see the ground-in dirt indicative of a hard-working man.

"Benjamin Shaw with the *Halifax Herald*. I'm trying to piece together what has happened. Mrs. Rice mentioned that you were here early this morning. Do you mind telling me what you know?"

"I'm not sure about having this splashed all over tomorrow's paper, Mr. Shaw. But the man from the *Digby Courier* has already been here and talked to everyone, so I guess word is bound to get out regardless."

Benjamin flipped to a blank page, stuck the tip of his charcoal pencil to his tongue, and nodded for Bernard to begin.

2: Who did this?

Bernard

Although it was cold, the sun was shining, and Bernard Parker had a list of errands he was going to complete in town. With both a letter and a few coins in his pocket, he was heading to the post office and then on to William Rice's shop for some tobacco.

He had made it as far as Walsh's mill near the electric station bridge, lost in his own thoughts, so did not hear at first when Peter Wheeler called out his name.

"Mr. Parker! Mr. Parker!"

Peter came running towards him down the hill from the direction of Omer Rice and the Kemptons' houses.

"Peter! What is all the excitement about?"

"Annie Kempton is lying on the floor of her house with her throat cut!" Peter shouted.

Bernard, thinking that he didn't hear the wild man properly, stood there staring, not saying a word.

"I said, Annie Kempton is lying on the floor of her house with her throat cut! You better go up!"

Bernard just stared, mouth agape. *Surely there must be some mistake!*

In an instant, his day's chore list left his mind, and he veered up the hill towards the Kempton farm.

He knocked gently on the farmhouse door, then entered to find Mrs. Rice and Louis Jeremy standing in the dining room. Clearly, Mrs. Rice had been crying. Louis was pacing.

He surveyed the dishevelled room, making a mental map.

He knelt down and picked up two pieces of tissue paper from the floor. The green one had not been used, but the yellow one was cut into strips and had notches cut out of it. It also had drops of blood on it.

In fact, when he scanned the room, he could see blood across everything, from the windowsills and panes to the frame of the door to the bedroom.

What in the Almighty's name had happened here?

Then Louis moved away from the stove and no longer blocked the view of the body lying on the floor. Bernard instinctively jerked backwards.

He regained his composure, then took off his coat, squatted on the floor next to Annie's head and reached out to gently stroke her beautiful jet-black hair. He blinked a few times to clear his eyes and slowed his breathing. Once he regained his composure, he asked, "What happened?"

Mrs. Rice knelt on the far side of Annie's body, pulled back the jacket, and placed her left hand on Annie's shoulder, gently rolling her back towards herself, revealing Annie's left side.

Bernard lowered his head towards the floor and looked up. "Heaven's sakes alive!"

He held back a sigh, and covered his mouth and nose, trying not to inhale the strong, iron-like odour. He blinked a few times, willing himself to look.

When he finally did, he saw a deep cut across her throat and, when the body was back in position, he noticed the pool of clotted blood on the floor that must have come from this wound.

He leaned in closer and gently touched Annie's forehead, where a bruise was starting to form. "It looks like she was hit in the head with some sort of club."

"I was thinking the same thing," said Omer Rice, as he came into the room. "There is a stick of stove wood over there on the floor that looks like it also has blood on it. It made me wonder if that was used."

Mrs. Rice gently placed Annie back on the floor and re-covered her with the coat. As she did so, she tried to wipe her tears on her shoulder.

Bernard jumped to his feet. "We can't just sit here. There must be something we can do!"

"I'm heading to town to send a telegram to Mrs. Kempton, and to call Dr. Lovett."

"Let's go check for footprints in the snow. We are fortunate to have snow on the ground, which should easily reveal where the perpetrator came from. Now is our chance to gather that evidence. Besides, we know a crowd of people is probably going to descend upon the house once word is fully out, so we best check for tracks now, before we can't, and that evidence is lost forever."

The others nodded.

"You're probably the best one to get the lay of the land, anyway, seeing you are the surveyor," Omer said.

Bernard pulled on his overcoat and went to the back door, to see what he could discover.

"I've found something!" he shouted, but turned to realize no one had followed him out.

Making a trail next to the tracks he had found, Bernard followed them until they ended at the pigpen behind the house. Annie, he presumed, had come out to feed the pigs, slipping on a pair of moccasins to do so.

Bernard made a footprint in the snow directly beside one that he had found to try to ascertain the size. The impression was slightly smaller than his own, so he guessed they were a size six, as his were sevens.

Seeing no other tracks in the vicinity, Bernard went back inside to report his findings.

The reporter

Benjamin realized he had become so enthralled in the man's story that he had forgotten to take any notes.

"Have you found any tracks the perpetrator may have made?" he asked Bernard, trying to piece together the clues, and ready to jot down his answer.

"No, not yet," Bernard said.

As Bernard was telling his story, more men had poured into the house, one after another. "What's happening?" asked Benjamin.

"Dr. Lovett has just returned. He and Constable Henshaw had to create a jury panel to examine the body," Omer Rice explained as he entered the kitchen.

"They are going to examine the body right here in the house?" This was Benjamin's first crime scene, and he wasn't sure of the procedure.

"Yes, they will lay Annie's body out to examine it," Omer explained. "Dr. Lovett has also telegraphed Halifax and asked them to send down a detective to help with the case."

"The dining room is getting pretty crowded, and the inquest is about to begin. We should go in to make sure we can hear." Bernard motioned to Benjamin to follow him.

Dr. Lovett

"Ladies and gentlemen!"

Once Dr. Lovett started to speak, a hush fell over the room. Although not quite 30, he was a politician in the making. Being in front of a crowd was in his blood. His grandfather had twice served as premier of Nova Scotia, prior to it becoming part of Canada.

"For those of you who don't know me, my name is Dr. Lovett, and I am the coroner for Digby County."

Dr. Lovett had only been in Bear River for less than four years, so many still didn't know he was the new doctor in town. Besides, most preferred to stay loyal to Dr. Ellison, who had been the town doctor for decades. Although Dr. Ellison was starting to phase into retirement, people didn't like it. Change was never a good thing.

Many residents recognized Dr. Lovett in the community, but mostly because of his family connections. Not long after arriving in Bear River, the doctor ardently wooed and subsequently married the daughter of Alphaeus Marshall. He was probably the most prominent businessman and shipbuilder in the village.

Mr. Marshall had a fondness for naming his ships after the members of his family, including one for Dr. Lovett's wife, Josephine. When the ships were to be launched, he sent away to Saint John to have a wooden likeness carved of that family member to adorn the front of the schooner.

Dr. Lovett wasn't sure if he was happy or disappointed the tradition didn't including naming ships after men!

"Thank you for gathering here on such a winter's day," he continued.

Winter was the one part of the job of a country doctor that Dr. Lovett thought he would never get used to. It was much easier to get around the streets in his hometown of Kentville, further up the Annapolis Valley, than in rural Nova Scotia.

Here in the country, he had to be prepared for anything. Behind his house he kept a stable with five horses and had hired stablemen. At least one was required to be there at any hour of the day, in case there was an emergency. Winter was the worst, as the stableman on duty had to prepare the sleigh. Sometimes, when the sleigh couldn't make it through the heavy drifts, Dr. Lovett had to continue without it, forging his own path on snowshoes. By the time he got to the patient, he would be cold, wet, and tired. But usually better off than those he was visiting.

At least the house today was on a well-trodden road in the village. Or it was certainly well trodden now.

"It is unfortunate that we have to meet under such circumstances. I have assembled a jury of twelve capable and honest men from the community who will witness our examination of poor Annie Kempton. Before we begin, I would like to call upon Reverend Ruggles, who happened to be selected for jury duty, to say a prayer."

The room was silent as Reverend Ruggles stepped forward to offer a word of prayer.

Dr. Lovett spent the next few minutes swearing in the various jury members, who then selected the Reverend as their foreman.

A good, honest man, thought Benjamin. *Probably a wise choice.*

"Now, gentlemen," the doctor said to the jury, "you are about to witness the examination of the body, and what you see may be distressing. Please take your time and step outside for a moment if you need some fresh air. Now, let us begin."

Dr. Lovett knelt behind Annie's body. The young girl lay on her side, her head dipped towards her chin, and both her elbows and knees bent at right angles before her. He removed both the handkerchief that shielded her face and the coat that covered her from the shoulders to below her hips.

Benjamin gasped, instinctively putting his hand over his mouth. It was his first time seeing a murder victim, and he wasn't prepared for the gruesomeness. Looking around the room, he realized he wasn't the only one in such shock. Women grasped a nearby elbow, and men shifted uncomfortably about.

Dr. Lovett took no notice and continued, "Right from the start, before looking too closely, I can see that there is a scratch on the nose and a wound on the left temple."

The jury gathered closer, many in front squatting so those in the back could see.

Benjamin wondered how they could stand being so close. He liked his comfortable distance.

"It's difficult to see much of anything else, as her head is down and curled under. I'm now checking to see if the body is still warm," the doctor explained, placing the palm of his hand on Annie's forehead. "Although I arrived at nine o'clock this morning, this is the first time I am checking her temperature. I did not want to do this without a proper jury here."

There was a murmur of agreement in the room.

"I'm not feeling any heat. And stiffness has set in already."

"What does that mean?" asked one of the jury members. "What does that mean for time of death?"

"The rule as to how long it takes for a body to get cold varies greatly."

"Indeed," said one of the jury members, pushing his way to the front of the group. "It's a phenomenon known as *rigor mortis*. If the body is cold and stiff, as she is now, we can assume death occurred at least ten hours ago."

"And you are?" Dr. Lovett asked, standing to face the man.

"Jury member. Charles Dunn," he said extending his hand.

"You are quite correct, Mr. Dunn," the doctor said. "But pray tell, how are you so familiar with the concept of *rigor mortis*?"

"Ah, yes," Dunn said. "I have quite a keen interest and knowledge in the area of detective work. My wife's cousin, in the Boston States, is a member of the American Detective Agency, and when we are down there visiting, he and I have spent a lot of time discussing his cases, and he has taught me everything I know."

With this, the room erupted into much excitement and awe at such a prestigious connection.

"Your skills should prove quite helpful, then, Mr. Dunn," Dr. Lovett said, "especially until the detective from Halifax arrives. Please take a seat next to me, and you can aid in the investigation."

Dunn pulled on his lapels, rocked back and forth on his heels and, with a pleased look on his face, made his way to Dr. Lovett's side.

"Now, where were we?" the doctor asked, resuming his kneeling position behind the body. "As I was mentioning, the time in which it takes for a body to go cold depends upon several factors."

"She was still quite warm when I arrived this morning, but the body was completely stiff," Omer Rice said from the back of the room.

"We shall take that into consideration," said Dunn, making notes in a book he had drawn from his pocket.

"Some factors which influence the cooling of the body include the temperature of the room. You can tell that it is fairly cold in here, as the fire was allowed to burn out, and it is winter. Another factor is the size of deceased. The more fat or fleshy tissue the deceased has, the longer they would retain heat."

"And, as you can see," interrupted Dunn, "Miss Kempton was quite fleshy. This means it would take longer for her body to cool. And for the fact that she is wearing clothes."

"Another important factor to remember here," continued Dr. Lovett, "is that one-fifth of the body's weight is blood, and Miss Kempton was definitely a full-blooded person. I would judge her to be about 140 pounds.

Using this calculation, she would have approximately 26 pounds of blood in her."

Benjamin looked around the room. The crowd was fully absorbed. He knew full well that many, if not most, did not understand a word the doctor was saying, but it sounded official, and, more importantly, Dr. Lovett appeared to know what he was talking about. Benjamin had no reason to doubt him, either.

"And when we look further below her body, we see a large pool of blood," the doctor continued. "Because her system lost so much blood, it would have quickened the cooling of the body."

"What is your best guess, Dr. Lovett?" Dunn asked.

"Going by the experience I had with the other case for which I was coroner, I would say that Miss Kempton died around one or two o'clock this morning."

"I concur," said Dunn, making a note in his pad.

A door slammed shut. A sea of faces turned towards the back of the room.

Benjamin turned his head towards the doorway at the sound of what could only be the complete agony of a father's heart breaking.

"Mr. Kempton!" Dr. Lovett stood again, and the crowd parted to let the bereaved man through.

He fell to the ground, placing his head on his daughter's shoulder and groaned louder. "Annie! My Annie!"

Dr. Lovett reached across her body and placed an empathetic hand on his shoulder.

"What happened? Who did this?"

"We will do all we can to find out!" said Dunn.

"We do have some news, sir," said Constable Henshaw, who had closely followed Isaac Kempton into the house. Although he had the title of constable, his role did not encompass detective work and arrests, but rather making summons and keeping the peace. "A telegram just arrived from Annapolis with news that two suspicious-looking Italians were found wandering the roads last night and have been arrested. They were obviously not from around here."

Shouts of hallelujahs filled the room.

"We should not get too excited, however," said Henshaw, trying to speak over the crowd. "I've been told they tell a fairly straight story, so they may not be implicated."

"We should carry on here, then, just in case," said Dunn.

"Do what ever you must to bring justice for my poor Annie."

Mr. Kempton heaved himself to standing. As he did, Benjamin heard a heavy scraping sound, followed by a thumping noise with each step as the man took a seat from where he could watch the proceedings. He noticed Mr. Kempton's pant leg rise as he sat. *Could it be he has a wooden leg?* He had heard rumours of the man losing it in a sawmill accident.

"At this point, I'm also going to call Dr. Ellison to come forward to share his notes from his examination of the body. As many of you may know, Dr. Ellison has been a practising doctor here in the village for over 40 years and arrived at the scene before myself."

"I'm so glad they could finally set aside their differences and work things out," whispered an older lady near Benjamin. Her gossip partner did not seem to know what she was talking about, so she enlightened her.

"Dr. Ellison didn't take too kindly to a new doctor coming to town, let alone one so young—only twenty-five years old! Thought he was trying to oust him from his position as primary doctor for the area, so Dr. Ellison made no overtures to friendship beyond professional courtesy. That was until the big event. Don't you remember?"

"I can't remember what I had for breakfast yesterday! Keep going," urged her friend.

"Well, a few winters ago, they met on a narrow, snow-drifted road. Both were on their sleighs, and each refused to give way to the other. They both stubbornly tried to pass, but the two sleighs became solidly jammed together. They had to work together to lift and push the sleighs, to release them from the lock. They had no choice but to converse and resolve their differences."

"That does sound vaguely familiar, now that you mention that."

"The two have been friends ever since."

Dr. Ellison worked his way through the crowd to the front of the room and addressed the crowd. "I was summoned first to the scene, for I believe there was a misconception that I am the county's coroner. As I was here, I was happy to lend my expertise to the examination."

"Dr. Ellison finished conducting his examination prior to our inquest. The victim's body was temporarily moved from here to be examined but was replaced as she was first found for the inquest. What were the first things you noticed, Dr. Ellison?"

"Upon first glace, I could only see a bruise on her forehead."

"Don't worry," interrupted Dunn, "I am recording all these notes."

Dr. Ellison continued, "There was a pool of blood around her neck and shoulders. This blood was starting to clot and extended ten to fourteen inches from the head, neck and shoulders. Both arterial and venous blood will clot when exposed to the air."

Benjamin prepared a fresh page in his notebook. He looked up and noticed a gentleman across from him doing the same thing. *It must be the reporter from the local "Digby Courier".* Benjamin thought he would just have to make sure his story came out first and included more details than his competitor's.

"I then looked at how the stiffness set in. The legs were partly drawn up, and the arms were extended at right angles. The head, as other witnesses had already established, was tucked down towards the left side. From this angle, still the only wound that could be seen was on her temple," Dr. Ellison said.

"Dr. Ellison, please describe for our records what the deceased was wearing."

"The victim is wearing an outer red wrapper, and underneath a white flannel shirt and white drawers slightly bunched up, and black stockings, no shoes. Her drawers are still closed and not disarranged. I can confidently say she was not violated."

A sigh of relief went through the crowd.

The same older woman leaned forward to talk to her friend. It was at times like this that Benjamin was happy that neither old people nor children knew how to whisper.

"That wall hanging there," she said, pointing to the needlepoint that read, 'Do Right and Fear Not.' "This young woman fought bravely for her chastity and honour. It would seem she died fighting for a righteous cause."

There was an amen from her friend, then the two faced forward to keep listening.

"Next I examined the wounds," continued Dr. Ellison. "From what I could determine there were five distinct wounds. The first was here on the left side of the forehead. It appeared to be cut downwards and was a half inch in length."

Dr. Ellison described how he lined the wood up against the wound. "It was exactly the wound that would be inflicted by such an instrument. The blow was given in a downwards motion and looked like it went through clear to the bone. Blood from a wound like this should pour down the face."

Benjamin winced at the description. "On the right side of the head, I saw another wound just above the ear. It was about an inch-and-a-half in length."

Dr. Ellison described how he had gently probed the wound with his finger to look for broken pieces of skull, but could find none.

Benjamin felt assured he had chosen the right profession. He took a deep breath and continued to listen.

"Once again, this was a downward blow, and could easily have been made by the corner of the same piece of wood. Wounds like this would probably cause the person to fall and to be unresponsive for quite a little while.

"Along the throat, I saw three distinct wounds. The first is below the Adam's apple and is three inches in length, and cut right through the windpipe. There is another wound along the throat, about four inches in length, but the cut appears to be only superficial. The third cut on the throat is four-and-a-half inches long and extends from the centre of the Adam's apple to right around under the jaw and up to the left ear. It severed all the large vessels and the carotid artery and went down to the spine. The cuts were made with a dull instrument. The first and the third wounds would have been enough to cause death."

At the description, Mr. Kempton let out another groan, and had to leave the room.

"I would estimate the time of death to be 15 to 20 hours ago, meaning around midnight."

"Thank you for that thorough examination," said Dr. Lovett. "Mr. Dunn, what is your suggestion for what we do next? I was thinking we should start calling upon witnesses."

"Grand idea," said Dunn. "Let's start with Peter Wheeler, who first found the body. Mr. Wheeler, please come forward and tell us your account."

Peter stood nervously at the front of the room, not used to being before a crowd. He clenched and unclenched his fists.

He was a short man, at only five foot three inches, but was thick-set with strong shoulders and arms from having worked both at sea and the logging camps. His hair was dark black with a slight inclination to curl, and his cheekbones were high. His eyes were of average size and would have looked even larger had it not been for the heavy brows that overshadowed them. His ears, Benjamin noted, were set well out from the head, but were not abnormally large.

It's his mouth that is the peculiar feature, thought Benjamin. It was an exquisite shape, but so small, almost like a woman's; and the lips were accentuated with a deep red colour.

Based on his weathered skin and hardened look, Benjamin wagered he was roughly 30 to 40 years old.

Peter took a deep breath and began. "Hello, I'm Peter Wheeler. I'm 26."

Benjamin raised an eyebrow. Life had not been kind to this fellow for him to look so old and yet be so young.

"I live with Tilly Comeau. I am the farmhand for the Kempton family. I work at the logging camps."

"He does more than just live with her!" whispered the gossipy woman near Benjamin.

"Mr. Wheeler, we don't need your life story. Just tell us what happened."

"I come up this morning to fetch the milk for Tilly and came in to find her dead on the floor with her throat cut!" Peter's voice cracked as he spoke.

Benjamin could hear people in the crowd whispering. They may as well have been talking, for their volume was just as loud. He wasn't sure who was saying what, for, to him, everyone looked exactly the same with their dark cloaks and bonnets and grey hair, or their woollen sack coats and moustaches.

"Who is he, again?"

Loudest of all, though were the two women near Benjamin. He leaned forward to try to pick out their conversation, as they seemed to know everything about everyone in town.

"Peter Wheeler. He's that foreign man. Come from away. He says he is from somewhere like Australia, or Portugal or Italy. Or was it Africa?"

"He's definitely not from here."

"Look at his skin! He's not black. He's not white. More of a combination of the two, I should think. Never have I ever before."

"Then what did you do when you found Miss Kempton on the floor?" questioned Dr. Lovett.

"I went down to get some help and stopped into Omer Rice's to tell him," Peter stated.

"I think he is a hired hand at the Kemptons'," whispered someone else.

"He's paying his rent to that French floozy in ways I can't mention," someone else hissed.

"When was the last time you saw Annie Kempton alive?" Dr. Lovett asked.

"I saw Annie sometime between four and five o'clock in the afternoon. She was going by our house and was by the bridge. I didn't speak to her, though."

"Was that the only time you saw her?"

"I saw her yesterday morning. I was passing along the road on my way to cut wood, and she called to me from the front door. I went in and stayed approximate half-an-hour," Peter said, oblivious to the murmurs in the crowd.

"Was anyone else around?"

"No, it was just the two of us."

"What happened during that visit?"

Annie

"Peter! Peter!" Annie called from the front door.

Peter stopped in his tracks. He knew there might be some jobs Annie needed help with. He went in the front door behind Annie and brushed the cold and snow off his jacket.

"Do you know if the sledding party coming from Digby tomorrow is going to be in the morning or afternoon?"

"I don't rightly know, Miss Annie. I'm sorry."

"Never mind, then. I'm just making my dinner," she said. "Thought you might be hungry. Want any beans with me?"

"Very kind of you, Miss Annie, but I'm heading home shortly. I'll eat there."

"Well, follow me into the dining room whilst I eat. I want to show you what I'm making!" Her enthusiasm was contagious.

"Look!" she said, pointing to a pile of paper flowers. "Aren't they just beautiful?"

"Very well done, Miss Annie. What are they for?"

"The coasting party! I'm planning on being there at the hotel for the party afterwards, and selling them. I think they will look divine!"

"I'm sure they will be very popular."

"Speaking of the hotel, pray tell me about Tilly's schedule there. Is she working there today, and for how long?"

"I'm not sure how long. I do know she's working there every day this week."

"I see," said Annie.

"What are you thinking?"

"Well, with Ma and Pa away, Tilly was going to come and stay with me at night so I wouldn't be alone. But she'd be awfully tired if she works all day at the hotel and then has to come here all night with me and walk back to the hotel in the morning. That seems like an awful lot of fuss."

"I'm sure she wouldn't mind," Peter said.

"Just tell her not to bother. Instead, I'll get Grace Morine to come up. It would be so much fun to have her come and stay!"

"Indeed, I shall pass along the message."

"My Pa always thinks I need to have someone stay with me. I'm more grown up than he thinks I am! One time when he was away, I stayed all by myself—but don't tell him I told you that! He would have an almighty conniption fit! I like to stay up late and enjoy the evening to myself."

"You are a young lady," Peter agreed.

"Did you know Pa and I had an awful row? It was an argument over some money Ma sent me from Boston. She usually gives me around $5 at a time. I think it's to make up for all the time that she isn't around, but I really don't mind. I didn't tell him that Ma had sent me money, because I knew he was going to take it from me. But he was bound to have his own way, and so he struck me! Can you believe it? I ran into the pantry, but he ran in after me, and struck me again!"

Peter just stood there, saying nothing, not sure whether to believe her story.

"Tucked away in the pantry was the smoothing iron, and I grabbed that in my hand and told him just what I would do with the iron if he didn't stop!"

"You are a feisty one, Miss Annie."

She just laughed.

"I best be going."

"Thank you, Peter. I must head out shortly myself. I need to walk into town to get some more paper to make some more flowers."

The reporter

Dunn continued the investigation. "And what were you doing last night, Mr. Wheeler?"

"I was home. I was supposed to go out to logging camp yesterday, but wasn't quite ready. I had to go into town to get some supplies. Last night I started cooking some meat for my stay out in the woods. It was such a cold night, that I wrapped up in some quilts in front of the fire. waiting for the meat to cook, and I fell asleep."

"Did you sleep all night?" Dunn asked.

"Well, no, because around twenty to two this morning I was awoken by the noise of some men outside carrying on. I got up and looked out the window, as they were making such a ruckus. I couldn't see which direction they came from or were going, but there were definitely three of them out there."

"Could you tell who they were?"

"It was pretty dark, but I could recognize the shape and details of some of them. I could definitely give a description. One was the height of Elmer Crabbe."

Benjamin followed the heads of the crowd who were scanning the room for this Elmer fellow. Thanks to the all-knowing older woman near him, Benjamin ascertained that Elmer was a 17-year-old lad from the village who worked out in the woods with Peter Wheeler. He wasn't currently in the room.

"The next one looked like Will Marshall, you know, the man who lost his wife? I recognized him from the logging camps. And the third one looked like Obadiah Chute's boy. Will? He's short and stout. One of them had on a long coat."

Again, Benjamin determined that none of these accused men were in the room. Although, he wasn't sure what they were being accused of— being loud when out for a midnight stroll?

"Because we live right at the crossroads, I often see people coming and going," Peter explained. "For example, I would often see Hardy Benson walking home with Annie."

When the older woman leaned over to talk to her friend, Benjamin listened intently. His years of reporting had taught him that it was the community, and especially the older women who missed nothing, who really knew what was going on.

"He's a nice lad. Good, wholesome family, there. Too bad he didn't make sure she was safely home last night," she said.

"After that, what happened?"

"I just stayed up and finished cooking my meat and napped on and off. I always sleep out there on the floor near the kitchen. It's much warmer there in the winter."

"I just want to circle back to something," said Dunn, tapping his pencil against his forehead. "When you came in, you said you could tell her throat was cut, yet the doctors examining her, as well as those in the room, determined that you could not see that wound because the angle in which the head had curled down and stiffened."

"Yes, but that wasn't the way I found her."

"What do you mean it wasn't the way you found her?"

"She was in a different position when I came in. Her arms were bent, and her forehead was down." As he spoke, he tried to contort his body. "It's easier if I show you."

Peter got down on his hands and knees next to Annie's body. He leaned forward with his arms bent in front of him, and his forehead resting on the floor.

He then stood back up, brushed himself off, and said, "I rocked her onto her side when I was checking to see if she was alive. I put her on her side."

"Thank you, Mr. Wheeler," said Dunn. "You are free to sit down, but please do not leave as we may have more questions for you. We shall have a short recess while we consult the witness list."

"I think we have our man!" a voice shouted from the back of the room. "He says he found her, and he's obviously lying!"

Peter stopped dead in his tracks, mouth agape, searching the crowd for whomever made the accusation.

Benjamin shook his head. *Where did that come from?*

The first slung comment incited a slew of others from the self-appointed jury.

The neighbouring women could not help but add their thoughts. "I've never trusted the man. Says he's Australian. Says he is British, then says he is Irish. Look at him. Does he look any of those?"

"If we can't trust where he's from, what can we trust?" asked her friend.

"Agreed. He's low cunning—clever but morally bad and dishonest. Idle, too!" Despite the cold wind outside, she produced a fan from her handbag and feverishly started waving it in front of her face.

"I've heard that before. Came here 12 years ago and never left. Not doing much of anything. I know he's gone to sea once or twice since, and has gone to work in the woods, but nothing consistent. He just idled his time away in Bear River." This remark was accompanied by a few tuts.

"I once heard that French Tilly Comeau woman saying that she had a hard time getting him to work and had to constantly get after him to do something."

"Oh, bet she got him to do something, alright!"

The two women laughed. When others turned to stare at them, they merely glared back.

"That woman has four children and not even married. We know how loose her morals are!"

"I heard Wheeler had a quick temper and was feisty. Small as he is, I wouldn't want to cross him."

"Agreed! Arrest the man now." Both women nodded, crossed their arms, and sat back, waiting for the scene to unfold before them.

Benjamin saw Peter look around the room frantically, searching for anyone who would defend him. He noticed a woman standing next to Peter, whom he presumed was his landlord. She reached out and squeezed his hand, giving him an encouraging smile.

"Let's not act too hastily," said Dunn. "That's the first rule of the American Detective Agency." As he spoke, he paced back and forth in front of the mantel. Benjamin believed Dunn fancied himself Sherlock Holmes and wondered when he would pull out a pipe.

Benjamin flipped back through his notes. How had they taken the step from A to B, from Peter finding the body to finding him guilty? *It wasn't so much of a step as it was a leap.*

Yes, the man found the body, and claimed that her throat was cut, despite no one readily being able to see the wound. Surely more evidence would need to be presented. However, the crowd, especially his two gossipy sources, seemed quite convinced already. They ought to know the inner workings of the town.

"Mr. Omer Rice. We would like to call you next to share your account."

Once the man was sworn in, he told of finding the body and described the condition of the room and how he helped clean up some of the mess before others arrived.

"You mentioned you put the chimney back on the lamp, placed the knives on a nearby chair, which have since been moved to the kitchen table, but you also made mention of a gold watch hanging from a nail on the mantelpiece. Where is that watch now? We do not see it here," said Dr. Lovett.

"I moved it to the closet in the hallway," said Omer. "I immediately recognized the watch as belonging to Tilly's son, Herbert Comeau. I saw him with it last fall. Then, later, when Tilly showed up at the house, she asked about the watch. Apparently, Herbert had loaned it to Annie last week. Tilly wanted the watch back, but I told her she couldn't have it."

The sea of heads nodded along with Omer Rice's testimony.

Why did 16-year-old Herbert loan his watch to Annie? Benjamin wondered. *Is he sweet on her, too, like this apparent Hardy Benson, who has yet to appear? Why would Omer Rice hide the watch? Was he trying to protect his neighbour from being implicated in something? Or was he holding on to it for evidence of something more sinister?* There must have been a good reason. However, if the doctor and the would-be detective did not think this an important line of inquiry, neither should he.

"There are two points I still cannot shake from my mind," said Dunn, addressing the room. "The first is that Peter is the one who gave the message to Miss Comeau." He made sure to emphasize the word 'miss', to draw attention to Tilly's lack of marital status. "Peter told *Miss* Comeau that Grace Morine would be going to the house to spend the night, so she need not bother going up."

The room agreed.

"Therefore, Peter knew that Annie would be in the house alone. This would establish a great opportunity for himself."

"What?" Peter asked incredulously, but Benjamin thought he may have been the only one to hear it through the ruckus of the crowd.

"Secondly," continued Dunn, "when Peter announced that Annie Kempton was dead, he said that her throat was cut. However, as two doctors and several witnesses have already determined, because of the position of her body, it was impossible to see any cuts on the throat. How did he therefore have this knowledge?"

Benjamin could feel the anger rising in the room. A few men moved closer to Peter, arms crossed, daring him to move. He was dwarfed by these men. Peter looked scared.

These are all valid points, thought Benjamin. *Peter seems to have information no one else was privy to. It is certainly a highly plausible explanation.*

"Arrest him!" shouted another. "We demand justice!"

"I'm afraid you leave us with no choice," said Dr. Lovett, addressing Peter. "Constable Henshaw, could you please come forward to make the arrest?"

Peter looked around frantically, shouting, "No! No! I didn't do it! It wasn't me! I'm innocent. Innocent, I say!"

No one listened. The louder he protested, the louder the crowd cried out for his arrest.

"Peter Wheeler," said Constable Henshaw, coming forward. A pair of iron manacles swung back and forth on his finger. "Peter Wheeler, I place you under arrest for the suspicion of murdering Annie Kempton."

Benjamin watched as Peter fell to his knees, begging for someone to listen. The men standing next to him, roughly hoisted him back to his feet.

"Please! When can I just go home?"

His cries went ignored.

"We will continue calling witnesses, to keep building our case against the prisoner," said Dr. Lovett, regaining control of the room.

Benjamin looked around in disbelief. He felt like he had blinked and missed something. Unaccustomed to being at murder inquests, he had no idea what was happening. He looked from face to face, and everyone displayed the same self-assured, angry expression. These people knew the community best and who was capable of what. Who was he to know any better? His role was to merely report.

Once everyone was silenced, and Peter stood chained in the corner, Dr. Lovett continued. "Next, we will call Matilda Comeau to give her statement."

"Please, Tilly! Tell them it wasn't me," pleaded Peter. A neighbouring man elbowed him so hard that he doubled over in pain.

When she was finally seated at the front of the room, the doctor asked Tilly to state her name and connection to the event.

"I live in Bear River. I live at the bottom of the hill by the bridge. Peter Wheeler has lived at my house for nearly twelve years. I knew Annie Kempton since she was a baby. I have often stayed with her when her parents were away but am not the only one who stays with her. I usually went, though, unless she let me know. The last time I went to stay was last Thursday. I didn't stay last night because Peter Wheeler told me that one of the Morine sisters would be staying with her. Any time I stayed up there with her, we never had any trouble, and no one came to the house when we were sleeping there."

With Peter arrested, Benjamin worried the two gossipy women near him would have nothing further to discuss. He was wrong.

"She should have been there last night and none of this would have happened! She should have been more trustworthy. Four children and no husband to show for it: just goes to prove her character," said the first woman, starting up her fan once again.

"She's also French."

"Born in Paris, I heard."

"She isn't entirely to blame here. That foreign man Peter Wheeler told her not to go up to stay," the second woman answered.

At that point, the two women brought their heads closer together and actually began whispering, and Benjamin could no longer hear their pearls of wisdom.

"And where were you, and especially your two sons, last night?" Dunn continued.

"Last night, my daughter, two sons, myself and Peter Wheeler all were sleeping at home. Peter slept in front of the kitchen stove, which is alongside of our bedroom door. He sleeps lengthwise with his head right beside my bedroom door, which is always opened about 18 inches, and his feet at the stove. My two sons sleep with me, and my daughter sleeps on the sofa in a separate room."

"And what happened last evening?"

"Hattie and I got home around six o'clock from working at the hotel. We went out again and then were back again at eight o'clock. I know it was this time because the hourly village bell had just rung. When we arrived home, Peter was there with Hardy Benson. Peter was making up his bed in the kitchen."

"Is it easy to slip out the door, if you are sleeping in the kitchen?" Dunn asked.

"There are three doors to our house. There's the main kitchen door, then the storm door on top of that. Then there is an outer storm porch and door that you go through to get outside. The inside door is fastened with a lock and key which makes a clicking noise. The storm door is also locked with a hook and eye, as does the porch door. I lock those doors, and Peter does the lock and key. So, to get out, you have to open three doors, all not ten feet from my head when I am sleeping. The storm door gives off an almighty squeak when it opens! And you really have to heave the storm door closed, especially in the winter."

Benjamin made a mental note to never live in rural Nova Scotia, especially in the winter. City dwelling suited him just fine, with his fireplace, bed, and properly-closing one-door system.

"On top of that," continued Tilly, "I have a really bad cough. I've had it for the past two years. Prevents me from sleeping good." As if on command, Tilly began a coughing fit which seemed to emanate from the bottom of her lungs. She took out her handkerchief to cover her mouth until someone passed her a cup of water.

"She wouldn't be so sickly if she had a proper man in the house to take care of the place. That's the Lord paying her back for her sinful ways," said the old woman into her fan.

Benjamin inched closer to the gossiping women so he would not miss any more of their analyses. Sensing his presence, they shuffled closer together and further away from him. Benjamin sighed, realizing he'd have to be stealthier next time.

"Are you sure the door was locked last night? And could someone get outside without you knowing?"

"Peter definitely locked the door last night after the children went to bed. And it would be impossible for anyone to get outside without me knowing."

Benjamin leaned forward, this time paying more attention to the action at the front of the room. *Why all these questions about getting out of the house? Where was this line of questioning heading?*

"What time did Peter go out? Did he go out again after you went to bed?"

That was it, thought Benjamin. *Did Peter sneak out in the middle of the night to kill Annie?*

"He most definitely did not go out again last night. I sent him up to the Kemptons' house around eight o'clock the next morning with the kettle to get milk. Sometimes I go, sometimes Hattie goes. We don't have our own cow, so we need to go there for milk. The children were getting ready for school, and Hattie and I were busy getting ready for work, so I asked Peter to go instead. I had to wake him up to go get it."

"How did you find out that Annie Kempton was dead?"

"Soon after I sent Peter up to get the milk, he was back like a bat on fire. Throwing open the door and yelling that Annie Kempton was up there dead. He told the boys to go sound the alarm and to go get the doctor. Peter went towards the mill to inform the men, and I went to get Louis Jeremy, my neighbour, who I thought would be of some help."

"Did Peter tell you how she died, or that he was afraid?"

"No, sir. He just said she was dead and laying in blood and never mentioned anything about being afraid."

The conversation turned to every item of clothing in Peter's wardrobe and established that Peter was wearing the same clothes today as he was yesterday.

Getting tired of the repetitive questions, Benjamin scanned the room, checking for people's reactions. From what he could tell, people were convinced of Peter's guilt. He couldn't help but wonder if they all felt like armchair or parlour detectives, as in one of Arthur Conan Doyle's mystery novels.

Tilly's 18-year-old daughter, Hattie, was called forth and was not only asked how she knew Annie, but also how she knew Peter Wheeler. She also spent twenty minutes discussing the doors in her house and if you could get out without anyone noticing.

Benjamin was about to raise his hand to suggest the entire group walk down the hill to test them out themselves, but then thought better of it. They would probably not catch his sarcasm, and it was cold outside. Two very valid reasons for not saying anything.

Hattie was then questioned at length as to whether the pork that Peter was cooking to take into the woods was really his pork. Hattie assured Dunn that the pork was indeed Peter's, given to him by her mother as it was left over from the hotel.

Benjamin squeezed his eyes shut and sighed. He wished they would just jump to the good parts.

The only thing Hattie's testimony established was that she had some of the pork, which did belong to Peter, for breakfast, and the whereabouts of not only her family, but other community members in the vicinity last night.

Apparently, Tilly and Hattie had arrived home from the hotel around six o'clock, and a few minutes later Peter and Herbert arrived with a sled full of wood. Together, they all went back towards town, where Peter met up with his logging friend, Hardy Benson, with whom he left. Everyone, including Hardy was back at Tilly's house by eight o'clock.

Benjamin sketched a timeline across the top of his page. It seemed pretty straightforward.

And yet Dunn and Lovett became fixated on other details.

"Let's call Hattie's brother forward," said Dr. Lovett, trying to get the proceedings back on track.

Benjamin wondered, however, what other evidence was needed. It seemed the case had already been solved.

He took a new pencil from his satchel and entitled the next page, 'Herbert Comeau'.

Herbert

Herbert was tired from a long day at school. He was cold, and he was hungry, and yet he still had chores to do. He arrived home to find the door locked and realized Peter must be out. Peter usually carried the house key during the day, since he was usually in and out, and in the vicinity.

Since his axe was inside, Herbert went to the front window. All the windows in the house were nailed shut with sticks across them, but he knew a trick. The glass was split into two pieces, and he had learned how to manoeuvre the glass so it would pop out.

To fit through, he had to take off his overcoat. He worked quickly in the frigid temperatures and pulled himself through to get his equipment. He returned the same way, putting the glass securely back in place. He then headed to the wooded area up the hill above his house to cut firewood.

Herbert had accumulated quite a pile of birch sticks and was in the rhythm of cutting when a voice from behind startled him. He turned around to find Peter Wheeler coming down the hill towards him.

"Let me help you with that," said Peter, piling the cut sticks onto the sled. "Where did the sled come from?"

"Louis Jeremy lent it to me. Where you coming from?"

"I was up to Stanley Rice's."

Peter said no more. Herbert assumed he was up getting the money that was owed to him, since Peter had worked several days in the woods for Rice and had yet to be paid.

"I have also been out checking my rabbit snares."

Herbert secured the logs on the sled, and he and Peter guided it back down the hill towards home.

The reporter

With more of the timeline established for Peter's whereabouts the day before, Dunn moved on to two of his favourite questions. Could someone quietly leave your house? And was the pork really Peter's?

Benjamin groaned at the thought of having to endure another fifteen minutes of this drivel. The woman in front of him turned around to glare at him, making Benjamin realize he was speaking out loud.

"Are you telling us that you met Peter Wheeler on the road coming from the direction of the Kemptons' house after five o'clock, and that he told you that he went to Stanley's Rice house for money?" Dunn summarized.

"Not quite, sir," Herbert said. "I said he was coming down the hill and that I supposed he gone to Stanley Rice's, but he never said he saw the man or anyone else, and I just assumed he was going to collect his money."

"We need to add Stanley Rice to confirm Peter's being there yesterday," Dunn said to Dr. Lovett.

The jury seemed to be ploughing through, and not taking any time for a break. Benjamin was getting tired and would have loved a chance to go to the privy, but he did not want to miss a word.

"We are starting to lose our light. It's getting cold, and it has been a long day. We are going to adjourn for today, but we are going to recon-vene tomorrow morning to continue taking witness statements," Dr. Lovett finally said.

Benjamin sighed with relief. He needed some time to write his story and send it through to the paper in Halifax.

"I would personally like to thank Mr. Dunn for lending his expertise to the inquest today. I know that a Halifax detective will be here tomorrow afternoon, so we have been lucky to have such guidance from right here in the area. Without him, I doubt we would have been so easily able to catch our perpetrator," the doctor added.

There was a thunderous round of applause.

Dunn grabbed his lapels, smiled, and rocked back and forth on his heels.

A particular verse from his Sunday school days came to Benjamin's mind: *Pride goeth before destruction, and a haughty spirit before a fall*.

Regardless, the community had acted quickly, come together, and caught the perpetrator, all in a matter of hours. What a day, and what a story it was going to make. The evidence obviously pointed towards Peter, so he wasn't sure what there would be left for the Halifax detective to do.

"We shall reconvene tomorrow morning at nine o'clock sharp in the upstairs hall on the Annapolis side," the doctor said.

Benjamin looked around, trying to ascertain the address, but it seemed everyone knew what he was talking about. He would just follow the crowd, as he was certain even more would show up the next day.

3: Liar!

The reporter

When Benjamin woke up, the sky was still dark and the room was cold. He did not like the idea of leaving the warm bed to get dressed. He stared at the hotel ceiling, replaying yesterday's events.

Peter went to a lot of trouble to orchestrate the entire event, from ensuring Annie was alone to being the first to discover the body. But what was the motivation? Or was it every man's basic carnal urges? Surely new evidence will come to light during the day's proceedings.

Benjamin went to the hotel's dining room for a cup of tea and toast. He looked around, now picturing Hattie here doing the laundry and washing, and Tilly the cleaning. It added a whole new personal touch to the place.

When he sat down, the waitstaff gave him a copy of a newspaper to read.

At first, he was disappointed that it was not his *Halifax Herald*, but the *Digby Courier*. But then he realized this was actually a good opportunity to see what the competition was saying about the events.

He didn't have to look far, as it was splashed across the front page. The headline read

> Bear River startled this morning –
> The details are sickening. –
> Worst that Digby County has ever seen and
> there have been few more revolting
> crimes in the rest of Canada.

Catchy. Benjamin did believe in a good dramatic headline. It helped with sales.

He read every word with great care. The story was obviously filed before the end of the day, and before Peter Wheeler was arrested.

The story exaggerated many of the details, but he could hardly fault them. He'd been known to embellish a few details here and there.

> It would appear as if the inhuman wretch, or wretches, had been secreted in the house before her return from town and had awaited the opportunity of night to commit the most brutal deed we have almost ever heard of. This is however only conjecture as the facts have not sufficiently been revealed. There were tracks showing blood leading from the house a short distance and this will form an important clue in the investigation.

Benjamin wondered if this reporter fancied himself the Watson to Dunn's Sherlock Holmes.

> The details are sickening and rank with the worse London slum scandals: A young girl, quiet, clever and intelligent and generally liked, frightfully maltreated and murdered in cold blood without the slightest cause or provocation. The perpetrator must be nearer brute than human; may he secure his deserts.

Benjamin looked at his pocket watch and realized he needed to get going, otherwise he was going to be late, especially since he had no idea where he was going.

His driver from the day before offered to take him down to the hall, but he said he preferred to walk, so he could get a better sense of the community he was writing about.

As he descended the hill, Benjamin really did get a good sense of the community being built like in the Swiss alps, on the hillsides surrounding the river valley. The homes were all quite magnificent, many with grand facades and vast verandas. He had been told that, despite being in the middle of nowhere and with a population of only 12,000, the community was quite affluent because of its six booming shipyards and lumber yards, All thanks to the Clarke brothers' enterprises.

Not only was this town industrious, but apparently it had a booming tourism market. The hotelier was trying to convince him to return in better weather to enjoy a hunting or fishing expedition.

He would first see how he made out being this far away from a city before committing to anything further. What would be worse? The freezing temperatures, or the incessant bugs? He probably would remain a city mouse.

As Benjamin neared Bear River's main street, he saw crowds of people milling about on the far side of the bridge. There were probably close to 100 people, all dressed in their finest suit jackets and caps, or woollen dresses with capes and hats at jaunty angles.

After crossing the bridge, Benjamin lifted his eyes to the hillside, taking in the view from the opposite side of the river. His tour guide of a driver was right. It was hard to see all the village from just one location.

Because he was not watching where he was going and was walking backwards, with his eyes to where the hill met the sky and the sparkling gold dome of a church steeple, he bumped rather awkwardly into someone behind him. He quickly turned to apologize, then realized it was something hard, round, black and iron sticking out in the middle of the sidewalk. He bent down to examine it more closely.

"It's a cannon," said a gentleman passing by.

"But it's standing straight up in the dirt."

"Indeed."

"But why?"

"Because it always has been." And with that, the man continued to the tall building nearby.

Benjamin realized that was the only explanation he was going to get, and chalked it up to another one of the interesting things that gave Bear River such charm.

He followed the crowd into the tall building with some connection to the Masonic Order, and upstairs to a broad room where the room was set up with a table for Dr. Lovett at the front. Chairs for the 12 jurymen were off to the side, and near the front stood another table. Behind that sat Peter Wheeler in manacles.

More than a few people in the room threw ugly slurs at him. "Murderer!" "You beast!" "Go back from where you came!" "You should never have come here in the first place!"

Peter kept his head lowered, refusing to make eye contact with anyone in the room.

Benjamin took a seat as near to the front as possible and steadied his notepad on his knee, ready for the day's action. Certainly, it couldn't prove to be more surprising than yesterday's. Could it?

He watched Dunn arrive and realize only one chair was at the table at the front. He dragged a chair from the jury box and placed it beside Dr. Lovett's. Benjamin wasn't sure if he felt sorry for the man, or if he was glad he was there to help. Probably a combination.

"Ladies and gentlemen," Dr. Lovett said, "we have a great many witnesses to get through today, so we shall get started right away. Once again, Mr. Dunn, with connections to the American Detective Agency has agreed to help us with our inquiry until Detective Power arrives from Halifax."

Detective Power. Benjamin knew that name well.

Many argued that Detective Power was one of the most illustrious police officers to serve thus far in Nova Scotia's history. As the Maritimes' only detective, it was said he tracked down more international crooks than any other detective on the North American continent.

Detective Power was known for having solved a robbery at the Halifax Fishwick Express Company, trailing a Nova Scotia bank robber to Michigan, and solving a two-year rash of Halifax house robberies.

Most notably, however, in 1883, he was credited with saving the life of Queen Victoria's grandson, His Royal Highness Prince George.

Benjamin remembered covering the story. Power, who had been made a detective the year before, appeared in Benjamin's office.

"I have saved the prince!"

Benjamin looked up from his desk to find a man looming in his doorway. He must have been six-foot-four and weighed no less than 260 pounds. He stood proudly, with his hands on his hips.

"Are you the most senior reporter?"

Without being invited in, the man marched into the room and sat in the chair opposite Benjamin's desk. "Get out your notepad, for you are going to want to take down every word I say."

Benjamin cleared his desk and duly produced a notebook, all the while trying to place the man. When he looked up, the visitor had placed a brown leather club on the desk before him.

Benjamin knew from previous experience that the club enclosed a steel spring with a one-inch ball bearing on the end. One flick of that, and a skull could be cracked. Fortunately, he did not know this from personal experience.

As the man arranged himself in the chair, he pulled back his jacket. On the inside of his breast pocket, Benjamin got a glimpse of a shiny metal insignia. That's when the gears in Benjamin's mind clicked into place and he realized with whom he was speaking.

"Detective Power! What can I do for you today?" he asked, smiling with relief.

"I saved the prince. And I'm here to tell you how, so you can write a story about me. It will be a great front-page story."

Benjamin leaned forward, pencil in hand, and without any prompting,

Detective Power began his tale.

"You see, His Royal Highness was anchored here in Halifax on board *HMS Canada*. We had to be extra careful, lest any Fenians—you know, the Irish Republican brotherhood, the terrorists behind the bombing campaign to free Ireland from British rule..."

Benjamin didn't have time to tell him that, yes, he was well aware, before the detective ploughed onward.

"Knowing the Prince was going to be in town, we needed to ensure the area was secure. I took this duty upon myself. I was determined that nothing would happen to His Royal Highness. Then, one day when I was out solving another crime, I happened to drop by a hotel near the waterfront, on Barrington Street, and discovered that two suspicious American visitors were staying there. I scanned the guest log, and two entries caught my attention. A Mr. Breckton and a Mr. Holmes were both visiting here from Boston, a known Fenian den, Irish supporting area, and with last names like that, they, too, must have had Irish connections. Besides, I was told that these men slept late into the day and were out at night. Up to no good, as one can imagine."

Benjamin wondered if these habits would describe many young adult males, but thought better of asking the question.

"The hotelier opened the room, whereupon I made a shocking discovery."

Benjamin waited for the man to continue.

"Whereupon I made a shocking discovery," repeated Detective Power, staring pointedly at the young reporter.

"What did you discover?" said Benjamin, catching on.

Power leaned forward in his chair for effect. "I discovered two suitcases, unlocked, stacked at the head of the bed. They were packed with 100 pounds of dynamite, fuses, an alarm clock and all the workings to create a crude time bomb. If detonated, there were enough explosives to level the hotel and every other building on the block!"

This caught Benjamin's attention, and he leaned forward needing to know more.

"I then did what any good detective would do and had them arrested! To add more to the evidence against them, within their belongings I found a stub saying they had stored packages at the train station. I also went there and discovered yet more incriminating belongings. It was a rubber diving suit. And if that wasn't enough, I discovered the day before that the men had had a boat tour of the Halifax Harbour."

"What do you think was the plan?"

"They were planning on diving out to the *HMS Canada,* where the prince was on board, and they were going to plant their bomb! And, they would have, if I hadn't discovered their plan!"

"What did the men say when they were arrested?"

"Naturally, they proclaimed their innocence, saying they were here to merely work in the gold mines, and that was the necessary equipment. Claimed that anyone could get dynamite these days. But of course, they would say that!"

"What happens next?"

"They will be going to court in a few months, mercy help them! But I shall be remembered as Detective Nic Power, who foiled the attempt to blow up the prince!"

"That is an incredible feat!"

"If you are going to take a photograph for your front-page story, I can direct you to my best side."

Benjamin was excited to see Detective Power again. The headlines about the assassination attempt had sold newspapers, and with him on this case, even more were bound to sell as well.

Benjamin wasn't so sure about the details of the assassination attempt, or if the gentlemen really had only been simple American miners. A few months later, the court only found the gentlemen guilty of improperly bringing dynamite across the border. There was no further mention of the plot to assassinate the prince. Those charges mysteriously disappeared.

But that version of the story was certainly not going to sell any newspapers, so Benjamin and his team only wrote a one-inch column with the update. No one was interested any longer. That's how it works.

Following that event, more and more stories about Detective Power's crime-fighting exploits came to light. He was always willing to share his stories, and the press was always willing to print them. The truth lay somewhere a bit distant from any story he told, Benjamin knew. But what did he mind? They were good stories, and they sold newspapers.

And now Detective Power would be the one overseeing the rest of the Annie Kempton murder investigation. At least Benjamin knew he would get an interview.

"Louis Jeremy, come forward, please," Dr. Lovett called over the hum of the crowded room.

When Louis was settled at the front of the room, he recounted having been told by Tilly earlier yesterday morning that Annie Kempton was dead with her throat cut. When he arrived at the house, although he could not see the wounds to her neck, Louis noticed blood on her face and some on the carpet closer to her throat.

"Did you hear any noise outside your window late last night?" asked Dr. Lovett.

"No, I heard nothing. Last night I slept upstairs at the back part of the house. If there was a lot of noise, surely it would have wakened me. I did hear something that I thought was hollering around nine o'clock last night, though."

"Curious," said Dunn, trying to reinsert himself into the investigation. "When you left the house early this morning, I heard that you found footprints. I know your people from the Reserve are good at following tracks, so what did you discover?"

Ignoring the barb, Louis said, "I noticed a track leading from the front door and I followed it down through the field to the road. I was trying to find out who made the track. All I could see was that it was made with larrigans. I'm not sure how fresh the track was, as snow had drifted in it. My best guess was that it was made yesterday morning."

"Have you ever had a conversation with Peter Wheeler about the murder?" Dunn asked.

"Yes."

A collective gasp could be heard in the room.

"He told me that he didn't know who murdered the girl."

"Liar!"

Benjamin turned around to try to figure out who was shouting, but couldn't pinpoint the culprit.

Louis continued, unperturbed. "He said whoever killed that girl went in there and played a trick on her. After the perpetrator found that he got himself so far, he tried to cover it up, and so he killed her. He said he pitied her. He said it must have been some tramps who done it. He also said that if he had done it, he would not have committed murder, for he would rather be in the penitentiary for 20 years than to be cast out of heaven."

An angry growl went through the audience. "He did it! He's all but confessed."

Benjamin had to agree. All the evidence pointed straight to Peter.

"Did he say anything else about the murder or the body?" Dr. Lovett continued over the unrest of the crowd.

"Yes. He said the way everyone saw the body is not the position she was in when he found her."

"Is that so? Can you go into more detail?"

"He got down on the floor and showed me the position she was in.

Said she was lying on her knees with her elbows and head on the floor, with the head to one side. But he didn't think it was good for people to go up there and see a corpse looking like that, so he laid her over to her side and put a coat overtop of her."

Benjamin could see Peter nodding along with Louis' testimony. *It matches Peter's description yesterday, but it still makes no sense. Why wouldn't he mention at the start that he moved the body? He is definitely hiding something.*

The crowd obviously thought so, too, as many were shouting, "Liar!"

"Where and when did this conversation happen?" Dunn asked, reinserting himself.

"Down to Tilly's house yesterday afternoon, before we headed up for the inquest. Hardy Benson was there, too."

Tilly's youngest son, 12-year-old Walter, was next called to the stand. He again testified that Peter was cooking pork that definitely belonged to him. His house had three doors leading to the outside, all of which made noise, and in fact were too heavy for Walter to handle on his own even if he were tall enough to reach the latches. He also confirmed that no key in their home fit any of the locks at the Kemptons' house.

Benjamin was glad his testimony didn't take too long, because the poor boy looked terrified at being on the witness stand. He also looked embarrassed when, at the end of his session, he was asked to sign his statement, and he had to admit he did not know how to sign his name and could only trace an 'X'.

"Next, we would like to call Bernard Parker to give his account," Dr. Lovett said, consulting reading off a list before him. When Parker was at the front of the room, he said, "State your name, your position and your connection with this case."

"Bernard Parker. I'm a land surveyor. I was one of the first on the scene, having run into Peter Wheeler at the bridge and being told that Annie Kempton was dead."

Bernard produced a map he had created that showed the footprints he discovered that led from the back door to the pigpen and back to the house.

"We have it under good authority," said Dunn, "that you returned to the Kemptons' house this morning to search for more tracks. What was the result of that search?"

Bernard

Rap! Rap! Bernard pounded on Omer Rice's front door.

"Omer!" he opened the door and peered in. Omer and his wife were at the breakfast table.

"Bernard. What's happening? Come in from the cold."

"I thought we could search through your fields and look for further tracks leading up to the Kemptons' place. I've invited Elmer Crabbe to join us. He'll be here any moment."

"That's a good idea," said Susan Rice. "You might want to check behind our place. I saw Peter Wheeler out back there on late Monday afternoon, the day before the unfortunate event. He was going along the old road that goes right through our orchard."

"What time was that?" Bernard asked.

"It was nearly dark. Around five o'clock?"

"That would have been nice to know," said Omer, glaring at his wife. "We've been out looking for tracks!"

Susan put her hands on her hips. "Well, you should have started with me in the first place." She brushed her hands on her apron, turned her back to the men, and began clearing away the breakfast dishes without another word.

"Are you coming then?" asked Bernard.

Omer took his coat from the hall tree, indicating his agreement.

On the front steps, they noticed a 17-year-old lad coming up the hill. "Elmer!" cried Bernard. "Good timing!"

Elmer approached the two older men, smiled, and pulled his cap down further on his head, tightening the ear lugs to block out the frigid winter-morning chill.

"Thanks for joining us," Bernard said.

"We logging men gotta stick together. Where were you thinking of starting?" Elmer asked.

"Getting our bearings, the Kemptons' place is about a quarter of a mile up the hill. I'd reckon, here at Omer's farm, we are halfway between the Kemptons' farm and Tilly Comeau's house at the bottom of the hill."

"Ever the surveyor," Omer chuckled, patting Bernard on the back.

"Let's head to the old road through the orchard, where your missus suggested we look," Bernard said.

"Wait!" Omer said, hurrying back into the house. He reappeared moments later with a corn broom.

"What's that for?" Elmer said. "You taking up women's work?"

"No, for clearing the snow. It snowed last night, and with the drifts, the prints were probably covered. This is to clear the area."

"Good thinking," Bernard said.

The three men set off towards the back of Omer's house. Moments later Bernard spotted tracks. He leaned over to inspect them further.

"Those are mine," said Elmer. "I came through this way on Monday, on the day of the murder. I was out hunting and cut through here. Let's try up over there," he said, pointing.

After they crossed Omer's back fields and came to the next field, they once again saw signs of footprints in the snow. Bernard bent down to examine them closer, careful not to destroy them.

"The top layer of snow here is crusted, but breaks through seven or eight inches deep, I believe," he said, using his hand as a make-shift ruler. "And because the snow is so deep, it's making a shorter stride, as well."

"These have to be Wheeler's tracks!" said Elmer.

Staying a distance from the tracks, the three men followed them until they took a sudden curve.

"That's curious," Bernard said.

"Not if you think about it," said Omer. "If you went straight up, you'd be seen by those houses over there. By turning here, you would remain hidden."

The others nodded.

A few moments later, Bernard stopped suddenly. "I think we've lost the tracks again. The wind would have swept right along here on the crest of the hill and covered those tracks last night. We are just hours too late."

Omer took the broom and gently started to brush away the light dusting of snow that covered the ground.

"I see something!" cried Bernard. "Keep going!"

For the next ten feet or so, Omer continued to sweep while Bernard and Elmer carefully followed along until they reached the logging road and the tracks disappeared, lost amongst several other sets of footprints.

Bernard stood in the middle of the logging road and circled around, until he finally spotted the trail they had been following. It led along the fence towards the Kemptons' old barn.

It was an old threshing barn with no doors, used to store hay. The front and back doors did not face the main road but were side on. They approached it.

"Look here at the entrance," Bernard said. "Here, in the soft snow that has blown in through the open door, there is a footprint. He must have come in here."

The men took shelter within the walls, wondering if Peter Wheeler had done the same. Bernard looked around for signs of disturbances but was interrupted by Omer shouting.

"I've found another track here at the back door!"

The others rushed over. It was the open back door, closer to the Kemptons' house.

"Just like the footprint going in on the front, there is one here in the soft snow coming out," said Omer.

"Great work!" Bernard said as the three picked up the trail again.

It took them towards the Kemptons' house and to the pigpen behind the house. It followed along the back of the pigpen, went into a small yard, and over a fence, down to the main lane and eventually to the road.

There they stopped again to discuss what they had seen.

"Did anyone see any rabbit snares along the tracks?" Bernard asked, tapping his index finger to his lips as he thought. "Peter said he was out checking his rabbit snares earlier that day, but I didn't see any. Did either of you?"

They shook their heads.

"Curious," he said again.

Nothing was adding up, or maybe it was all adding up.

The reporter

By the time Bernard had finished describing the various paths and pointing them out on the map he had created for the inquest, Benjamin's head was spinning. The important thing, he thought, was that tracks were found going through the fields behind Omer Rice's house, up to the main road in a circuitous route, probably to avoid detection from neighbours. The tracks followed the road, went across to the Kemptons' thresher barn, then through the barn, and over towards the Kemptons' house, back around the pig pen, and either out to the main road or down the steep hill to the river.

The tracks were supposedly Peter Wheeler's.

"Knowing that you would need the exact specifications of those tracks, I went out and measured them myself," said Dunn. He took a piece of paper out of his breast pocket and handed it to Dr. Lovett, who read it and made notes in his journal.

"Did you and Peter Wheeler ever have any conversation about the murder or the events that happened that night?" the doctor asked.

"Yes," said Bernard. "I asked him where Hardy Benson was throughout all this."

Benjamin looked up sharply. *Why Hardy Benson all of a sudden? Who was he and what did he have to do with anything?*

"And what did Peter respond?"

"He said that Hardy Benson had been up to his place. But then I asked him what time he left, and Peter said it was handy to nine o'clock that night."

"What is he insinuating?" grumbled a man in the crowd. "Asking where Hardy Benson was? He is a fine young lad from an upstanding family."

Mutters of agreement rippled through the assembly.

As the discussion grew, Dr. Lovett tried to regain order. He pulled out his pocket watch, realizing it was already past four o'clock. The light was fading outside. There wasn't much point in calling another witness; however, there were still quite a few testimonies to hear. Time was of the essence.

"This inquest is adjourned until half-past seven this evening. We will take a break until then."

He wasn't sure how many people heard him, but he closed his notebook and started clearing off the table. This signalled to the crowd that it was time to leave.

Benjamin realized the train from Halifax would arrive soon and Dr. Lovett probably wanted to be there to meet Detective Power when he arrived and give him the full attention and welcome the great man would expect. It would be an honour to have such a man in the community, despite the circumstances.

On his way out, Benjamin wanted to interview some of the community members to get their feel for the case. He made eye contact with two older gentlemen across the room, who smiled at him, giving Benjamin the invitation he needed. He walked over, introduced himself, stated his purpose, and began asking questions.

"Gentlemen, what are your thoughts about Peter Wheeler as the murderer of Annie Kempton?" he asked getting right to the point.

"For the most part, ask me last week, and I would have said he was a quiet, inoffensive, hard-working fellow. Never one to be idle, that's for sure. He is Spanish, though."

"I thought he was Portuguese," said the other.

"Not sure. From somewhere over there. Not from around here. Not one of us. Regardless, it was a big shock to Bear River. Not just the murder, but that someone like Peter, who lived among us for so long, could do such a thing."

"This whole case brings back the memories of another tragic event about twenty years ago. We were all hoping to forget that."

"What happened then?" asked Benjamin.

"David Robbins murdered his wife, Emeline, back in 1875."

"I have vague memories of that," Benjamin said. "I had just started as a reporter with the *Herald* that year. But remind me of the details."

"Well, Robbins and his wife were never known to agree. In fact, ask most of his neighbours and they would have called him an old crank." As he said this, the man stepped closer and lowered his voice, lest the others still milling about should accuse him of gossiping.

"This particular night, he crept into the room where his wife was sleeping and shot her in the head with a rifle! She didn't die, and crawled to the kitchen, probably attempting to escape, where the crazed man took a mallet for splitting shingles and continued to beat her in the head with it until she truly was dead."

"The poor woman! What happened then?" Benjamin asked.

"Robbins hid in the woods from the authorities for nine days. Rumour has it he came back for his wife's funeral, watching the entire affair from behind a stone wall not 100 yards from the house."

"The nerve! Was he caught then?"

"No, from there, the madman burned down his brother-in-law's barn, and while everyone in the community was trying to save that barn, Robbins went and burned down the barn of another relative! He then got his gun and shot the cattle of a neighbour who displeased him. By this point, the community was terrified. Everyone was afraid to venture outside, especially alone, and anyone who had ever quarrelled with Robbins was afraid to sleep."

"Was he ever caught?"

"Yes, by luck. Early one morning, Robbins was discovered out in the woods, asleep, with a loaded gun at his elbow. They arrested him and took him to Digby, where he was tried and condemned to death."

"As the story goes, the night he was arrested, his hair was jet black, but on the day of his execution, it turned snow white!"

"So great was the judgment towards the man that, on the night before his execution, the authorities had to call in the militia to prevent hundreds of men who had flocked in from far and wide from tearing down the jailhouse fence so they could witness the hanging. The man's last night on earth was full of the cries of the angry mob outside, who were thirsting for his blood."

"What an ordeal! And were you part of that angry mob? You seem quite sure of the details," suggested Benjamin.

The two men smiled at him, tapped their noses reminding him to mind his own business, turned and walked away.

~

Later that evening, Dr. Lovett resumed his position at the front of the room, but this time, Dunn was sitting back with the other jury members. To Benjamin, he looked a little disgruntled. His services and so-called expertise were no longer needed, now that Detective Power had arrived.

With the room full to capacity and overflowing, Dr. Lovett stood to call the inquest to order. As he did so, Detective Power cut through the crowd, which parted before him like the Red Sea.

He stood at the front of the room, legs spread wide and hands behind his back, which made him look all the more imposing. He wore a navy, double-breasted sack coat and dark, firmly-pressed trousers, topped off with a navy hat with gold braid along the peak.

Benjamin looked up and caught the man's eye. Detective Power winked in recognition. Benjamin smiled. The man did look sharp and imposing, but that was to be expected. Given that he might have been one of the few gentlemen with a career that paid $40 a year just in a clothing allowance, he certainly should.

Benjamin felt proud knowing this distinguished character. Theirs had certainly been a mutually beneficial relationship over the past few years —one selling stories, the other his image.

"Detective Power! Join us please," the doctor said.

Detective Power made a grand show of taking the seat at the head table once occupied by Dunn.

"Pray, continue," he said to the room at large. "Dr. Lovett has been so kind as to offer a synopsis, and Mr. Dunn has graciously shared his notes with me, so I feel fully brought up to speed on the case." He waved the action forward.

"In that case," said Dr. Lovett, "I call Grace Morine to offer her account."

The young woman timidly made her way to the front of the room. Benjamin thought she looked absolutely terrified to be in front of so many people. Tear stains streaked her cheeks.

"Now, Miss Morine, please tell us who you are and what you know of these matters," said Dr. Lovett, gently.

The young girl stood trembling at the stand. She clutched a linen handkerchief and began to speak in a quiet, quavering voice. Silence fell on the room as everyone strained to hear her testimony.

"My name is Grace Morine, and I was intimately acquainted with Annie Kempton, as we were great friends." Grace began crying again, but dabbed her eyes with her handkerchief in an attempt to regain her composure.

Grace

Annie Kempton raised her feet in the air and threw her head back. Her dark hair blew behind her in the wind, and her laugh emanated from deep within.

"This is the most fantastical thing I have ever done in my life!" she cried when she reached the bottom of the hill.

Still laughing, she dismounted the bicycle, and smiled over at Hardy Benson, who had ridden down beside her.

He beamed. "I told you it would be fun!"

Annie leaned the handlebars over to Herbert Comeau, who was waiting at the bottom of the hill for the bicycle. Hardy and Herbert began the uphill cycle so they could once again enjoy the coast back down.

When they were alone, her best friend Grace, who had also been waiting at the bottom of the hill, turned to Annie. "You really shouldn't be riding like that," she scolded.

"And why shouldn't I?" Annie asked.

"It's not ladylike. What would your mother say if she were here? It's not dignified, Annie!"

"Mother isn't here. She's in the Boston States with my sister. What she doesn't know won't kill her."

"Well, you might have gotten yourself killed!"

"Grace, you ought to try it. It's so liberating. I have never felt such freedom in my life."

"You just like it because it means you can ride down the hill with Hardy, and not have a chaperone."

"Take that back!"

"I will not! You know it's true. Next, you'll be going off on one of those tandem bikes together. Then the two of you really will be the talk of the town. First comes love, then comes marriage… then comes the baby in the baby carriage!"

"I'm only 14. Don't be planning too far ahead!"

"You know you like Hardy, Annie!"

Saving her from having to admit anything, Peter Wheeler walked by. "You looked like you were having fun, Annie."

"Oh, Peter! It was glorious! It was like I was flying like a bird." Then, realizing she was talking to her father's sometimes farm hand, she stopped herself. "Oh, but you won't tell Pa, will you?"

Peter winked. "Mum is the word. Your secret is safe with me."

"You should really try it sometime, Peter."

"No, thank you!" he said adamantly.

"Come on! Everybody and their mother rides a wheel. Except for maybe Grace."

Grace harrumphed and crossed her arms. Annie elbowed her in jest.

"I know far too many stories of calamities that have happened on those contraptions," Peter said. "Just last week in Digby, that man was riding on the public pier there, and when he dismounted, he accidentally went over the side of the wharf."

"He would have fallen into the ocean, though, surely. A bit cold, is all," said Grace.

"It was low tide! Fell 15 feet onto the beach. Luckily, he didn't break any bones. Dusted himself off and climbed back up and rode home."

Annie and Grace gasped and then laughed at the thought.

"Then, how about what happened here last week," Peter continued, "when that party of young lads from Annapolis came riding to take advantage of all our hills!"

Grace winced, having heard the story at school.

"Exactly," said Peter. "Two were thrown off the tandem bike, and luckily, only slightly hurt. But when their friend, who was also hurtling down the hill, saw them, he tried to stop by putting his foot in the wheel and was thrown, somersaulted through the air, struck his head, and lost consciousness."

"I've heard all this. You don't need to go into the gory details," said Annie.

"And what have you learned from the experience?" Grace asked, hands on hips.

"Not to stick your foot in the wheel to stop the bike!" she said.

Peter and Grace groaned.

4: My tracks were there

At the inquest, Dr. Lovett looked at Detective Power, inclining his head in the young woman's direction. Did Power want to interview her?

Power shook his head, so Dr. Lovett continued. "When did you last see your friend?"

"It was Monday afternoon, the afternoon before her murder," she said with a sob. "It was between half-past three and four o'clock. I had asked her to go to the post office with me, but she said she couldn't for she had to do a few errands and was to go right back home."

"During this time, did Miss Kempton ask you to stay the night with her?"

"No," said Grace, "nor at any other time has she."

"Caught in a lie!" Rolled-up newspapers and other items hurtled to-wards Peter Wheeler. Benjamin had to duck because the assailants were somewhere close behind him.

Peter kept his head down and did not react, further inciting the crowd.

Grace began sobbing again, and Dr. Lovett dismissed her.

"That's all the evidence we need. Throw him in jail, now!" a strong male voice called out from behind Benjamin.

He turned to look but couldn't distinguish one man from another. They were all dressed in the same black suit jackets and had the same moustache and slicked-back hair. They all wore the same angry look on their faces.

Next on the docket was Stanley Rice. He testified that Peter worked for him as a cook at his lumber camp and did so not more than three weeks ago. Stanley owed him $2. He had told Peter to pick up the pay-ment at the mill, not at his house. Although Peter had said he had gone up to Stanley's house around five o'clock on the evening of the murder, Stanley stated that Peter did not go there to collect money.

The news of this sent the gallery into a further frenzy. Men were jumping onto their seats and shouting. This included the lead vocalist be-hind Benjamin. "I call for his immediate execution! The man is an in-fernal liar! He wasn't collecting money; he was murdering that poor young thing!"

Benjamin watched as Stanley looked around the room, and it was al-most as if he was enjoying the attention, and the power of bringing the room, literally, to its feet. The lad looked to be in his early twenties, and this was probably the most excitement he had ever had.

Stanley then briefly discussed having been sent a letter by the local magistrate on behalf of Peter Wheeler.

"I owed him a balance of $2 for his work in the woods, and he sued me. The letter said I had 15 days to pay him back, and so far, it's only been about a week. Because of money differences in the past, Peter has come to me for his pay. But just not this day in question."

"There's more, that I should mention," said Stanley leaning forward. He lowered his voice, so the crowd had to quieten to hear the news. "When we were out to the camps, I would often hear Peter talk about An-nie Kempton."

"What would he say?" asked Dr. Lovett.

"He'd say a bunch of stuff." Realizing Dr. Lovett was pressing for more details, Stanley continued. "Whenever we talked about girls, he would al-ways talk about Annie. He said he would like to screw her the first chance he got and was going to, the very first chance."

As the crowd erupted, Stanley added, "He said he would rather be with Annie than any other girl in Bear River!"

"Release him, and let us execute him, if you are not going to! The evil brute!" shouted the man behind Benjamin.

Mr. Kempton, sitting in the front row of the proceedings, burst into tears, moaning loudly as his heart broke again.

Stanley fed the crowd more. "He would say things like this once or twice a week, but sometimes it could but up to three times a day! She was always on his mind."

"Recess! Five-minute recess!" Dr. Lovett cried over the crowd.

It was going to be a long evening.

After allowing the crowd to calm down and retake their seats, Dr. Lovett restarted the proceedings. He recalled Bernard Parker.

During the break between the afternoon's session and this evening's, Parker had gone back out, measured more of the tracks and created an entirely new map which he presented. He had heard the confusion about what exactly was where, and who found and saw what, where, and de-cided to make a better map. Knowing this was something he could easily do to help the case, he had gone home at suppertime and drawn the map on the only thing he had available—brown wrapping paper.

Benjamin's eyes glazed over as he tried to follow all the dots and lines which connected various points. He would have to go up there himself, he thought, to walk around and get a true sense for the surroundings.

Following Bernard was his 23-year-old brother, Charlie, who also worked with Peter Wheeler out at the logging camps. He picked up where Stanley Rice had left off.

"Last summer I heard Peter say, 'You see if I don't have it in her inside a year.' He was talking about Annie Kempton."

After having just settled, the crowd erupted again, demanding for immediate justice.

"When and where did he say this?"

"We were outside, walking along the road. Peter had just been making fun of me. He was saying that I was no good. He didn't come right out and say it, but he meant sexually. Then he said that Annie Kempton had said as much to Hattie Comeau, who had repeated it to him. Peter then asked me why I hadn't bothered Annie before this, and I said I had no desire to. He then said I didn't know anything about girls, but he had been around a lot of girls and knew all about them."

"That's the first thing he's said that I believe!" shouted the man behind Benjamin. His statement was met by laughter and a round of applause.

"That's when Peter said he was going to have it sometime with her, anyway. He was referring to Annie, of course. He said the best way to get her was to take her down, and if she was a decent girl, she wouldn't tell on you," said Herbert. "It would spoil their womanhood if they told on you."

There were a few disgusted groans and comments in the crowd. Peter Wheeler looked even worse than before.

Next to give his evidence was another young man, Elmer Crabbe. He recounted the story of looking for footprints in the snow with Omer Rice and Bernard Parker. He then added another layer of detail which had yet to come out in the evidence.

Elmer

When they got to top of the hill where it intersected with the main road, Elmer stopped his companions. "Here," he said. "It happened, here!"

"What happened where?" asked Omer. He didn't want to stop for stories but wanted to keep following Peter Wheeler's tracks through the snow.

"I saw Peter Wheeler from this spot on Monday afternoon, around half-past five, right before the murder."

"You are just telling us this now?" Bernard asked. "This is important information to help us follow his tracks. Where was he? What was he doing?"

"He was standing over there by Mr. Kempton's threshing barn. I had been out hunting all day and was standing down here by these two big rocks on the side of the hill. Peter was walking over there by the barn, and I was headed that way."

"Did he see you? What did he look like?" asked Bernard.

"Well, he didn't have nothing in his hands, nor was he carrying nothing on his shoulders. I called out to him in a pretty loud voice and asked him where he was going."

"What did he say?" asked Bernard.

"He didn't answer me. He didn't even stop. He turned his head and just went on. I couldn't see if he went into the barn or not, though. I never saw him again after that."

"Do you think he really didn't hear you, or was he just ignoring you?" Omer asked.

"I don't know how he could not have heard me."

"Let's re-enact it," Bernard suggested. "I'll walk over there and stop where you said you saw Peter. Elmer, you stay here and call out to me, as you did to him on Monday."

When they had finished the experiment, Elmer counted 118 paces between where he and Elmer stood.

"I'm not sure how he could not have heard you. I could distinctly hear you from there," Bernard said.

The reporter

"Was that the last time you saw Peter Wheeler before he was arrested?" Dr. Lovett asked Elmer.

"No," Elmer said. "I saw him again later that night at the bridge, when he was there with Tilly and Hattie and the likes."

"Did you have any conversation with him? Did you ask him if he heard you earlier that day or not?"

"I said to him, 'Peter was that you on this hill?' and he said, 'Yes, and was that you with the gun on your shoulder?' and I said, yes. That was all that was said. I have no idea if he heard me or not."

Elmer stood to leave the chair at the front, to go sign his mark on the evidence page, but as he did so, he looked over at Peter.

"I do know one more thing," he said. "Peter is wearing the same pants now as he was wearing then. I don't think the man owns many clothes."

Benjamin thought about Elmer's comment about the clothes. Several people had given evidence that Peter did not own many clothes, that he only owned one coat, and that he was still wearing today what he wore when he was arrested, which is what he was wearing the night before the murder.

The calling of the next witness interrupted his thoughts.

Hardy Benson strolled casually to the front of the room. The boy, for that is what Benjamin thought he looked like, was cool, calm, and collected. He took the seat at the front of the room and looked Dr. Lovett directly in the eyes.

"My name is Harding Theodore Benson, and I am 15 years old, rising 16," he said confidently.

"The poor lad," whispered one lady sitting close to Benjamin. "He must be heartbroken. Annie was his sweetheart."

Benjamin couldn't be sure if it was the same older lady from the previous day. They all looked the same to him.

"Can you please tell us about what happened on the Monday night, the night before the murder? When was the last time you saw Annie Kempton alive?" asked Dr. Lovett.

"It was probably four o'clock in the afternoon. She was walking across the bridge towards the store, and I was coming home from school."

"And what about Peter Wheeler? We understand you were with him later that night."

"Yes, I seen him. I seen him up handy by the bridge and decided to walk with him back towards Tilly Comeau's house. I was wondering if I might see Annie around there. We've been keeping company for a while, and I was in the habit of walking her home. She usually retired around nine or ten o'clock at night," he said lowering his head.

"Had you made arrangements to meet Annie there at the bridge that night?"

"No, sir."

"Did Peter say anything to you that night about Annie Kempton?"

"Not really," said Hardy. "He just said that Tilly had been going to go up to the Kemptons' house to stay with Annie while her father was in the woods. Then he said it was too much for Tilly to be going up there to stay, because as soon as she woke up there, she would have to come back down to the house, get her breakfast, and then walk into work."

"What time did you leave Tilly Comeau's house that night?"

"It was probably a little after nine o'clock. I didn't hear the bell ring, nor the drum beat at quarter to eight."

Benjamin had been told the story about the bell and had heard and seen it himself. On Bell Road, between Tilly's house and the hotel, there was a tall pole, attached to which was a large, cast-iron bell. Every work-day, on the hour, a group of men were commissioned to ring the bell, signalling to labouring men the time, letting them know what time they could knock off work. The bell also served as the Bear River fire alarm.

As for the drum beating, Benjamin realized there was an active militia group stationed on the outskirts of Bear River. He figured they practised a drum routine every night at a set time.

"After I left Peter at Tilly's house, I went home," Hardy continued.

"How did you hear about Annie's death?"

"I heard of the murder from little Walter Comeau. I was heading to school when I met him on the bridge. I went up to the schoolhouse to let everyone know, and then I went back home to tell my mother, and then I started up to the Kemptons' house. When I was on the road, I ran into Peter. He said Annie was dead, told me how sorry he was, and he started to cry."

"Sorry that he killed her? I bet they weren't real tears!" shouted the same voice from behind Benjamin.

"Peter said nothing further about the murder," Hardy said. "I have not talked to him since. But I did see him describe the position in which he found the body and how he moved it and threw a coat over it."

After a few more general questions, Hardy returned to his seat.

Dr. Lovett wrapped up the evening, explaining there were still more witnesses to move through, so he scheduled a third day of the inquest to start the next morning.

Benjamin was happy there would be another day, for perhaps more information would come out. There were still so many questions going through his mind.

Annie was last seen leaving the store downtown between four and five o'clock in the evening in question. Where was she after that? She had obviously been working on her flowers. Her clothes were strewn over the chair, but what else was she doing?

Would she really go all day and not secure anyone to stay with her that night?

The body was hardly cold when she was discovered around eight o'clock in the morning. According to the doctor's evidence, it would seem

Peter killed her at midnight. What would have kept her up that late in a cold room? Were she and Peter visiting at first, and then things turned sour? More importantly, why did Peter kill someone he apparently knew so well? What exactly had happened on that night?

Benjamin had so many questions.

He emerged from his own thoughts and looked around to see most of the crowd had dispersed—all but one of the most important people in the room. He jumped to his feet and rushed to the table at the front where Peter Wheeler remained.

Constable Henshaw approached to take the prisoner back to the cell especially fitted within his own house.

"Excuse me, Mr. Wheeler," said Benjamin, "I'm with the *Halifax Herald*, and wondered if I could ask you a few questions."

Benjamin looked up at Constable Henshaw, who nodded, and then looked to Peter, who also nodded. All three men sat down.

He crossed his arms and glared intently at the accused.

How could Peter sit there so calmly, knowing what he had done to that poor girl?

The next thing that struck him was how small Peter Wheeler actually was. Benjamin was by no means a large or tall man, but he felt so across from the man who measured slightly more than five feet in height.

Although he was small, his biceps and shoulders were well formed from the years of manual labour. He easily possessed the strength to commit the deed.

Benjamin rested his elbows on the table and leaned forward. "How could you have done this, Peter?"

Peter closed his eyes and took a few moments before responding. "I am innocent," he said looking Benjamin right in the eyes. "I would give all I had not to be the one who found her. Then, I wouldn't be in this awful mess. It's all so stressful."

Benjamin could have sworn he saw the man's eyes pool with tears. "You are feeling the stress?"

"I feel such a strain knowing the whole community—which I have been a part of for the past 12 years—thinks I am guilty." He put his head in his hands and sighed deeply.

Benjamin stared intently at Peter. The townspeople were right. Just by looking at him, he couldn't tell exactly where he had come from. He definitely wasn't a typical white European descendent. His skin was on the darker side, making him look Spanish or Italian. He was definitely someone who had come from away, without roots in the community, let alone the province.

"What happened on that Monday, right before the murder?"

Peter rolled his eyes up to the left, as if recalling the day's events in his mind. "I started the day making bread. Tilly was feeling poorly, and she was away at work, so I was making the bread."

"I mean later. Many witnesses testified seeing your tracks in the area. How do you explain that?" Benjamin could hear the edge to his own voice.

"It's true. My tracks were there."

Benjamin was a bit taken aback by the open admission. Maybe he would get a confession from the man after all. He said nothing and let Peter continue.

"That first part of the evening, I was out setting rabbit snares. I can take anyone to them, if they would just let me out of these," he said raising his hands and shaking the manacles in the air, letting the rattling noise fill the room.

"But you were said to have made comments about Annie Kempton."

"She was Hardy's girl. He used to go see her, but I never knew him to go and see her when she was alone, though."

"But you were sweet on her, weren't you?" pressed Benjamin.

"No! I was the family's farmhand. Known her most of her life."

At this, Peter's voice trailed off and he looked up, trying to blink back tears. "I ask you this. If she were killed early in the evening, then how did she have time to make the flowers? See, when I was there at noon, she had only made one bunch of flowers, and she ran out of paper. People saw her going to the store at five o'clock to buy more paper. If she didn't get paper until the evening, and she was killed early in the evening, like some are suggesting, how did she manage to make six more flowers in the span of a few minutes?"

The logic is infallible, thought Benjamin. *If the man is guilty, he certainly has a powerful control over his thoughts and emotions.*

"And her clothes don't make sense," Wheeler continued, evidently happy to have someone listen to his thoughts.

"How so?"

"Annie always looked out the pantry window before she let anyone in. That's what she always told me. So, the theory that she was only partially dressed when she opened the door is highly improbable."

"You knew Annie well, then?"

"She was so kind-hearted, but strong! Was she ever strong, which is why I wasn't surprised to see from the state of the room that she had

74

kicked up a fight. I knew her strength because we once wrestled together for fun."

Benjamin raised an eyebrow, wondering about the appropriateness of that comment.

"She might have been strong, but she wasn't overly brave. She would come to me sometimes, and I'd have to help her out of some fixes."

"What do you mean by that? What fixes?"

Peter

"Peter! Peter!"

Hattie Comeau threw open the inner door of their tiny house to find Peter sitting by the fire. She was out of breath, and Annie Kempton was fast on her heels. A few moments later, Tilly appeared in the doorway.

Hattie threw out a high-speed, out-of-breath string of words.

"Hattie, slow down! I can't make hide nor hair of what you are saying."

"Peter, you must come with us now, back up to my place. We need your help. Someone or something is in my house!"

Peter raised an eyebrow and looked up at Tilly. She nodded.

He stood. "What happened? What has you all frightened?" he asked pulling on his overcoat.

As the four of them walked up the hill towards the Kemptons' house, Annie filled him in on the details. "Well, Hattie and I had just finished coasting, so we went and got Tilly to come up to my house. You know the latch on the door is so tricky! The catch had fallen down again, and I couldn't open the door. So, I didn't know how we were going to get in."

"What did you do?" Peter asked.

"Tilly said we should just come back down to her place, but I said I would find another way to get in."

"Bound and determined, that one," Tilly said from behind.

"I said I would go through my bedroom window. So Tilly put the sled there under the window, and I stood on it to hoist myself up, to crawl through. But when I opened the window, I heard a noise coming from inside the house."

"It's true! We all heard it," added Hattie, pointing to her mother and Annie.

"It was so loud! Sounded like someone was running across the hall!" Annie said.

"Could it have been some mice, or barn cats?" Peter asked.

"I tried to tell her not to go in the house, but she wouldn't listen," Tilly said. "She was in there, standing in the bedroom. I could hear the running, too!"

"Heavens!" cried Peter. "What happened then?"

"I pulled her back through the window," Tilly said, "and we high-tailed it out of there."

"That's when we came down to get you," Hattie added.

By this point, they had reached the Kemptons' house. Peter fiddled with the main door, thumping it and jiggling the handle until they eventually heard the latch give way.

He went in, took matches from his coat pocket and lit the lamp above the mantelpiece. He held the lamp tightly and began to walk from room to room in search of anyone who might be hiding.

"All clear," he finally shouted. "If anyone was here, they are now gone."

"I think we all ought to stay here tonight," Tilly said. "Peter, you stay here with Annie, and I'll go down and bring up the other children."

"Oh, please don't tell Pa," Annie pleaded. "He will never let me do anything on my own again. It was just a noise, and no harm has come of it!"

Tilly put her hands on her hips and glared at Annie, but eventually acquiesced.

The reporter

"And less than two weeks later, Annie is dead, and I'm in an awful fix," Peter lamented.

Benjamin looked up from his notes. *There is some sense to what he was saying, but yet, so much evidence points to Peter.*

"There are rumours they will find human blood on your clothes. What do you say to that?"

"They will never find human blood on my clothes," Peter said. "The only way it could possibly be there if I got some when I was placing the coat over Annie's body."

Benjamin had seen the murder scene. There was blood everywhere. The girl's throat was cut. If this was the case, then surely the murderer would have had blood on him. So far, not the minutest amount of blood had been found on Peter's clothes. Because he owned so few clothes, he could not have gone home to change them, let alone burn them.

It isn't adding up.

"You sound pretty confident that they won't find any blood."

"I only own the one coat, and they will not find human blood on it. Rabbit blood is another matter. A week ago, a friend and I were out hunting and we shot a rabbit. I carried it back, so some drops may have gotten on my trousers because of that."

"I guess we will let the evidence speak for itself," Benjamin said, less confidently. As hard as he tried to fight it off, a seed of doubt was sprouting in his mind.

"There seems to be so much mystery about you and who you are. You are obviously not what you seem, and doesn't look like you have too many friends around here."

"I've always been one to look after myself. I've had to since a small age. With so many siblings and my mama dead so young, I had no choice."

"You had a lot of brothers and sisters?" Benjamin had never thought about him as having a family.

"Yes, there were 16 of us. Eight boys and eight girls. My poor mama never had a spare moment. No wonder she died so young."

"Where exactly are you from, Peter?"

"Mauritius."

"Where?" Benjamin searched the recesses of his mind, back to the days he studied geography in school, but came up with nothing.

"It's the most beautiful place in the world. It's a tropical paradise. Bright blue water, white sand beaches, and sugar cane as far as the eye can see."

"But where is it?"

"It's a small island in the Indian Ocean, off the coast of Madagascar, about 1,200 miles east of Africa. Did you ever hear tell of the dodo bird? That's where it lived."

Benjamin nodded. "Ever see one?"

"Not alive. Went extinct two hundred years before my time," Peter said with a chuckle.

"Tell me about it."

"What? The dodo bird?"

"No, your life. Who are you? No one can figure out how you came to live in Bear River at such a young age."

Peter

I was born in 1869 in Port Louis, the capital of Mauritius. It is a giant port, with hundreds of ships coming in every year from all over the world. It was exciting place for a child, hearing all the different languages and seeing people from all over the world.

Mauritius was always a smelting pot. The Dutch were there first, and then the French. Those who survived the cyclones, droughts and all the rats brought slaves from the mainland of Africa, as well as from India. Other people moved in from China. Eventually the British took over.

That's where my father comes in. His name was Louis, and he was of Irish and French descent, I think born in Australia. He was an officer in the British army. He did really well for himself and was decorated with medals. I think one was the Victoria Cross.

One night some friends who were in the army with him beat him up. He died the next morning. I don't know all the details. I was too young.

My mother was Emily. I think she was also French and Irish, but you never know in Mauritius! She was the most kind and beautiful woman you could ever imagine. She died when I was only eight, and it all happened so suddenly. I was with her when she died. I just have vague memories of her now. But I know I'm going to see her soon.

My uncle, Captain David Stephenson Wheeler, took me on his ship, a beautiful three-masted barquentine, called the *Lochiel*. I had never left Mauritius before, and you can imagine my delight at being on the open water, sailing into ports around the world. It changed my life forever, and I fell in love with the seafaring life.

We called at London, and from there we sailed to the northwest coast of France. I was so used to hearing all the French in Mauritius, I could easily get by here. After France, we sailed to a Scottish port near Glasgow.

I often had news from my family in Mauritius. But come to think of it, I haven't heard from home at all since I came to Nova Scotia.

I stayed in Scotland for eight whole months, in the hospital. I had injured my foot, and it took that long in hospital for me to recover. It was a really nice hospital, but I missed my life by the sea.

After that, I worked for awhile at the Dunbarton shipyards outside Glasgow. I learned so much here. But I grew restless again, and a great opportunity came my way.

In 1884, I was 15. I boarded another barque, this one called the *Carpacian*. It was laden with coal and bound for Barbados. It took us six weeks to cross the ocean.

I loved Barbados. It reminded me so much of home in Mauritius, it being an island country with a similar climate. The aquamarine water, the fresh tropical air, and the palm trees....I was so homesick.

I decided to stay awhile. I found a home with a working man and his family. It was so close to the beach that I could hear the ocean at night.

However, I didn't stay long there. I met a sea captain, and he convinced me to come to sea once more. This time, we were bound to Digby, Nova Scotia on the *Edmond*.

There were fellows onboard from Digby and Weymouth. They talked up the place so much, and made it seem like it would be the best place in the world to live. They described the nearby ocean, the beautiful sloping hills and forests, and bustling towns and ports. So, when we arrived in Digby, I decided to stay awhile. A crewman said his mother in Bear River took in boarders, so I went to seek her out.

They were right. There was something special about coming up the Bay of Fundy. The dramatic changings of the tides, rugged coastlines, and beautiful farmyards.

Of course, we arrived in October, so I had yet to experience a Nova Scotian winter when I made my decision to stay. I had felt cold in Scotland, but never to the extent that I have ever experienced here! I just closed my eyes and dreamed of my days on the beach in Mauritius.

Isaac Kempton hired me on, so I needed a place that was close by. That's when I started boarding with Tilly Comeau, just down the hill from the Kempton place. I've stayed with Tilly and worked for Mr. Kempton ever since.

I keep myself busy. But I guess you could say I've just had a simple, labourer's life, not really anything noteworthy. I just plod along and get done what needs to be done to survive.

Over the years, I have had my misfortunes, and been laid up with sickness a few times. Sometimes this kept me from work for long periods, but I have to say, of all the misfortunes I've encountered, this, that I am now charged with, is the worst.

The reporter

Benjamin looked up from his notes, realizing that Peter had come to the end of his monologue. He hadn't interrupted, mesmerized by the tale.

For the first time, he looked at Peter—actually looked at him. He saw a young, orphaned boy. Peter had never belonged and never been cared for. And now, only Tilly, in a sea of hundreds, stood beside him.

Benjamin felt sorry for him. *What if this man is innocent? What if Peter is being blamed for something he didn't do, all because he was not born into the group?*

The shock of the realization hit Benjamin, nearly taking his breath away. He pushed his chair back, stammered a few words, and quickly retreated from the room to be alone with his thoughts.

5: No doubt in my mind

When Benjamin awoke, he could see his breath in the air. It was going to be another cold winter's day. He willed himself out of bed, despite the few hours he had spent sleeping in it.

He had been up most of the night, tossing and turning, or pacing the floor, thinking about Peter Wheeler. He had neglected to take into consideration that here was a real man with real feelings. Someone who kept protesting his innocence. *Is there any merit to it? Has the community jumped to conclusions without looking in other quarters?*

But the evidence was there. People in small communities tend to know their neighbours the best. He would just have to wait to see what else the inquest revealed, especially with Detective Power now at the helm.

He hurried to get himself ready so he could be at the hall the moment the doors opened so he could secure a good seat—a better spot than the reporter from the *Digby Courier. At least my paper is printed every day, whereas the Courier only hits the stands once a week.*

Bear River seemed like a small village in the middle of nowhere, but Benjamin had been surprised to hear that nearly 1,200 people lived there. If everyone there attended the inquest, plus people coming from Digby, Annapolis and beyond, the room would be overflowing.

Seated and ready in position, he turned towards the back of the room when he heard a gasp.

Mr. Kempton hobbled into the room, a woman hanging onto his elbow. This must be Mrs. Kempton, fresh off the boat, back from the Boston States. She clutched a handkerchief in her hand, and her whimpers could be heard as she made her way to the reserved seats at the front.

Behind the couple was what appeared to be their eldest child, Annie's brother. He had been out in the woods with his father, coming home when they got the news. He walked in with his head down until he got to the front of the room. He looked up to see Peter Wheeler sitting at the table in front of him.

Suddenly, his pale face turned bright red. He rushed the table, tried to reach across to hit or strangle Peter.

"You killed my baby sister!" he shouted. "Murderer! You should be put to death right here and right now!"

Mr. Kempton pulled his son back as Constable Henshaw rushed to separate the two men.

In a calm, flat voice, Peter said, "I did not kill her. It wasn't me."

"Liar!" the son shouted again, as his father pushed him into his seat.

Emotions are high everywhere, thought Benjamin.

When the jury, the prisoner, and Detective Power were all in position, Dr. Lovett called the inquest to order.

Dr. Ellison was the first witness called. He recounted the details of the autopsy he had performed at the house on Tuesday afternoon.

What a way to start the morning, thought Benjamin.

He obviously wasn't the only one, as several women had to excuse themselves from the room, being unable to handle the gruesome details. Somehow, Mrs. Kempton remained. It was probably the first time she had heard the details.

Following Dr. Ellison's testimony, Dr. Lovett called for a quick recess, after which he called Sadie Morine to the front of the room. There were so many Morines in Bear River, and they all seemed to have a lot of daughters. Benjamin was having a hard time keeping all the characters straight. Apparently, Dr. Lovett did as well, for he began by calling Sadie by her sister's name until he was corrected.

This Sadie Morine was a cousin to Grace Morine—the one who Peter said was going to stay with Annie that night. Sadie was 11 years old and lived a half-hour's walk from the Kemptons' house, up the hill, on the same road.

Sadie recounted everything she had seen on the Monday afternoon, including Annie walking towards home around half-past four. When Sadie returned home around six o'clock, she had to pass the Kemptons' house, but did not see anyone coming or going at that time.

She did, however, see Peter Wheeler. He started in the field off to the side of the road, crossed over the road in front of her, and carried on towards Mr. Kempton's barn. She saw him cross the field and continue to the back of the barn, go over the fence, and head down towards the Kemptons' house and behind the pigpen.

"He only stopped once the whole time he was walking, and that was behind the pigpen. I had a clear view of him, but was too far to call out to him," she said.

"Did he go through the barn?"

"No, I'm absolutely certain he did not go through the barn. He went around the barn."

Wait a minute, thought Benjamin. *These sounded like the tracks that the men followed the day after the murder. Here this child is saying she saw him walking exactly that route. If he walked that route late afternoon, how could those have been the tracks Wheeler made when he supposedly went to kill Annie? If Peter didn't go through the barn, who did?*

Benjamin cut off his train of thought. He didn't like where his mind was going. It was as if, after meeting Peter the night before, his mind had now opened to new possibilities and questions.

"Do you know Elmer Crabbe?" asked Dr. Lovett.

Sadie nodded and instantly lowered her head, looking at her feet.

He continued, "Did you see him that afternoon as well?"

"I did see him around the same time. He was off down in the hollow before I got to Mr. Kempton's barn, lower down the hill from where I saw Peter Wheeler."

"Did you have a conversation with Elmer Crabbe?"

Sadie kept her eyes down and hesitated before answering. "No, we shared no words, but..." Her voice trailed off.

"But what?"

"He whistled at me, and I got really scared."

There were a few tuts that went through the crowd. Some surmised the girl was exaggerating and defended Elmer's character.

Benjamin turned when he heard Elmer yell, "Hey, now!"

Someone pulled the lad back into his seat, elbowing him to be quiet.

"What did you do then?" asked Dr. Lovett.

"I went on a little further to get out of sight, but then I stopped and waited. I knew my brother and sister were coming down to meet me, so I stood and waited for them. I was scared to go on by myself."

"What route did Mr. Crabbe take?"

"He was first on the road, and then went down into the hollow that runs alongside the road. This is right before you get the Kemptons'. I didn't see him come back up from the hollow."

"Did you hear Crabbe call out to Peter Wheeler?"

"No, I heard nothing."

"Where did you go after that?" Dr. Lovett continued.

"When my brother and sister met me, we just went back home. Mother asked me what had taken me so long, but I didn't want to tell her.

We got home around six o'clock."

He sounds like a fine outstanding citizen, Benjamin thought. *Whistling at and scaring small children.*

Dr. Lovett read back Sadie's statement to her and had her make her mark at the bottom of the page. He then called John Brooks to the front of the room.

"My name is John Brooks. I live in the lower half of the Reserve here in Bear River," he said. "I attend to Mr. Kempton's barn, so I know the family and the house quite well."

"How do you get there?"

"Sometimes I go right across the river that is between us and strike the road in the hollow by his house, or other times I go up further and cross up and come up behind Kemptons' barn. My boys, one is 16 and one is eight, they go twice a day, morning and evening, to help with farm chores, too. They go the same ways."

"Where is your house situated in relation to the Kemptons'?"

"My house is directly opposite the Kempton house, just on the other side of the river. My house is on the side of the hill, and my windows look directly towards theirs. There is nothing obstructing the view between our houses. Also, my bed is next to the window that faces the Kemptons' house."

"Monday night, the night of the murder, tell us what you could see from your house."

"As soon as it got dark, around five or six o'clock or so, I struck a light in my house. I saw a light coming from the Kemptons' house at the same time. The blind must have been up because I could so plainly see the light. I couldn't see into the room, but the light was coming from the dining room—the room where the body was found."

"And did you see the light go out?" asked Dr. Lovett.

"I was working in my house that night until about ten o'clock and the light was bright and steady up until then. I went to bed around eleven o'clock and it was still on then."

"Did you see it again after that?"

"Yes," continued Brooks. "I got up around two o'clock to see to my little boy who was sick. I looked out the window then, too, and could see a dim light still burning at the Kemptons' house. Then, I got up between three and four o'clock in the morning to strike the fire, and the light was still there in the same room. That was the last time I noticed it."

"Did you see any movement?"

"No, I never noticed any movement. However, my little boy had been out coasting that night, and the next morning he said to me that there must have been people over at the Kemptons' place because he saw the light moving and it looked like people were dancing."

"What time was this?"

"He goes to bed between nine and ten o'clock, so was before then."

"Do you know these times for sure, or are you just guessing?"

"We had a clock, but it doesn't give the correct time. So, I guess I was judging by my own time."

Dr. Lovett dismissed John Brooks, and called for a recess, with the inquest to resume at half-past three that afternoon.

Having heard so much about it during the various witness testimonies, Benjamin decided to head out into the cold and find Troops' restaurant by the bridge to get a bite to eat. He had heard the building was built on stilts to allow for the flow of the river under it at high tide, as many of the other shops and buildings were along the bridge. If it wasn't too cold, he would take time to investigate for himself. Just another part of Bear River's charm, he thought.

When the afternoon session resumed, Isaac Kempton hobbled his way to the front of the room. When he announced he was the father of Annie Kempton, now deceased, his voice quavered, and Benjamin saw women dabbing their eyes with their handkerchiefs.

Mr. Kempton explained how his wife had been away in the States, and he was in the woods, so he had arranged for Tilly Comeau to stay with Annie. There was no payment exchanged, as Tilly would come get milk from them when she needed it.

"I last saw my daughter alive on Monday morning when I left for the woods, and then saw her lying dead on my floor when I returned on Tuesday afternoon."

Benjamin heard Mrs. Kempton sobbing in the front row.

"When I left her on Monday morning, she said she wasn't going to go to school that day. She had gotten her boots a little damp the evening before and wanted to dry them. I suggested to her that she go down to Clarke's store and buy a new pair of overshoes. Then I left for the woods."

"Was Annie in the habit of milking your cow?"

"She would milk the cow if I wasn't home, except when Tilly was expected to stay, as she would do the milking. I get about three pints every morning, or a little less, like a quart at night."

Benjamin tapped his pencil to his lips, thinking about these words.

Omer Rice milked the cow Tuesday morning, saying he got an awful lot of milk that morning. The thought behind this was that the cow had not been milked the previous evening. Annie would milk the cow unless Tilly was coming. So, if Annie didn't milk the cow on Monday night, did this mean she really was expecting Tilly to come and milk the cow?

Benjamin scratched his head, trying to make sense of it all. *If only the cow could talk.*

Keeping on the theme of the cow, Dr. Lovett recalled Omer Rice to discuss how much milk he got when he milked her Tuesday morning, after the body was discovered. Two quarts.

Benjamin quickly did some calculations in the margin of his notepad. Mr. Kempton usually got one-and-a half quarts, or three pints, every morning, but this particular morning, Omer Rice got two quarts, or four pints.

This was a big enough difference in the quantity of milk, worth noting. The other farmers in the room seemed to agree.

The cow couldn't have been milked Monday night.

After Omer Rice, his wife, Susan described the murder scene in great detail, she being one of the first to arrive: how she discovered the room in disarray, and the condition of the body. She recounted having seen Peter at five o'clock going past her field in the opposite direction to the Kemptons'.

The final witnesses called forth were Stella, Percy, and Charles Rice, Stanley Rice's younger siblings and father. Although Peter had claimed he was going there to collect money owed, no one in the household actually saw him.

Dr. Lovett left his position behind the table and came around front to address the crowded room. "Ladies and gentlemen, gentlemen of the jury, that brings to a close the list of witnesses we had hoped to interview for this inquest. Now, we will ask the jury to retire to a room downstairs so they can deliberate."

Detective Power and Dr. Lovett solemnly led the twelve men from the room amidst shouted instructions. "Hang him now!" "Find him guilty, or don't come back!"

Benjamin didn't need to turn around. He knew that voice by heart, now.

Peter remained, head down, motionless, at the front of the room.

Benjamin sat and waited for the jury to return. He wished he could have been in the room to hear the conversation. Was Dunn leading the discussion and influencing the outcome? He was pretty sure their minds were already made up.

But yet, Benjamin continued to have that niggling feeling. *Are there others who could have committed the murder? Are there tramps in the area, as Peter had suggested?*

But yet, too much evidence is stacking up against Peter, he thought. Peter told Tilly not to go to the house to stay with Annie, the cow wasn't milked that evening, Peter was seen in the vicinity of the Kemptons' house, and the other logging men testified to hearing Peter talk salaciously about Annie.

These facts only added to the already well-grounded opinion that Peter was definitely the guilty party.

Even if doubts had started to creep into his mind, doubts and theories did not make people feel at ease. More importantly, they did not sell papers. He needed to keep the end goal in sight, and especially keep ahead of the *Courier*.

Before long, the door at the back of the room swung open, and the jury marched back in, taking their seats at the front of the room.

Dr. Lovett stood and addressed the crowd. "When the verdict is read, I would like to request that you, ladies and gentlemen, act with the utmost decorum. Please do not make any demonstration. Please, listen in silence."

He then asked the jury foreman to read the verdict.

Foreman Reverend Ruggles stood, holding a piece of paper in his hands. "Before I read out the verdict," he began, "I would like to announce that the funeral service for Poor Annie Kempton will take place tomorrow afternoon."

Then, in his loud preacher's voice, he read, "We do upon oath, say that Annie Kempton, between the hour of five o'clock in the afternoon of Monday, the 27th day of January, and the hour of eight o'clock in the morning of Tuesday, 28th day of January, was violently assaulted and struck on the forehead with several heavy blows and had her throat cut in several places, causing her death."

That is interesting, thought Benjamin. *The doctor had clearly said the murder had happened between midnight and two o'clock in the morning. Why the sudden change to extend that to five o'clock the evening before?* This widened range could only mean that new evidence or theories were going to be explored in the coming weeks.

Reverend Ruggles cleared his throat and continued, "And we further say that the said Annie Kempton was thereby feloniously killed and murdered at her father's residence in Bear River. And we suspect Peter Wheeler of Bear River to be guilty of said murder of Annie Kempton."

The verdict was no surprise to Benjamin, but what did surprise him was that the room remained in complete silence, and perfect order prevailed. *In many other places less favoured than Nova Scotia*, he thought, *Wheeler would be torn from the officers of the law and lynched.*

Dr. Lovett addressed the jury. "Thank you for your duty, gentlemen."

To the whole room he said, "The prisoner will be transported immediately to the Digby jail. The preliminary trial will then begin within the next two weeks. I have it on good authority that the Annapolis firm of Mills and Ruggles are willing to defend the prisoner."

Most of his words fell on deaf ears, as people were quietly commenting to each other on the verdict. But Benjamin caught them all. It was interesting that in advance of the jury's verdict, a defence team had already been secured. It was as if they had pre-determined the outcome. Not that it had been hard to guess.

He was also surprised the jury had named a suspect. *Isn't the point of a coroner's inquest to determine how a death occurred? Did she die by suicide, accident, or homicide?* It wasn't supposed to be looking for the guilty party, let alone arresting anyone. *How did this inquest get so off track?*

Around him, Benjamin could hear snippets of conversation. He sat and listened as the spectators filed out of the room. He waited especially for the jury members to walk by, curious as to what they would say.

"Of course, that foreign man killed her!"

Then, above everything else, he could hear Detective Power's voice cutting through the crowd. "I never had a doubt that that Peter Wheeler was the murderer. That was obvious from the start!"

The detective had been relatively quiet throughout the inquest, sitting with arms crossed and surveying the crowded room, letting Dr. Lovett take charge of the questioning. There was no doubt, however, that he had been working hard behind the scenes, asking his own questions, and conducting his own investigation.

6: This was your idea

As was his custom, Benjamin started his morning at the Bear River Hotel restaurant with his cup of tea, poring over the newspaper. He wanted to make sure his stories were getting adequate attention and good placement.

In the centre of the table was a vase full of beautiful pink and white paper flowers. Benjamin made mention of these to the waiter.

"Tragic, really," the man said. "Annie Kempton herself made them for the sleighing party that was to be held here earlier this week. We kept them out in her honour."

"Indeed tragic, which makes them all the more beautiful."

The waiter refilled Benjamin's teacup and laid down a copy of the *Digby Courier* beside him. "Some morning reading, sir. It's Friday, so we have copies of the weekly paper for you today."

The man probably didn't realize Benjamin was the competition to the local paper. He smiled and thanked him anyway.

He took the opportunity to devour the article about the murder, comparing it to his own. This journalist certainly had a way of cutting to the chase. Reporters' names were never attached to the articles, so Benjamin still had no idea the man's name, but knew his face well.

He followed along with his finger as he read, not wanting to miss a single word.

> Wheeler has kept up his bold front through all the investigation. If he is guilty, as certainly is very probable, he is remarkably cool and an audacious villain. He has not borne an entirely credible record in Bear River, but no one hardly thought the man possible of such fearful conduct. The Bear River people want justice, and their investigation has been only to that end. Wheeler is having only his dues. He has been interviewed by pressmen and tells such a story as criminals always do. If it turns out to be true, all will be well; but meantime such a case of brutal butchery needs

to be given no leniency.

Benjamin folded up that newspaper and turned to find his own headline in the *Halifax Herald*: "The Coroner's Verdict on Poor Annie Kempton – The Jury Pronounce It Murder and Suspect Wheeler."

Not bad, he thought. A headline like that would cause the newspapers to fly off the shelves.

He knew what else sold papers—interviews with Detective Power. Benjamin laid down his napkin, pushed his chair back, and went off in search of the detective.

After wandering around town, Benjamin managed to find the detective at one of the other hotels in the village. He did not have to exert much enticement, and soon the two men were sitting together to discuss the case.

"How have you found your time in Bear River?"

"I shall leave tomorrow, on the first of February. Three days are all that were needed to draw this case to a close and for me to fully grasp the situation."

"What can you tell our readers about what is happening with the case?"

"I have been working hard behind the scenes, in preparation for the preliminary trial which will be happening here next week. I cannot say too much in advance of that, but what I can tell you is that I have discovered some very important evidence against Wheeler."

"Can you give us an inkling of what that evidence is?"

"I shall say nothing until I am called forth as a witness. But what I can tell you, and if you print it, I shall say it is only rumours, is that there is new blood evidence found on Wheeler's clothes, which was not at first exhibited. And that we found a button that corresponds with his coat."

"I don't remember a button coming up in the inquest," Benjamin said.

Detective Power raised an eyebrow as if demanding to know why he was being questioned.

"I mean to say, that that is great detective work!" Benjamin hastily added.

"Regardless, the chain of evidence is strong enough, even without any new evidence. But we have plenty of it. I will prove that the man is guilty. Besides, other strong evidence has just come out this morning. You will be one of the first to know."

"This morning?"

"Yes, I accompanied Constable Henshaw as he took our prisoner to the jail in Digby. While we were driving, Wheeler turned to me in the carriage and said that something didn't come out in the inquest. When I pressed him further, he said it was something that he felt would do him some good."

"What was it?"

"It was a story about him and another lad on the night of the murder. He refused to name the other young man, but when I came back to Bear River this morning, I put my investigative powers to the test and discovered it was, as I had suspected, Hardy Benson."

"What happened? What is this new evidence?"

Hardy

"What's the time?" Hardy Benson asked Peter.

Hardy and Peter were standing outside of the Comeau house, having just come from walking into town with the family. The two men decided to head back earlier than the rest.

"I reckon it's around half-past seven," Peter replied.

Hardy kept looking up towards the Kemptons' house in hopes Annie might come walking down the hill. "When is Tilly going up to stay with Annie?"

"She's not, after all. When I was up there this morning, she told me to tell Tilly not to bother coming. Annie knew that Tilly was working all week at the hotel, and she'd have to work all day, go up to the house to stay with Annie, wake up, come back down to her own house, have breakfast, and walk back over to the hotel again and work all day. Annie figured it was too much for Tilly."

Hardy nodded.

"Instead, she said Grace Morine is going to come over to stay with her."

"Do you think Annie is home yet? Or is Grace up with her, yet? I can just make out a faint light in the window up there and looks like someone is moving around. Maybe we should go up and pay a call."

"What? Go up and visit Annie now?"

"Yeah, we could find out if she's going to the meeting tonight over at the Salvation Army. That starts relatively soon. Come on, let's go!" Hardy said.

"I don't know, Hardy. I'm busy getting ready to go to camp tomorrow."

"We'll just go for a minute to find out about her plans."

"Fine," said Peter, giving in. "But just for a quick visit."

The two trudged up the hill through the snow and arrived at the gate that was a stone's throw from the Kemptons' front door. Peter stepped towards the house but noticed that Hardy had not gone beyond the gate.

"Let's go, then," Peter said.

"No, just you go."

"This was your idea."

"I have on my old clothes. You go in and ask her if she's coming out. Be a pal and go in for me. I don't like to go in. But don't let Annie know I'm here," Hardy said.

Peter sighed and ran around the corner of the house to the back door. After about two or three minutes, he returned. Hardy was pacing at the gate. Peter ran up and put his arms around Hardy.

"What happened? Is she coming? What is she doing?"

"Let me answer, boy!" said Peter. "She is in there making her paper flowers. I asked her if she was going to the meeting, but she asked why I wanted to know. I just said, because."

"Is Grace there with her?"

"No, she is alone."

"What did she say about going out?"

"She said she would get ready right away," Peter said.

Hardy beamed. "Don't let on we were up here," he said.

"Why?"

"I don't want anyone to know that I come up here at night when Annie is alone," he said.

"Don't worry, my lad," Peter said to the young teenager in love. "I'll never tell on you. But if I were going with a girl, and I found out she was coming out, I would wait for her."

"Some other time," he said with a shrug.

Peter and Hardy headed back down the hill towards the Comeau house and turned around to see if the light was out and if Annie was on her way, but it was still burning bright.

"Come on, let's go wait inside at Tilly's. It's about eight o'clock. She'll probably be down later," Peter said.

Half an hour later, there was still no sign of Annie. Tilly returned and Hardy left.

The reporter

"That's quite the tale!" said Benjamin. "What did Hardy Benson have to say when you questioned him?"

"He did admit to going up there but tells a much different version of events. According to Benson, it was Wheeler's idea to go up to see Annie, but Benson refused to go in. He said Wheeler was in the house for about fifteen minutes, compared to the three minutes that Wheeler claimed."

"Curious," said Benjamin. "How do you figure out who is telling the truth?"

"Benson said that when Wheeler came out of the house, he ran towards him and put his arms around him. As they walked back down the hill, Wheeler told Benson not to tell anyone that they had been at the Kemptons' house. Then, Wheeler told Benson that Annie was there by herself, and he should go back and stay with her."

"What did Hardy say to that?"

"Said he wasn't going to do that and went back home. Respectable lad. He had made an oath to Mrs. Kempton to never visit Annie while she was alone. He will have reason to remember all his life that it pays to keep a promise made to a good woman. For, had he listened to Wheeler's counsel, he might now be behind bars, charged with the murder of the girl he loved!"

The thought had crossed Benjamin's mind, too. He wondered if therefore Peter had told this tale as a way to implicate Hardy. The plan seemed to have backfired.

"Why didn't any of this come out before?"

"Apparently, right after the murder, Wheeler cautioned Benson not to say anything about them being up there, as there were two knives on the floor, and it would appear as if they had each used a knife."

"But if Benson did nothing wrong, why wouldn't he have said all of this during the inquest?"

"You must remember," said Detective Power, "he is only a young lad, barely 16 years. Wheeler is more than a decade his senior. In Benson's defence, the boy said he answered all the questions that were asked of him and merely withheld the rest for fear that, as Wheeler had told him, he might be blamed."

"I'm assuming this adds to the chain of evidence against Wheeler," Benjamin said.

"It certainly does, and when you put it all together as a complete story, you will see there is no other conclusion.

"Would you please oblige us by sharing your chain of evidence?" Benjamin asked. He felt he, too, needed to be convinced.

"I would be delighted to," said the detective, leaning back in his chair.

"It all starts with Mr. Kempton being away from the house and arranging for Tilly Comeau to sleep there in his absence. Wheeler's story is that he was around the Kemptons' house before noon, and that Annie said to tell Tilly she was no longer required, as Grace Morine was going to stay instead. Wheeler then told the same story to Hardy Benson—who comes from a very respectable family, by the way. By telling this to both Tilly and Hardy Benson, he was paving the way to have the poor girl alone."

Benjamin nodded.

"Then, late in the afternoon, Wheeler is seen going towards the Kempton house, but he does not go there straight. He took a circuitous route, going the back of the hill so that he could reach there without passing a house and without being seen. However, he *was* seen by Elmer Crabbe, and then by the young Morine girl. This was around half-past five."

This is all true, Benjamin thought, *according to witness accounts.*

"For half an hour, Wheeler is lost to view, but in 30 or 35 minutes, he is seen again, this time by a Comeau boy at six o'clock, who is cutting wood near the Kemptons' house. Wheeler says he went to Stanley Rice's house to collect money."

Detective Power leaned forward and tapped on Benjamin's notepad, ensuring he would get the next details recorded properly. "However, the Rice family all swear that Peter Wheeler was not there. Wheeler claims he had been setting rabbit snares, which is evidently a lie, for no trace of rabbit snares was to be found."

Benjamin nodded again, not wanting to interrupt.

"This means, then, that there is more than half an hour from the time the man and the girl saw Wheeler at the back of the Kempton house till he came upon the Comeau boy alongside the road."

Detective Power raised a finger to emphasize his words.

"There was ample time to commit the murder."

He let the statement hang in the air, and smugly nodded his head.

"And what did Wheeler do after had had committed the murder?" Benjamin asked.

"Wheeler helped the boy get his wood into the house, and then went on to the village with Tilly and her family. There, he met Hardy Benson, and he turned away from the others for a walk with Benson. Wheeler then suggested that the two of them go up to Annie's house, and when they got there, Benson refused to go in and instead waited at the gate."

"Was the murder actually committed after eight o'clock, then?"

"Wait and see," said Detective Power, cautioning Benjamin not to interrupt. "Wheeler then disappears into the house. Benson waits for Peter at the gate, as directed. He may not have thought much of it at the time, but Benson says it was called forcibly to his mind afterwards that Wheeler appeared very nervous and seemed strangely broken up. Then, Benson says that Wheeler put his arms around him and said, 'The little Satan is in the house all alone!' Then the two left the scene of the murder and went back to the Comeau house."

"He did not say that!"

"Benson swears it is the truth. Those were Peter Wheeler's words. This part of the story came out much later, after Benson's first telling."

"This is worse than I had thought," Benjamin said.

"Wheeler then tried to convince Hardy to go back and stay with Annie, as she was alone. However, Wheeler knew that Benson was a kind and bashful person and would refuse to do so, therefore it was safe to suggest. It was when they got back to the Comeau house that Wheeler said to Tilly that she need not go up to stay with Annie, for Grace was there. This was said in Benson's hearing."

"I certainly did not know all the facts when I first formulated my opinion," Benjamin said.

"None of us did, but I am certain beyond doubt that we have the truth of the matter now, and my theory is built upon these facts."

"What is your conclusion, then, of what happened?"

"I believe that we can prove that Wheeler stunned or killed Annie Kempton on that first visit, between half-past five and six o'clock in the evening, and that the second time, while Benson waited outside, he cut her throat to make sure of his work if she was not already dead, for dead men tell no tales. Or because he thought by using the knives upon her, he might thereby disarm suspicion."

"And we already know what happens in the morning."

"Indeed," said the detective. "In the morning, earlier than usual and contrary to his usual custom, Wheeler offered to go for the milk. He reached the house, and everyone knows how he made his pretend discovery and how he announced it. It was not natural, the way he spoke of the awful event. It was not natural that he should handle the body as he says he did and throw his coat over it. Many men would be more startled at suddenly and unexpectedly coming upon a dead dog."

"Now that you mention it....," said Benjamin, pausing to get a fresh notebook.

"After the discovery, Benson appears in the story again. Wheeler orders Benson not to tell anyone, for their life, that they were near the house, as they would be blamed because of the two knives found.

Wheeler told Benson just to say they had seen a light in the distance, rather than that he was at the house. Adding to that, right before Benson is to go on the stand, Benson swears that Wheeler sent a boy to him with a message, telling him again to only mention the light."

"And you think the assault was committed during the first visit to the Kempton house?" Benjamin asked.

"I have no doubt of it," Detective Power said confidently. "I think the knife was used on the second visit while Hardy waited at the gate. One reason I have for this belief is because only a very small quantity of blood was found—not more than a square foot on the floor. There was nothing like the quantity that would have been shed had the poor girl's throat been cut when she was still alive."

Benjamin admonished himself for not having seen the truth of this before. He had become so swept up in Peter's personal tale that he failed to see the evidence laid out as a whole.

"The doctors will probably ask to examine the body further to determine the condition of it when the cutting was done, and to learn whether the blows on the head were sufficient to cause death."

"What are your particular reasons for thinking Peter killed the girl in the evening rather than at midnight, as the doctors mentioned?"

"There has been a great deal of speculation as to the time when the crime was committed. Some thought it was during the night, others in the morning when Peter went for the milk. After going over the ground carefully, I am of the opinion that Annie Kempton was killed by Wheeler between half-past five and six o'clock in the evening."

"What are your reasons?"

"The Kemptons' custom was to milk the cow between six and seven o'clock and it was Annie's business to milk. In the morning, after the tragedy, the cow gave twice the quantity of milk of the day previously and of the day that followed the discovery. The cow had not been milked."

Benjamin nodded. He didn't know much about cows, but this sounded plausible.

"The time is further shown by the fact that the beans the girl had put in the oven for her supper were still there when the body was found in the morning. Another reason for thinking as I do is that the girl was dressed in the costume she would wear in her household duties. Her clothing showed she had not yet gone to bed, as she had on a wrapper, and inside garments. Her back hair was done up just as it was on the street."

"What do you think will happen from here?"

"I think that, at the preliminary examination, which starts at the end of the week, the chain of evidence will be complete."

"Do you have any doubts?"

"I do not have the slightest doubt of the guilt of the accused and that he did the murder between half-past five and six o'clock in the evening, to cover up the traces of his attempt at another crime, or in anger at his failure."

"How do you feel the inquiry was conducted?"

"Dr. Lovett performed his duties to perfection," the detective said.

Benjamin flipped back through his pages of notes and started to write some concluding thoughts. His mind was racing with new questions. Detective Power made a powerful case, but there were still unanswered questions.

It had snowed overnight. Couldn't Wheeler's tracks have been covered up?

The coroner and doctor said the murder had happened between midnight and two o'clock in the morning, but yet, Detective Power figured out a different timeline for the murder. The detective placed the murder seven hours earlier, around dusk. Who was right?

Was the detective more concerned about finding Peter guilty than looking for other leads?

But what did he know about detective work? If Detective Power said Wheeler was guilty, then he had to be. *He was right, there was so much evidence stacked against him. It made sense once you put all the pieces together.*

Detective Power saw that Benjamin had finished writing and said, "Read it back to me."

Normally, Benjamin would not agree to such a request, but he always did so for the detective. Not only did the man like to be in control of his image in the media, but if he was happy, he always provided the paper with great content that their readers flocked to get.

"Mr. Power did effective work, and once more showed himself an accomplished detective. He has not the slightest doubt that Peter Wheeler is guilty of the murder, and that a chain of circumstantial evidence will be forged which will certainly end in the prisoner's conviction."

Detective Power leaned back in his chair, and steepled his fingers, pressing his index fingers against his lips. He took a deep breath, held it a moment, released it, and finally said, "I like it."

Benjamin smiled. They were both happy.

7: Larrigan boots

It was Sunday afternoon, and the village of Bear River was starting to quieten again. With the inquest over, and the preliminary trial not set to start for five days, the sensation-seekers had returned home, only to prepare to come back for the trial.

With a few hours before his train to Halifax, Benjamin decided to go to Annie's funeral service that afternoon in the Methodist church.

He walked down the hill from his hotel, across the bridge into Annapolis County, and back up to the small, white church on the crest of the hill, just below the schoolhouse. As usual during his time in Bear River, Benjamin didn't have to ask for directions. He merely followed the stream of people like a sheep or one ant in a line.

As he entered the church doors, a distinguished-looking gentleman approached. "Excuse me, sir. We are endeavouring to collect funds to place a memorial in the Mount Hope Cemetery, here in the village, in honour of Annie Kempton. We are asking one hundred men to contribute a mere dollar each. Would you be willing to add your dollar to show your appreciation for her valour and commemorate her virtue?"

With a delivery like that, Benjamin could hardly resist, nor would he have. He reached into his inner jacket pocket to pull out his billfold and handed the man a note.

"My pleasure to contribute," he said.

"Thank you, sir," the gentleman replied. "Annie Kempton was a real heroine whose deeds through this may not appear as history, but yet they are worthy of recognition because of their virtuousness. Is not a person who considers the honour of virtue before life, a hero? There are everyday heroes who walk amongst us with their heroism unknown. We think Annie Kempton was such a hero. Her name should be recorded in honour."

"Do you have much further to raise to reach your goal?"

"I believe by the end of the week we will have had our needs met."

"Thank you, sir," said Benjamin, reaching out to shake the man's hand. He then made his way into the sanctuary to get a seat, and to allow the gentleman to continue canvasing for his noble cause.

"For he has set a day when he will judge the world with justice by the man he has appointed!" declared the reverend from the pulpit, reading from the book of Acts.

Benjamin listened intently to the sermon, which he deemed to have been one of the most scholarly ones he had heard in a while. The reverend not only gave a glowing tribute to Annie, extolling her courage and virtue, but also shared the lessons to be learned from the whole sordid affair. Most specifically, the minister addressed the many youths in the congregation, telling them there were examples to profit by and, more importantly, roads in life that should be shunned.

The minister concluded the service with a few anecdotes about Annie, highlighting her joy for life.

Annie

"Now off you go!" said Annie, sending a group of small children on a task. "Remember! They have to be just the right size."

"What are you doing, Annie?" asked Grace Morine, who had come up behind her.

Annie just smiled her mischievous grin.

"Annie? Should I even ask?" Grace asked.

"I was just telling them the legend about the giant oak tree outside the school. No one had ever seen fit to tell them the story, and so I thought it was my duty to educate them."

"Which one? The tale of it being 500 years old?"

"No, about how, back in the old days, Mr. Harris' grandfather walked to Bear River from Halifax. The man must have walked and walked for days just to get here. And as he walked, he used an oaken walking stick as his cane."

Grace looked mystified.

"What do you mean? You've never heard this story either?" Annie asked

Grace's silence encouraged Annie to continue. "So, Mr. Harris, walks all this way from Halifax, and when he finally gets here, he decides to rest. He takes his oak walking stick and sticks it in the ground right over there," she said, pointing to the tree. "And that walking stick has grown into the grand old tree we now have in our school yard, and it's why we call it the Oakdene Academy."

"That is so not true," Grace said.

"How do you know?"

Before the argument could continue, the group of young children returned. Each held a couple of sticks in their fists, which they had collected from the ground beneath the massive tree.

"Tell me what you are telling them now!"

"Wait and see," Annie said, leading the group back to sit under the
shelter of the tree.

She stood beside the tree and said, "Now, children, if you take these
sticks that you have collected from this very tree, and stick them into the
ground, just as Mr. Harris' grandfather did all those years ago, then those
sticks, too, will grow into trees, just like this one!"

Grace groaned and rolled her eyes, which just made Annie laugh and
be more determined to help the children dig holes for their sticks.

The reporter

A few younger children in the congregation giggled at the story, remembering how they went back to check every day to see how much their
stick had grown.

Regardless of whether it was true, it still made a great story, and made
the children love Annie even more.

With a heavy heart and a feeling he had truly gotten to know not only
Annie Kempton but the residents of Bear River, Benjamin took his leave.
He found the same driver to take him to the station for the trek back to
Halifax.

After a few days of rest, he would be back in Bear River again.

~

Benjamin came down the steps of the train onto the platform of the
Digby station. Despite the cold, and it being mid-week, there were quite a
few people milling about on the platform. It seemed like he had hardly
been home before he turned around and travelled the 130-mile journey
back to the area. The last journey, however, he had only gone as far as
Bear River. This time, he came all the way into the town of Digby. He had
some research to do.

He pulled the collar of his wool coat up and tightened his scarf around
his neck. From the station he could see the Annapolis Basin and could

feel the cold wind coming off the Bay of Fundy just beyond that.

Digby was the main commercial and transportation hub for the area. Not only did the Dominion Atlantic Railway pass through town on its way to Yarmouth, in the south, but there was a deal of ship traffic. The wharves were full of fishing vessels, and steamers made daily runs between Annapolis Royal and Saint John, New Brunswick, and trips twice a week to Boston.

Benjamin wasn't quite sure where he was going, so stopped to ask the station master for directions to the courthouse and jail.

"Oh!" the man replied. "You're one of them! Come to get a look at the infamous Peter Wheeler, accused of murder, have you? I have been directing people all day."

Benjamin merely nodded and followed the man's finger, which pointed up the hill, just beyond the station.

Benjamin could see two buildings standing out from amongst the sea captain houses that overlooked the water. Rather than hire a carriage, he decided to walk the ten minutes to get a better sense of the lay of the land.

As he walked up the hill, he saw four grand buildings in a row. To the far left was the spire of what he was told was the Anglican Church. Next was a solid, classy-looking brick building with a wooden cupola on top. It was the Digby Academy, only opened a couple of years prior. Next came the courthouse.

Then, finally, in front of him stood the Digby County jail. It was a two-story wooden building, which paled in comparison to the grand schoolhouse. Benjamin wondered how the community felt, having the school right next to where they housed hardened criminals such as Peter Wheeler. He would have to remember to investigate that further.

The jail actually took up the basement of the large building. The sheriff and his family lived in the grand wooden building above. In front of the building there was a covered porch. A white picket fence encircled the property.

Benjamin climbed the stairs to the main doors, knocked and entered. Inside, he immediately recognized the reporter from the *Digby Courier*. His heart sank. The competition. He had managed to avoid the man all week until now, and he was trapped.

"Sabean. Simon Sabean," he said reaching out his hand, as if reading Benjamin's mind. Benjamin forced a smile and introduced himself.

"I suppose you too, are here to see the prisoner," Simon said. "People have been coming here all week, trying to get in to see Peter Wheeler, but they have been turning them all away. Lucky for us, this morning they are just letting in members of the press."

Benjamin could never figure out people's morbid fascination with death and murder. He did know, however, that the more sensational the story, the more newspapers they sold. The public loved any titillating crimes, especially ones with sexual references or violence. Anything that was out of societal conventions made it all the more exciting.

"I am hoping to catch a quick word with Wheeler."

"That's all you'll get, anyway," said the reporter. looking at his pocket watch. "They need to leave in an hour, to get to Bear River in time for the start of the preliminary trial." He gestured with his head toward where Peter was being held. "What's your take on all this?"

Benjamin hated to admit it, but the more they talked, the more he liked the man. "My opinion about the murder?"

"Regarding the man's guilt. I have just come from interviewing him. He is certainly acting with a great deal of self-control and courage. He tried to assure me numerous times of his innocence. Kept going on about how he was being unjustly treated and having to bear the blame of an-other's crime. Can you imagine? The nerve!"

Benjamin just nodded, not wanting to interrupt the flow.

"The network of circumstantial evidence points in the strongest way to Wheeler, with a clarity seldom surpassed in criminal cases."

"I have to admit, I was as convinced as you, at first, of his guilt," Benjamin said.

"At first?" The reporter gave him a look of incredulousness.

"And then Detective Power explained his well-laid-out theory, suppor-ted by circumstantial evidence, as you say."

"But?"

"But there are just a few niggling bits in my mind. Inconsistencies that just don't seem to add up."

Simon stared open-mouthed at Benjamin, before emitting a loud guf-faw. He slapped Benjamin hard on the back. "You had me there for a mo-ment, old chap! Made me believe you thought Peter Wheeler was actually innocent!"

Benjamin smiled, reminding himself to keep his internal dialogue just that. *Internal*.

"I think Wheeler knows his time will soon be up, for he is becoming more anxious. I feel strongly he is implicating himself with contradic-tions in his story," Simon added confidently.

"I guess we will find out soon enough," said Benjamin, stepping around him to make his way towards the prisoner's cell.

"I'll save you a seat!" called Simon over his shoulder.

~

"Mercy sakes alive!" Benjamin cried when his carriage finally pulled up the steep hill into the grounds of the Bear River Exhibition.

Outside the large red barn, that was primarily used for agricultural fairs, were dozens and dozens of teams of horses. Drivers were trying to manoeuvre around each other, lest their reins or wheels become entangled. A few members of the community attempted to direct traffic and help the visitors hitch up in an orderly fashion.

Benjamin jumped down and pushed his way through the crowd, attempting to find Simon from the *Digby Courier*, to see if he was a man of his word and had indeed saved him a seat.

When he entered the barn, however, he stood in shock. There were hundreds and hundreds of people, maybe close to one thousand, who had come out to witness the preliminary trial. Benjamin wondered if everyone in the entire province was in that one room, as it indeed felt that way. No wonder the men outside had talked about having to add buttresses to the end of the building, lest it burst at the seams.

Benjamin kept inching his way to the front. When he was nearly there, Simon stood and waved a handkerchief in the air as a signal.

"I wasn't sure how much longer I could save this seat! If you didn't come soon, I feared I would be the next one murdered, just for the bench!" Simon laughed, but quickly covered his mouth, realizing the crassness of his statement.

Benjamin patted him on the back and offered his gratitude.

Shortly thereafter, Justice Wallace Purdy, the local justice of the peace, appeared at the front. He was an unusually tall man, and his presence filled the room. The community described him as a nobleman who used plenty of the Queen's English. He was also known to be impartial and fair in his judgment.

Justice Purdy bowed his head, closed his eyes, and pressed an index finger to his forehead. Benjamin could almost read his mind, trying to figure out how these proceedings were to happen with so many people. There was no way that people beyond the first third of the room would even hear.

Benjamin looked over again at Simon next to him and smiled in thankfulness.

In his loud, booming voice, Justice Purdy brought the session to order.

Benjamin was not sure who was a bigger or more intimidating man, Justice Purdy or Detective Power. He vowed never to be on the wrong side of the law with either of them.

Seated at a table behind the magistrate was the crown prosecutor, Albert Copp, from Digby. Not only was the man a prominent lawyer, but he also had political aspirations. He had been nominated for the head of the Liberal party for Digby County for an election that would be held later that year. Word on the street was that he was a shoo-in.

Sitting beside Peter Wheeler was Henry Ruggles, a lawyer practising with the Mills and Ruggles firm in Annapolis Royal. He was to represent Peter throughout the trial. Benjamin doubted that Ruggles would be making any money taking on this case. He had overheard Ruggles say he only did so because he took pity on Peter with him being a foreigner and being alone in the world.

Sitting off to the side was the court clerk, taking the minutes of the proceedings. Benjamin also recognized him as the man heading up the committee to get a memorial stone for Annie, who had spoken to him at the funeral service.

Benjamin sighed, knowing this was going to be a long morning, and it would also be loud, and therefore hard for him to concentrate. Those in the front would be whispering to the people behind them, relaying what was said, as if it were the childhood game. The one positive is that, with all the bodies in the hall, he would not be cold.

Justice Purdy first called on Dr. Lovett "Dr. Lovett, can you please outline the details of your report that you presented at the inquest last week?"

"Objection!" Ruggles shouted, jumping to his feet.

Benjamin looked to his neighbour with raised eyebrows. The day's proceedings were already off to an interesting start.

"Explain," said Justice Purdy.

"I have two points to make regarding the doctor's report. First, the evidence presented at the inquest was done in a different county to where we are today."

Benjamin inhaled quickly. He had not seen that coming. The lawyer certainly did have a point about introducing evidence from a different county. The inquest had started at the Kempton home in Digby County and finished at the hall in Annapolis County. This was the trouble with having the county line go down the middle of the town, he thought.

"Second, when Dr. Ellison wrote his report about the condition of the body, Peter Wheeler was not present, and therefore did not have the opportunity to be cross-examined. Because of these two points, the coroner's report should not be admissible in this trial."

"I acknowledge your argument, and agree with your reasoning," the judge said, as Copp scowled from the prosecution table. "Therefore, I will not allow this evidence to affect my judgment."

"Thank you, Squire Purdy."

Dr. Lovett proceeded with his report, talking about the position of the body when found, the garments on the victim, and where blood was found. He also amended his statement.

Originally, the doctor had reported that Annie had died twelve hours previously, but now said she might have been killed 48 hours earlier, instead.

Benjamin couldn't help but wonder if this change was urged on by Detective Power, so that it better matched his theory.

"I cannot judge definitely," the doctor explained. "The time it takes for a body to cool after death varies according to the temperature of the surrounding atmosphere and varies with different people. I had tested the temperature of the body with my hand, but this would only have given me a relative idea."

"At this point, was the body completely cooled or was there a slight degree of heat that remained?" asked Ruggles for the defence.

"I could not say. For if blood had been taken from the body at the time of death, the body would cool somewhat more rapidly. I might have noticed a degree of heat; she was almost cold."

The doctor also added the possibility that Annie Kempton may have already been dead when her throat was cut.

"Would it have been possible," asked Ruggles in his cross examination, "for the victim to have died in the cramped-up position in which she was found, with her arms and legs bent?"

"It would have been possible, I believe. However, the body was moved before I had a chance to fully see and examine it. The house was full of people by the time I got there."

When Ruggles finished, Copp jumped to his feet.

"From what you are describing, there wasn't very much blood at the scene. Can you say that the cause of death was the cut to the throat?"

"There were bruises on the head as well. I do not think there was enough blood to show that death had definitely been caused by the cuts."

"And for someone of Annie's heft, how long would have that taken for her body to cool?" asked Copp.

"It might have taken 12, 24 or 48 hours, or less than any of these, to cool."

That was precise. Benjamin laughed inaudibly, but he wrote it down anyway. If the doctor could not pinpoint the time of death based on cooling, then there certainly could have been time for Peter to have killed Annie earlier in the evening, as Detective Power had suggested.

The next few witnesses reported the same information that they had presented at the inquest. Throughout it all, Peter sat at the table next to his defence counsel, leaning forward, taking in every word.

"He certainly is putting a lot of trust in his counsel," said Simon, elbowing Benjamin and gesturing towards the front of the room. "Seems like a lost cause, though."

"By English law, a man is entitled to a fair trial. Wheeler should have one, too, regardless of where he is from," Benjamin reminded him. "The justice system is essentially accountable for two lives here—Annie Kempton's and now, Peter Wheeler's. Nothing should be done with uncertainty."

"True," Simon agreed. "But the evidence points so strongly towards Wheeler's guilt that it seems there is no way he will be able to escape conviction. This would be justice."

Before Benjamin could respond, Justice Purdy continued with the next witness. Everything seemed the same until Omer Rice began an account of an event that had happened after the inquest.

At the inquest he had talked about having gone looking for footprints in the snow with the other two men the morning before the inquest; however, this time he talked about going again afterwards with Detective Power. This must have been some of the new evidence the detective had alluded to.

Omer

"Where exactly did you see the tracks, gentlemen? Please direct me right away," Detective Power ordered.

Once again, Omer grabbed the corn broom and slung it over his shoulder. "You going to be okay in this deep snow?"

"Never you mind me. I am made of hardy stuff!"

"At least let me carry your bag. We are more used to traipsing through the snow than you are," said Bernard Parker, reaching out his hand.

Reluctantly, Detective Power handed over his satchel. Then he followed the men across the field behind Omer's barn.

When they had followed the tracks to the top of the hill, Detective Power commanded the group to stop. "Here is a good place," he said kneeling beside the prints. "Pass me my satchel."

After Omer had swept away some of the snow that had drifted into the prints, the detective took his measurer from his bag.

"Ten inches," he said measuring the track from heel to toe.

"I concur," Bernard said.

Next, the detective pulled out a pair of worn, oiled-leather work boots, stitched together like a pair of moccasins.

"Whose larrigans are those?" Omer asked.

"I took them from Wheeler when he was imprisoned."

Detective Power then placed the boot on the snow beside the footprint. "I judge these to be the same size."

Omer and Bernard nodded.

"We need to be certain," the detective said. He put his hand inside the boot and pressed it down into the snow next to the existing footprint. He then took out his ruler and measured again, determining this new print to also be ten inches.

Then, he took the boot and placed it overtop the old footprint. Once again, he put his hand inside the boot and pressed down. "Just as I thought. They are the same size. These tracks were made by these boots. These tracks are definitely made by Peter Wheeler."

The two men stared in amazement, excited to witness such detective work.

"Let's test the tracks in a few other places along the trail to compare, but I am confident the results will be the same," the detective said. "We will also compare the stride, but we already know what we will find."

After determining that the stride length and the size of the footprints were consistent throughout the trail, Detective Power congratulated the men for having collected such valuable evidence.

As they returned to the road, Elmer Crabbe came up the hill and joined them.

"Thank you for meeting us, Mr. Crabbe," Detective Power said. "Now, I would like you to show me where you were standing when you saw Peter Wheeler."

He stood in Peter's position and listened for Elmer to call out to him.

"Hello Peter! Where are you going?" called Elmer.

"I can hear you plain enough," the detective said.

"So could I," Bernard confirmed.

"Definitely solid evidence," said the detective.

He continued to follow the tracks down the hill towards the Kemptons' house, with the other three men in tow.

The reporter

"Mr. Rice, you mention tracking, measuring and examining these larrigan tracks," Ruggles said in his cross examination.

"Yes, they were a match to Peter Wheeler's boots," Omer Rice said.

"So you say. How common are larrigan boots in these parts?"

"A great many people around here wear larrigans," he confessed. "Especially in the wintertime."

"Are there any distinguishing marks on the bottom of these boots? Like a heel or tread?"

"No, they are soft-bottomed shoes. They have no treads, and they have no heels. They are like moccasins, made for walking in the snow. Lumbermen and trappers tend to wear them a lot around here. The print of one pair of larrigans looks like another in terms of shape and everything except for size."

"Does Mr. Kempton wear larrigans on his own land?" Ruggles asked.

"I think he does. Or at least he does on one foot. I don't know what he wears on his wooden leg."

"So, I repeat: the tracks could have been made by anyone."

"They were a match to Peter Wheeler's boots when we measured them," Omer fired back.

"No further questions," Ruggles said.

After three and a half hours, the judge released Omer Rice from his testimony. By this time, dusk was falling, so Justice Purdy adjourned for the day, calling for a ten o'clock start for the following morning.

This began the mass exodus, and a tangle of carriages trying to exit the grounds, only to repeat the process the next day.

8: Put it down right!

By the time Benjamin had walked from the Bear River Hotel to the exhibition hall for the second day of the preliminary trial, snow was already coming down heavily. Word in town was that it was going to be quite the storm. Last night it had rained slightly, and then the temperature dropped, causing ice to freeze on the roads.

Benjamin could barely get his grip walking up the hill towards the hall. It was like walking on a sheet of glass. He wished that one of the numerous teams that passed would stop to offer him a ride, but he was to have no such luck.

Judging by the number of teams passing him on the road, the weather wasn't going to deter people from coming to the trial. With it being winter and much of the community farmers, there was little else to do at this time of year. People who arrived late would be forced to turn back or wait outside in the snow for any news from the overcrowded hall.

Benjamin made his way to the front of the crowded room where, once again, Simon had saved him a seat. One of these mornings, Benjamin vowed, he would get there first.

He sat back and did what he loved the most—listen to the discussions happening around him. Two women beside him were having an involved discussion. He couldn't quite discern their ages, for their bonnets blocked their faces, and women of all ages dressed alike in Bear River.

"Wheeler must have a fair trial. It's only right," said the first woman.

"No doubt he will be found guilty, though. All the evidence points in that direction," answered the second.

"I don't see any other possible outcome."

"I, for one, think he might actually be innocent."

Benjamin nodded. The same thought had passed his mind.

The first woman gasped. "What? Has the devil possessed your soul, too? I cannot believe you would even say such a thing! How can you not see what the rest of clearly do? Be careful of saying that too loudly."

The second woman hung her head.

"It doesn't matter how eloquently he may plead his innocence in the jail cell, we all know he is guilty of this most heinous crime," insisted the first.

Peter Wheeler certainly does not have many friends in this crowd, Benjamin thought. He looked at the man, already seated at the front of the room. Peter appeared anxious and unsettled, his eyes darting everywhere. This was a much different display than during the inquest, when he sat calm, cool and collected next to his counsel.

Dr. Ellison was the first witness of the day. Like Dr. Lovett, he outlined his report, describing the condition of the body when he examined it. His evidence was practically the same as had been given at the inquest.

He described the five distinct wounds he discovered on the body: one on the forehead, one on the right side above the ear, and three cuts on the throat. Two of the cuts were superficial, while the third was two-and-a-half inches deep, cut the windpipe and jugular vein and would have caused death. Most importantly, he assured the room that Annie had not been outraged or violated.

"Would the blows to the head be enough to kill her?" Copp asked. "Or would the effect be to stagger her and that is about all?"

"It might have knocked her down and she would be totally insensible," Dr. Ellison replied. "Or it might have fractured a vein or an artery and caused compression or a concussion of the brain from the shock of one of these blows."

"There seems to have been little blood from the throat cuts," Copp said. "Can you please explain?"

"If the victim had received a shock from a blow on the head, the throat wounds would have bled very little 'til a reaction took place. Annie Kempton was a robust girl. I think she probably rallied from the shock from the blow to the head, and then got up and wandered around a bit and fell down again. That is, provided the blow to the head did not render her a serious concussion to the brain."

"What position do you think the body was in when the cuts were made?"

"I think she would have been lying prone, straight out and face down," said Dr. Ellison.

"Could these cuts to the throat have been inflicted had the girl been on her hands and knees?" Attorney Ruggles asked in his cross examination.

"Yes, they could have."

"And how many hours earlier do you think the murder took place?"

"I did not test the temperature of the body. The fleshier a person, the longer it takes for the body to cool."

"How many hours?" Ruggles insisted.

"Well, I examined the body in the afternoon. I would say between 15 to 20 hours."

Benjamin did the calculations. This would have been between eight o'clock to midnight, and closer to what he had originally stated. A smaller window than Dr. Lovett's 24 to 48 hours. With these medical discrepancies, it meant they were not certain of the time of death, and it could still leave a window of opportunity for Peter to have committed the murder.

Following the doctor's testimony, Bernard Parker presented yet more maps and plans, this time including one of the interior of the house. Then William Rice spoke of how Annie was in his shop between four and five o'clock, buying tissue paper. This further helped establish the timeline of the murder, for Annie had not had time to use all the paper before she was killed, meaning the assault was committed shortly after she arrived home.

The morning progressed with witnesses stating what time they had last seen Annie alive, and Grace Morine adamantly stating she had no agreement with her to stay the night. Others testified as to what time they saw Peter in the area, while the young Brooks boy from across the river talked about having seen a moving light at the Kempton house.

The court sessions proceeded morning, noon, and night and nothing new was presented.

After a long day, with little new to report, Benjamin was excited when Tilly finally took the stand. She always had something interesting to say and did so in her sassy way. Many called her a viper. Benjamin knew he would not want to cross her.

Throughout the past few weeks, Tilly had been defending Peter to everyone. Some claimed the pair were too intimate from a moral point of view, but Tilly said Peter was more like her son. She loved him like one of her own but wasn't above scolding him when he needed it.

Others thought Tilly was just protecting Peter, but Tilly kept repeating that she would turn in her own brother if he were guilty.

No matter what people said about Tilly, they couldn't take away the fact she was industrious, and hard-working.

With Tilly in the witness chair, Attorney Copp turned to the clerk. "Can you please read back the witness's sworn testimony? I want to make sure we have the right sentiment for what she is saying."

After the reading, Attorney Ruggles made a few suggestions for alternate wordings, to which Copp adamantly disagreed.

Tilly could take it no longer. "Put it down right," she said. "I want you fellows to know just what I say. Don't rush the clerk. You don't ever give him enough time to write."

She glared at the lawyers, and they stopped mid-sentence, mouths agape, looking at her. The clerk stopped writing, looked up at her, and smiled. The crowd howled with laughter.

When the matter had finally been sorted, Copp asked Tilly about what time Benson left her house the night before the murder.

"I can't really say."

"You can't?"

"No, I can't say. I might say nine o'clock, and someone else would say eight. And then I would be called a liar!"

Copp turned his back to Tilly and tried not to laugh at her earnest responses. The crowd did not hold back.

After a long day, Benjamin set foot outside, only to be greeted by at least eight inches of snow. Feeling deflated, he had no idea how he would make the trek back down the hill to the hotel.

Eventually, a sleigh going by stopped to offer him a ride, and Benjamin quickly jumped on board. He cuddled under the bear skin blanket, even if just for the five minutes to his destination.

~

The following day, Benjamin vowed to be at the hall even earlier, so he could be the one to secure the seat for the *Digby Courier* reporter and himself.

"I, at least, made it here in one piece," Simon said when he arrived.

"What do you mean, 'at least'?"

"Wheeler, apparently, is being harassed by the local lumbermen as he's being taken from his cell to the trial here. It's all men he knew and worked with, but they are also loyal to the Kemptons and are trying to avenge her honour. My source told me tons of these lumbermen flocked in from the woods and caused Wheeler many an anxious moment as they closed in on him."

"I hope Constable Henshaw could do something about it."

"There's only so much he can do when a crowd descends. But who can blame them? I guess they were trying to snatch Wheeler from custody. Word has it they had a barrel with spikes nailed into it. They planned on rolling him down the hill!"

"No! That sounds awful!" Benjamin cried.

"Not as awful as having your throat cut in your own house!"

"I suppose."

"Going to be an interesting day today, I think," Simon said.

"What makes you say so?" Benjamin hoped he was right. If there was nothing new to report, it made for an uneventful news day.

"Hardy Benson is testifying this afternoon. He's the most important witness for the prosecution, now."

"That is true! Such a position to be in for such a young lad. Not even 16 years old and it seems the weight of the case lies on his shoulders. I do not envy him. Must be difficult testifying against Wheeler, for they were quite the chums, I heard," Benjamin said.

"His conscience and moral compass are strong, and he knows he must do what is right."

Benjamin thought about that for a moment and wondered how much of that was true. *Does Hardy know more about what happened that night? Did he really go straight home after leaving Tilly's house?* He didn't have time to come to any conclusions, as his thoughts were interrupted by the gavel banging to signal court was open.

By the time the afternoon came, Benjamin was ready for the anticipated excitement of Hardy's testimony. As Hardy walked to the front, Peter looked up for one of the first times. He leaned forward, staring at the lad, but Hardy continued walking, purposely avoiding looking at the prisoner.

"I remember that fateful Monday," began Hardy, once he was sworn in. "How could I forget?"

He described seeing Annie in the village around four o'clock. He then saw Peter later in the day, when Peter told him Grace Morine was staying with Annie. This was when Peter urged Hardy to go up to visit Annie. Hardy refused to go in, but Peter tried to convince him.

"The Satan is home, come on!" said Hardy, dramatizing Peter's voice.

A gasp went through the room. This evidence had not been presented at the inquest. Although many had read about it in the newspaper, it was the first time to hear it for themselves.

"I then asked him if Grace was there, and he said she wasn't. He then told me not to tell Tilly that we had been up there."

"Disgraceful!" shouted a few voices from the back.

"That's evidence enough!" shouted another.

"When we got halfway back down the hill," Hardy continued, "Peter said to me that I should probably go back to Annie's. But I refused because I was not in the habit of doing so. So, we instead went back to

Tilly's house."

"Respectable lad!" said the same voice from behind Benjamin.

"That's what being honest and straightforward is about!" his neighbour agreed.

"What happened the next morning?" Copp asked.

"I saw Peter the next morning after the body was discovered. He said to me that poor Annie was dead, and that he was so sorry, and he commenced to cry. Then after that, he said, 'Poor Annie's dead. For God's sake! Don't tell that you or I were up there last night, for you know there were two knives on the floor, and they will think you and I did it!' I assured him I wouldn't say a word."

More angry shouts echoed across the crowded room. There were accusations of Peter trying to hide his crime, and influence and implicate a poor boy.

When Copp finished with Hardy, he gestured to Ruggles to continue with his line of questioning for the defence. Ruggles shook his head, indicating he did not wish to cross-examine this witness.

Probably wise, Benjamin thought. *What more could you say?*

The final witness of the preliminary trial, the son of Constable Henshaw, was 16 years old, and friends with Hardy Benson.

"What evidence do you have to give that is connected with the case?" Attorney Copp asked.

"Last week, when Wheeler was staying in the cell within our house, under my father's custody, he called me over to the door of the cell. In a low voice, he asked me to go give a message to Hardy Benson. This was before Hardy testified at the inquest."

"And what was the nature of this message?" Copp asked.

"He said to tell Hardy that, when he got up on the stand, to say they were out on the road that night near the electric light station, and that the light in the Kemptons' house was going back and forth as if someone was walking in front of it. Wheeler then said to tell Hardy that he would be swearing the same thing."

"What did you do?"

"I did not deliver the message," the young man said.

"Another fine lad!" said the disembodied voice from behind.

"Good, honest boys we have here in Bear River!" his friend agreed.

When the teenager had left the witness chair at the front of the room, Copp addressed Justice Purdy. "The prosecution's case rests. We will call no further witnesses."

Justice Purdy announced a short recess, and when he returned, he announced his decision.

"Ladies and gentleman," he said, his voice reaching all corners of the hall, "thank you for your participation in this preliminary trial. I have reviewed all the evidence that has been presented and declare that we have sufficient evidence to set the matter down for trial before a Justice of the Superior Court. I hereby announce that Peter Wheeler will be committed for trial for the murder of Annie Kempton. This trial will happen in the June session of the Supreme Court."

Without allowing for further questions, Justice Purdy gathered his papers and left the hall through a door at the front.

Peter stood, open-mouthed, unable to say a word. Benjamin watched him close his eyes, take a deep breath and put his hands on the table to steady himself.

Simon turned to Benjamin. "That was quite the whirlwind! Three days and 25 witnesses. My hand could certainly take a break! I can't say that I am surprised about the outcome. The whole process was conducted in a very creditable manner. I am quite impressed, especially in comparison to some other court cases I have witnessed. Ruggles did try to fight his case inch by inch. It was a valiant effort on behalf of Wheeler."

Benjamin just stood there, not saying anything. Another immediate verdict. *How could Justice Purdy have weighed all the facts in that amount of time?* His head spun with a hundred unanswered questions.

"I think the people of Bear River can start to feel vindicated," Simon continued. "They felt from the beginning that Peter Wheeler was the guilty party, and the results of this trial just go to prove they were right all along. The English blood that courses through the veins of every true man here has been aroused like never before."

Benjamin looked at him with a raised eyebrow. It sounded more like a political speech from the capital.

"The circumstantial evidence certainly is strong here. I bet most people believe the case is already settled. I don't think we have hardly ever known of a case in which suspicion was so clear and the evidence so convicting," Simon said.

"Yet, it is still circumstantial evidence only," Benjamin reminded him. "While it does point strongly to Wheeler being the murderer, I'm not sure it is by any means strong enough to secure his conviction."

"Don't be too sure. I have heard a rumour that the Crown is holding back some points that will only come out at the Supreme Court trial in June. I guess just the bare minimum was given so that Wheeler could be remanded to jail until then. Detective Power has not even been called to testify yet, and I've heard he has some valuable evidence."

"Yes, that is true," said Benjamin, not letting on that he was on fairly close terms with the esteemed detective and had already conducted several interviews with him on the topic.

"It's a shame that the next court session is not until June, for it would be nice to have the trial completed much earlier than that."

"Why is that?" Benjamin asked.

"The expenses of keeping Wheeler in jail for that long will be so heavy on the county. And if we can lessen those expenses by making the trial earlier, the better. We aren't so affluent as you city folk might be! I wonder if they could do a spring session in March or April. Yes, that would be much better."

Benjamin tried to wrap his head around the whole ordeal. *The community has it so firmly settled in their minds that Peter was the murderer, they can see or think about nothing else.* He wondered if their feelings had also overcome their better judgment. *Although the circumstantial evidence does point strongly to Wheeler, there were no positive testimonies saying he actually did the deed. Regardless, Wheeler will have a hard time disproving some of the statements alleged against him, especially as some of his stories kept changing.*

On top of that, his appearance certainly didn't help him. For such an affluent community, Wheeler was pretty unrefined and rough. And to many eyes, that was enough to see him capable of committing such a crime.

Benjamin remembered how he, too, had been so caught up in the whirlwind of events, the community gossip, and the pull of Detective Power's fame to give it much thought of his own. He needed to take another step back.

"Time will tell, I guess." he said aloud, keeping his inner monologue to himself.

"Indeed," Simon answered. "What I do know is that all of this makes such sad history. The fact that such a deed was possible in our own country, let alone our own county, says something. The terrible nature of the situation shows something of what Socialism has yet to do in restricting the individual for the good of the many."

Benjamin started to pack up his belongings and put on his coat. He did not want to get into a political discussion.

"We are painfully reminded of man's worst nature. The punishment of justice cannot repair the harm of what has already been done."

Benjamin nodded. Finally, something upon which he could agree.

9: A speedy trial is the answer

It had been nearly a month since Benjamin left Bear River to return home to Halifax. He knew nothing would happen with the trial over the course of the next few months, but that didn't stop him from wondering what was happening in the bustling village in the middle of the woods.

Have the residents gone back to their daily lives, secure in the fact justice had been met? How is Peter Wheeler faring in his Digby jail cell? Has he broken down and confessed to the crime? Has new evidence turned up?

He could not stop himself from thinking about the story.

Out of curiosity, on his lunch break, Benjamin went to a newsstand in search of the *Digby Courier*. Simon was always writing something of a mix between local news and his own soapbox editorials. If nothing else, it might help dull the February winter blues.

Benjamin spread the tabloid across his desk. Flipping through, he was soon rewarded. A headline immediately caught his attention.

> Bear River Tragedy. The possibility of Wheeler's not being the guilty man, and an Indian instead.

Below that, it indicated that the story was a discovery from the Yarmouth paper.

Yarmouth, located 64 miles from Digby, and approximately 70 miles from Bear River, was a seafaring hub and notable shipbuilding town at the south-western tip of Nova Scotia. Steamships transported visitors between Boston and Nova Scotia, and the railway easily connected passengers with the rest of the province.

Benjamin had to know more, for fear of missing out on an important lead in the case. He went to the main office to use the telephone and dialed his contact in Yarmouth.

The honourable Loran Baker was a prominent businessman, politician and probably one of the most influential men in Yarmouth. Besides his long list of accomplishments, he was also the first to bring the telephone to the town when he connected his home and office.

Using the telephone was much easier than wiring a telegram and waiting for a limited response. Now with calling, Benjamin could get answers more accurately. Besides, he had forged a strong relationship with Baker's secretary, who answered the phone, and regularly acted as an unnamed source for his stories from that part of the province.

"Miss Starr!" he said when she answered the phone. "Just whom I was hoping to reach! It's Benjamin Shaw calling from the *Halifax Herald*, and I was hoping you might be willing to shed some light on some events that are transpiring there in Yarmouth."

"I was wondering when you were going to call," she said with a giggle.

"It's regarding the Peter Wheeler case, and possible new information and clues regarding one Joseph Pictou. It was a connection discovered by the *Yarmouth Times*, I heard. What can you tell me?"

"I am not sure if you could rightly call it a clue, but it is a story that definitely deserves some consideration."

"Do tell me what you have learned. All off the record, of course."

"Of course," she said, not needing any further prompting. "It all began on Tuesday, January 28, the morning when Annie Kempton's body was discovered."

~

"And that about sums up the tale," Miss Starr explained.

Benjamin scratched his head wondering how this banal tale had gotten so blown out of proportion. In essence, a man from the Reserve left Bear River early the morning after the murder and appeared on the Yarmouth doorstep of some former Bear River residents. When he heard about Annie Kempton's murder, he turned ghostly white and left without a word.

Apparently, it was enough to arouse the family's suspicion, and they went to the Yarmouth chief of police, and the *Yarmouth Times* got wind of the story, and it went from there.

"Whatever came of it? Was the man from the Reserve arrested under suspicion of the murder of Annie Kempton? That would also confirm some of the community gossip about the murder."

"Honestly, the paper didn't make an opinion on the matter one way or another. They merely presented the facts of the story. Might be worth investigating, nonetheless," Miss Starr said. "But who am I to know anything?" She laughed again.

"Indeed. However, I fear it might be too late. The night of the murder, Peter Wheeler claimed he saw three men outside his house at midnight. One of them, apparently, could have matched a description for this man. That should have been followed up long before now."

"All just rumours at this point."

"True enough. These days, it's hard to know what fact or fiction is. Just the other day we had word from someone here in Halifax saying they knew Peter Wheeler from his seafaring days. Apparently, he was on board a vessel with him when Wheeler attempted to murder one of the crew. Turned out to be an utter fabrication, but, unfortunately, I did not find this out until after we printed it!"

"I'll say this," Miss Star said, "if Peter Wheeler is innocent, he is a greatly misjudged man and a martyr alive. If, however, he is guilty, he is certainly one of the biggest scoundrels and most plausible hypocrites that ever existed."

"I hope we will be able to determine the truth, regardless of who suffers."

~

"Mr. Shaw?"

A young apprentice stuck his head in around the corner into Benjamin's office. Benjamin looked up from what he was writing.

"There is a gentleman here to see you."

"Who is he?"

"I'm not sure, sir, but he looks very fancy."

Benjamin sighed. The lad would never make a good reporter if he was unable to ask questions and pry out the details.

"Send him in."

Benjamin stood as a very prominent figure indeed appeared in his doorway. "Mr. Clarke!" he said, coming around to the other side of his desk to shake the man's hand, and usher him towards a chair.

"You do know who I am!"

"Of course, sir. I recognized you immediately as Mr. Clarke from Bear River."

Before him stood one of the Clarke brothers, either Wallace or Willard, but he wasn't sure exactly which one. In 1880, they had formed a partnership called Clarke Brothers, which had grown to become the most extensive business in the area, grossing over $200,000 a year. Besides their dry goods shop, they operated numerous warehouses, a lumber business which was purported to be the largest in the province, mills, and other businesses to support the shipping industry.

They were, indeed, the most notable, prominent, and wealthy clan in the Bear River area, if not beyond. It was, therefore, both an honour and a shock to have one of the Clarke brothers standing in his humble newspaper office.

"I had some business here in town these past few days, so thought I would pay a call, rather than writing of my discontent."

Benjamin was caught off guard. "I'm not sure what you are speaking of," he stammered.

"I shall only take but a minute of your time," he said, refusing to sit.

"How can I help you, then, sir?"

"It is about the coverage of the Annie Kempton ordeal in the newspapers. I am not pleased about how you are presenting the village of Bear River."

"Pray continue."

"There have been many columns in your paper insinuating that the people of Bear River have come to a rash conclusion in regard to the guilt or innocence of Peter Wheeler."

Benjamin said nothing, but let the gentleman continue.

"We have indeed given him a fair trial. I would not hesitate to wager that nearly all, if not everyone who attended the preliminary trial, if not the inquest, clearly see that there is very little if any need of further search for the guilty one."

Mr. Clarke opened his suit jacket and removed a folded newspaper clipping from his inner pocket. "These columns are full of unjust statements. The reporter says, and I quote, 'Surely the only evidence against Wheeler is his statement to Tilly Comeau that Annie told him that Grace Morine was going to stay with her that night.' This proves that this reporter truly was not there at the trial."

Benjamin tried to lean closer to have a better look at the newspaper article.

"I suggest that I represent our community when I say it was this reporter's mind that must be very weak. For if he had heard the evidence in the examination, he would understand that this is about the weakest evidence in the case, just a commencement or starting point of the great and strong chain of evidence that points to Peter Wheeler as being the murderer of poor Annie Kempton."

Benjamin nodded, reflecting upon the hours of testimony he had twice sat through.

The man went through the entire chain of evidence that pointed to Wheeler's guilt, from his threatening statements, his circuitous route through the woods, his lies about the rabbit snares and having visited Stanley Rice for money, and finally his telling Tilly Comeau that Annie did not want her there that night.

"Wheeler had the nerve to say that Hardy Benson asked him to go to see if Annie was alone. He then appeared surprised on seeing a light on in the Kempton house, and left Benson in the road while he went in the house, then came out and told Benson she was alone, but did not tell Tilly this. The next morning, Wheeler went in and stated her throat was cut when it could not be seen, because of the way she way lying, by anyone who entered the house."

By this point, Mr. Clarke was out of breath, and had run out of fingers, listing off the various points of evidence against Peter Wheeler.

"A thorough summary of the chain of evidence," Benjamin said. He almost suggested that Mr. Clarke apply for a job working with Detective Power but thought better of it.

"Wheeler then told Hardy Benson not to tell that they were there the evening before. And that is just some of the evidence that leads us in Bear River to believe that Peter Wheeler is the murderer."

Realizing there was still more, Benjamin decided to sit, even if the older man would not.

"Further, we have reason to believe that if Wheeler had been left alone, without the protection of his lawyer and not locked away in a cell, he would have confessed his crime before this and thereby saved the rate-payers of our county of the unnecessary expense."

"Indeed," said Benjamin, not sure what else to say.

"The blood of Annie Kempton is crying for justice on her murderer, and for her sake, as well as for the living, it is our duty to try to ascertain by facts and circumstances, in every way we can, just who did the deed. We cannot expect justice from those who are blocking the way and warning Wheeler not to confess or say anything to anyone."

A small part of Benjamin was actually happy to hear this part. It was nice to hear that Peter Wheeler did have a few friends and people who were trying to help and support him. Whether he was guilty or not, as a foreigner, he had seemed completely alone.

"So, for the reporter to have the gall to say there was only one piece of evidence is outrageous. His powers of observation are obviously very weak and limited."

A bit harsh, thought Benjamin, *but probably a fair point*.

"This reporter must be awfully tender-hearted to say he thinks it would be cruel to try the man on such slight grounds. It is unfair to say that the community wants a quick trial before the feeling of such hasty assumptions of his guilt dies out."

Benjamin had heard rumours that many officials were trying to get the trial moved up from June to earlier in the spring. He thought it had to do with the cost of keeping the prisoner in jail, but he conceded the man might have a point. Better to try Wheeler now, while the sentiment of his guilt and the evidence was still top of mind.

Mr. Clarke waved the newspaper clipping in the air. "I believe I have voiced the sentiment of the people of Bear River village adequately. I hope your newspaper will learn from this discussion, and refrain from such reporting."

Benjamin once again leaned forward to try to look at the clipping. None of this article sounded familiar. This time, Mr. Clarke noticed him trying to look, and passed the clipping to Benjamin, who quickly scanned the column.

"I'm afraid, sir," he said, "that this is not a clipping from our newspaper." Benjamin looked intently at the typeset and figured it must be from the *St John Daily Sun* across the bay in New Brunswick.

"Oh," said Mr. Clarke. After a moment he took back the clipping and returned it to his breast pocket. "Pray I do not see such reporting from your paper, or I shall return."

With that, Mr. Clarke turned on his heel and marched out of the office.

Benjamin sighed with relief. This case was taking everything out of everyone. A speedy trial might be just the answer.

~

It was a slow news day and Benjamin's mind wandered again to Bear River, wondering what was happening there. The June trial was still over six weeks away, and Peter Wheeler had been sitting in a Digby jail cell since the end of January, waiting for the next step.

Wanting to maintain readers' interest in the story for when the trial did recommence, Benjamin decided to visit the Halifax police station in search of Detective Power, to see if he could secure an interview.

He grabbed his overcoat and hat and walked down to Barrington Street, one of the major streets in the city. There, he jumped aboard the horse-drawn trolley to take him to the station on Spring Garden Road. Later, in the summer, the city was planning on replacing the horses with electric versions of the streetcars. He would miss the familiar sights and smells of the horses.

But progress was impossible without change.

When he arrived at the police station, Detective Power immediately called for him to enter his office. Any chance he had to speak with the press was a good day.

"Detective Power," Benjamin said reaching out his hand. "I am hoping to get an update from you about the Annie Kempton case. How are things progressing and would you say we are right on schedule for the trial?"

The detective motioned for Benjamin to sit down.

On the desk, Benjamin noticed materials laid out, including scissors and glue. It looked as if Detective Power was cutting out clippings and gluing them into a scrapbook.

He noticed Benjamin eyeing them inquisitively, so explained, "I have an avid interest in want-ad posters from around North America, so whenever I can get my hands on one, I like to cut it out and keep it in this book for future reference."

Knowing it would be a long conversation if they went down that road, Benjamin brought the detective back on task. "The Annie Kempton case?"

"Ah, yes! I have it under good authority that the prosecution has been working hard to prepare their case so that all will be ready on time. I have prepared my list of witnesses which totals well over 30 people."

Detective Power has been busy, thought Benjamin.

"No efforts have been spared, and I can assure you it will be very thorough."

"Absolutely, our readers would expect nothing less. This case most definitely demands the most careful consideration."

"I have also met extensively with our attorney general, James Longley. He will be a great asset, providing legal advice to our prosecution team. He is also, conveniently, from Annapolis County, in close enough proximity to Bear River."

Longley had been a reporter and managing editor for several newspapers before pursuing his law degree. Benjamin liked when he was involved in cases and stories, for he understood how the press worked. That made the reporter's job easier.

"Longley made a special visit to the scene of the murder to collect his own personal observations. The man takes his job very seriously! All I can say is that there is considerable evidence that has yet to be presented. It is very damaging to the prisoner."

"I have heard it said that since there has been such a long gap of time since the preliminary trial, the public might be having some doubts now, or are questioning what the outcome will be," Benjamin suggested.

Detective Power glared. "For this case, there is only one possible outcome, and once that is settled, there will be a much greater sense of satisfaction from the public."

"I'm sure the defence has some points in their favour."

"A calm, clear trial will be the only means to bring out the facts," said the detective.

"And how is Wheeler handling the news? Have you had any word from Digby?"

"He was just informed of the trial date of June 9. According to Sheriff VanBlarcom down there, he took the news with indifference. He apparently says he is ready for it. I would say, however, that he now appreciates something of the seriousness of his position, now that an official date has been set. VanBlarcom has been asked to keep a close eye on him until the time of the trial. We would not like to see him perform any hasty measures upon himself which would prevent us from fulfilling the law ourselves."

"Yes, I suppose he could always try to take his own life as a way of avoiding the trial and probable hanging. I had never really thought of that."

"And that is why I am the detective!"

Benjamin smiled and nodded.

"Otherwise, things are not going well for our man Wheeler. When I spoke with Sheriff VanBlarcom, he mentioned he was having trouble with members of the public coming to visit the prisoner."

Peter

Peter leaned back against the cold wall. He tried to shift his weight from side to side to get comfortable on the hard wooden plank bed and straw mattress. It was no use. Nothing seemed worth trying any more.

He picked up the book that Sheriff VanBlarcom had kindly loaned him and tried to concentrate on a few pages. He was well fed, well read and still alive. He would take one day at time. Some days were worse than others.

He had just started reading when he heard footsteps and chatter coming down the hallway. It was usually a sign that the day was going to get worse.

He thought about pretending to be asleep, but then figured the chain around his ankle that was connected to the middle of the floor of the cell would probably rattle too much if he moved and would give up his pretense.

He decided to stay in position and take whatever was coming. Maybe he would be pleasantly surprised.

Thanks to the looking glass hanging on the cell wall, he could catch a glimpse of who was coming, before they could see him. From the way they walked, he could usually tell if they would be friend or foe. He couldn't tell by the way they were dressed, for those who were dressed the fanciest often shouted the loudest and flung the worst insults.

Truth be told, Peter didn't mind the visitors, for the most part. Many were kind. People who would have never paid attention to him in his former life were now treating him like royalty, lavishing him with attention. Some guests even brought their fancy Kodak equipment to take a picture of him in his cell.

He knew it was mostly morbid curiosity that brought them. They wanted to see what a convicted murderer tethered in chains looked like. He had never thought he would see one, either.

"There he is!"

A group of five men and women, dressed in their finest clothes, stopped in the hallway and peered through the bars. Peter felt like a circus freak left on display for the entertainment of those who wanted to tour the jail with too much money and too much time on their hands.

"There's the murderer! He's the one who violated and murdered that poor child!"

"Demon! Monster!" they shouted.

Peter had learned not to respond. It only made them yell more and stay longer.

"Do you speak English? Why don't you go back from where you came?"

Peter ran his hands over his now bald head. They shaved him since he came to prison. The thought was that if he tried to escape, he would be more recognizable.

Peter wondered why he would try to escape. He was probably safer inside the prison.

"You foreigner! You are no better than a dog!"

Peter grunted.

"So, he does understand! You are going to hell, you terrible, heinous beast!"

Peter lowered his head and tried to block out the sound of their words. It was indeed the rich folk who were the worst.

"We hope you feel every bit of your hanging! You don't deserve to be another day on the planet!"

Then, one of the men reached into the basket carried by the woman next to him. He pulled out a handful of rotten fruit and stones and began to throw them at Peter through the bars. Peter, hindered by the leg iron, tried unsuccessfully to dodge them.

When the larger rocks began hitting the walls, the noise alerted the attention of the aged sheriff. He sauntered down the hallway and eventually put an end to the assault, sending the visitors on their way. Out on the streets, this posse would instantly revert to the refined citizens they were.

Sheriff VanBlarcom looked at the small man huddled on the bed. "Seems like they have it in for you."

"I am condemned even before going to trial."

The reporter

"Your honour, I would like to petition the court to have a change of venue for the upcoming trial."

Henry Ruggles was addressing the court on behalf of his client, Peter Wheeler, a few weeks before the Supreme Court trial was to begin. It was a special session of the spring court, and Ruggles had made the trek to the Halifax courthouse to plead his client's case.

Because the petition was being heard in the city, Benjamin could attend. He had taken a shortcut through the city's old burial ground, dodged through the wrought iron gate, and rushed up the stone steps of the courthouse.

Out of habit, before he entered, Benjamin ran his fingers through the sandstone blocks that covered the building. It was almost like a crew of worms had carved tunnels on the surface of every brick, giving it a unique effect. He found it therapeutic and calming to run his fingers through the bricks, centring his mind, before he entered.

Once he had learned where the hearing was, he slipped quietly into the courtroom, to discover that Simon, his friend from the *Digby Courier*, was once again there ahead of him. Benjamin nodded in his direction but decided to sit on the other side of the courtroom. He wanted to be left alone with his own thoughts this morning.

Overseeing the court proceedings was Justice Charles Townshend, the Supreme Court judge who would also be presiding over the trial later in June. Benjamin had heard it said that, by blood, outlook, religion, and education, Charles Townshend was a true specimen of the old-regime elite in the Maritimes. His grandfather had also been a judge, and he was connected to a great number of legal dynasties in the province, especially in Amherst, from where he had come. The combination of his family prestige, economic growth of the area, and Townshend's own talent brought him an extensive clientele in his years as a lawyer.

Justice Townshend had been a judge now for almost ten years, and had already gained a reputation of being conservative, yet wise and thoughtful, and his legal opinions were well-respected. Sitting at the bench now, he appeared almost regal.

Benjamin was very interested to hear what would transpire from the proceedings.

"I am petitioning for a change of venue," continued defence lawyer Ruggles, "and would like to have the trial moved from Digby to Yarmouth, or to any other place your honour may deem fit to decide."

"And what are reasons behind your petition?" asked the judge.

"The reason for this is that we, the defence, fear the public of Digby County have been influenced into a prejudiced opinion through the opinions expressed in the local press at the time of the preliminary trial, and that therefore Peter Wheeler would not be given fair treatment at the hands of a Digby County jury."

Benjamin had not predicted this line of reasoning. He looked over at his colleague, who kept his head down and looked as though he was muttering to himself. He had to admit the community had already made up their minds that Peter was guilty. But was the newspaper encouraging those sentiments, or reflecting what was happening there?

"Your Honour, I request to be allowed to present my evidence."

"You may proceed."

Ruggles pulled a wooden crate from beneath his table and placed it on the table. From inside that, he pulled out a stack of newspapers. One by one, he took the newspapers and read selections he had previously underlined.

"Reading first selections from the *Digby Courier*.

"Headline: Circumstantial Evidence Against Peter Wheeler stronger than ever and everything points to his being guilty.

"Headline: Peter Wheeler, the man who first found the body, arrested on suspicion and found guilty by the coroner's inquest. Everything points to his being the guilty person.

"And reading from selected columns:

"'The sentiment against Peter Wheeler has been very strong and things pointed badly for him from the first. Suspicion rested on him for three reasons.'

"'The network of circumstantial evidence that has been gathering ever since the discovery of the murder involves Peter Wheeler more and more in the strongest of suspicion and point to him with a clearness seldom surpassed in criminal cases as the guilty party.'

"'The evidence points so strongly to Wheeler's guilt that it is thought he cannot escape the conviction which would be only justice.'

"These passages clearly show a bias against the accused."

Benjamin looked over at Simon. He was madly scribbling notes, no doubt writing a rebuttal.

"The Yarmouth press has acted much in the same way with their sensational and, frankly, careless printing of the story implying Joseph Pictou from the Bear River Reserve was also involved in the murder. They have also written about Peter Wheeler's guilt in their papers."

Ruggles returned to his table and picked up a stack of handwritten notes.

"I will now produce affidavits from several prominent citizens in Digby County who are habitual readers of the *Digby Courier*."

Ruggles read each of the letters slowly, pausing to let the words linger in the air. In essence, these gentlemen indicated that there was indeed prejudice against Wheeler in the county and that it would be difficult, if not impossible, to get an unprejudiced jury.

"Now, reading this affidavit from someone in Annapolis County. Mr. Alcorn writes that after the coroner's inquest, he heard one of the inquest jury members say, 'Of course the goddamned bastard killed her!' My apologies, for reading such language aloud in court," Ruggles said when he heard several people gasp at the obscene language.

"This gentleman continues, saying that he had also heard other members of the jury say they had no doubt Wheeler was the murderer," Ruggles said.

Benjamin nodded. He had heard as much during the inquest. It did not come as a surprise.

"Further," continued Ruggles, "we have other affidavits which I would like to now read, which show that local residents have been going to

Wheeler's cell and are using insulting language and going so far in some instances as to denounce him as the murderer."

Benjamin knew this to be true, having heard of several of these occurrences from Detective Power.

"My next affidavit is concerning someone who says that the evidence was only circumstantial and not strong and therefore it would be impossible to obtain a fair trial in Digby."

Detective Power did lay out a very strong chain of circumstantial evidence that was hard to ignore, thought Benjamin. *There were no actual witnesses, however.*

"For these reasons, we would like to petition the court for a change of venue for the trial to prevent it from occurring in Digby County."

When Ruggles had finished, a lawyer assigned to represent the prosecution came to his feet. "The prosecution objects. We have several affidavits of our own that express the exact opposite sentiment, showing there is in fact no prejudice against the accused. We find these claims of the defence to be outlandish and a change of venue unnecessary. The place and time of the trial should stand as first appointed."

Judge Townshend took a few moments to compose his thoughts before he spoke.

"Thank you, gentlemen," he began. "With regard to the comments of the press, it is not too late to move against the publishers of the newspapers. The comments were of a most outrageous nature and a prosecution would teach the papers a lesson."

Benjamin looked over and could see Simon's body tensing. His face was turning red. He still refused to look up.

"The Halifax papers are equally to blame," continued the judge.

Benjamin stared, astonished. Where was this coming from? The complaints had been solely made about the *Digby Courier*.

"The papers out of Halifax ought to have known better. In fact, all press in Nova Scotia should be better than this. Soon our provincial papers will be as bad as those of the United States, where a man is tried by the newspapers before his case is given to the jury. This should not be happening in our country, let alone our province of Nova Scotia," said the judge.

Benjamin was ashamed and felt duly scolded.

"We shall take a recess, and I shall issue my verdict at a later time."

Before Justice Townshend had left the courtroom, Simon leapt to his feet and hurried out the door. Benjamin found him pacing back and forth in the hallway, obviously still angry and upset.

"Can you believe it? Can you believe what he said about us?"

Benjamin wanted to respond that it was mostly about the *Digby Courier* and not his paper but thought better of it. Instead, he ushered Simon outside, where they could talk more openly. He half considered suggesting to the man that he should try running his fingers through the wormeaten mazes on the brick facing but thought better of it.

"Most of his Lordship's blame fell to the *Courier*! I could not believe it so! I think the attitude of our paper in regard to the murder has been fair and reasonable from the first to last! We do not make a specialty of reporting crimes, and prefer reprinting matter, but we have given the facts in this case as far as they could be obtained."

"I'm sure you have," said Benjamin, unsure of what else to say.

"We were the first to publish the news of the murder to the world, even putting out an extra on the same day the deed was discovered and, ever since then, the only opinion we have expressed in regard to Wheeler is that the circumstantial evidence against him is very strong. The defence itself cannot deny this."

It was worded a bit more strongly than that, Benjamin thought. He was unsure, however, what he would have done in the same situation, so reserved judgment.

"We have said, too, that there were points of doubt about the case, and we have repeatedly expressed our hope that a thorough and impartial trial may be given."

"That is true."

"We all keep the case at the top of the mind, enlarging every point, drawing out stories of suggestiveness and somewhat unnecessary sensationalism. We know that this is what the readers want to know, and frankly, what sells papers."

"That is definitely true."

"Then blaming the Yarmouth press!" Simon said. "They were treated in the same manner! Claiming the prejudice was rampant there, as well. I seriously doubt that the press in Yarmouth has handled the case with any difference in partiality and fairness than we have at the *Courier*."

Benjamin thought about this. With newspapers not only from across the province, but across the country and into the States, printing stories about Peter Wheeler and the murder, he wondered if there truly was an area that was untainted or had not yet heard of the story. *Could a place be found that has not been touched or prejudiced by the newspapers?*

"Really, if you think about it," Simon continued, "we haven't said too much about the case, but rather, too little. Our readers would appreciate a detailed account of what is happening. Not everyone can attend the trials, so we are providing them with the next best thing."

"We definitely live in an era when interest in crime is heightened. Arthur Conan Doyle's novels have helped with that. Everyone wants to be a detective now!" Benjamin said.

"I cannot predict the feelings of Digby County residents regarding Wheeler, but I can say that I feel, in my heart of hearts, The *Courier* has done nothing but present the case in a fair manner."

Benjamin put his arm around the man's shoulder in solidarity and led him back into the courtroom to hear the verdict.

When Judge Townshend returned to the bench, he addressed those in attendance. "My duty is to see, if possible, that the trial, in which the prisoner's life is at stake, takes place before a jury untainted with prejudice or foregone conclusions. After what I have heard and read, it is impossible for me to think such a jury can be obtained locally. When the feelings of the community, whence the jurors must be taken, have been so excited and worked upon by the press, it is always to the disadvantage of the accused."

He then looked up from his notes and said, "In making my decision, I would like to make it very clear that my ruling is no reflection on the people of the district. I know this could happen in any county or area of the province when there is a fearful crime and an alleged perpetrator."

Justice Townshend put on his glasses and began reading his official statement.

"Upon hearing read the notice of motion on behalf of Peter Wheeler that the place of trial for Peter Wheeler of Digby, a prisoner in the common jail at Digby, on the charge of murdering one Annie Kempton, be changed from Digby. It is expedient to the ends of justice that the trial of the said Peter Wheeler on the aforementioned charge should be held in some county other than the county of Digby, in which the offence was supposed to have been committed and would otherwise be triable. The trial shall be held in Kentville, in the County of Kings."

There were a few grumbles in the crowd, many displeased about the announcement.

"I do further order," the judge continued, "that the sheriff of the County of Digby and the keeper of the common jail at Digby do forthwith deliver the said Peter Wheeler to the common jail in Kentville in the County of Kings and deliver him to the keeper of said common jail in Kentville. I do order and command the keeper of the common jail in Kentville to receive the said Peter Wheeler into his custody and there safely keep him until he shall be thence delivered by the due course of law."

The judge outlined that, while the affidavits showed evidence from both sides, they left one in doubt as to the true state of feeling existing in the county toward the prisoner.

Benjamin could not disregard that the newspapers, including his own, might have influenced the opinions of its readers. But surely he was less biased in his reporting—only delivering the facts as they were known at the time when he wrote each article.

Regardless, the next steps were to move Peter Wheeler from Digby to Kentville. Then the other pieces would fall into place.

~

It was a beautiful day, and the sun was shining brightly. The trip up from Halifax had been a beautiful one.

When the train reached the Annapolis Valley, Benjamin could see the famous apple blossoms in all their glory. They were so abundant that Benjamin could almost smell them through the closed windows and hear the roar of the bees going through the branches.

It was little things like this that Benjamin missed, living in the city.

When the train finally pulled into the Kentville station, it was nearly supper time. He had heard that Peter Wheeler would be arriving in Kentville sometime that evening, but he wasn't sure of the exact time. To not miss Peter's appearance, Benjamin decided to find something to eat in the station restaurant. That way, he could keep an eye out on the arrivals.

Benjamin was midway through his coffee and sandwich when he heard a train whistle blow. He heard the station master announce that it was the express train from Yarmouth. *That has to be it!*

He downed the rest of his coffee, threw some money on the table and rushed out to the platform.

When the doors opened, Benjamin immediately recognized Sheriff VanBlarcom from the Digby jail. At seventy-four years of age, VanBlarcom was one of the most prestigious men from that area. He had started life as a shingle manufacturer, but later became a provincial representative for the House of Assembly for the area.

VanBlarcom also had a scrupulous business record and was renowned for saving public money by detecting and bringing to light fraud being practised by contractors. The most notable one was during the construction of the Western Counties Railway.

Behind the sheriff came Peter Wheeler.

Benjamin patted himself on the back for his good detective work. The exact date of his removal to Kentville was kept a secret so there wouldn't be a large, raucous crowd to meet them. However, Benjamin had managed to find out the information. Maybe Detective Power was rubbing off on him.

Peter was neatly dressed in a black suit and, apart from being a little pale, showed no sign whatsoever of the severe mental strain or near nervous collapse to which the other papers had referred.

It was obvious that none of the other bystanders recognized Peter, for no one remarked on his presence.

Benjamin kept back, careful not to be observed, to watch the interaction.

The prisoner and his keeper made their way to the platform, and Benjamin watched as Sheriff VanBlarcom searched the faces of those who were waiting, as if looking for someone. Eventually he smiled and walked towards a distinguished-looking, balding man with a white beard.

The entire time, Peter was no more than two inches away from the sheriff.

"Sheriff Belcher!" the sheriff said, extending his hand. "This is our man, Peter Wheeler, who will now become a guest of your fine establishment."

Peter put out his hand to shake it but realized his faux pas and quickly dropped it.

Benjamin watched as the three men crossed the tracks, and headed down the street towards the jailhouse, which was almost in view of the station.

Later, Benjamin wandered around town, ducking in and out of the various shops, enjoying the streetscape. Kentville was easy to navigate, with basically only four streets making a square. As it was the main shire district for shopping and services, the streets were always full of people running errands and conducting business. He loved the small-town feeling, but not enough to move there.

After about an hour, Benjamin walked towards the courthouse and jail. They were separate wooden structures that sat near the railway tracks. The original structure had housed both jail and courthouse, but when they rebuilt after a fire less than 50 years earlier, they had separated them into two buildings.

Benjamin hesitantly opened the jailhouse door. Inside he found the two sheriffs, VanBlarcom and Belcher, sitting and chatting over a cup of tea in the parlour off the main entrance.

"Excuse me, gentlemen," he said from the doorway. "My name is Benjamin Shaw, and I am with the *Halifax Herald*. I was wondering if there was any way to have a private interview with one of your prisoners."

Sheriff Belcher raised an eyebrow towards his colleague.

Sheriff VanBlarcom nodded. "I recognize him from the Digby courthouse."

"In that case," Sheriff Belcher said, standing, "I shall take you right to him. He is just getting settled in his new quarters. No one else seems to realize he is here yet."

"Thank you, sir."

Benjamin followed the sheriff down the long hallway to a cell door, which he opened with one of the keys on a ring he carried.

"Peter Wheeler, you have a visitor." Then, to Benjamin, he said, "You have ten minutes."

Benjamin walked into the cell, and the sheriff locked the door behind him and disappeared. At least Peter wasn't known for being violent or taking fits of rage, or at least not yet.

"Hello, Peter. I'm Benjamin—"

"I remember you. You are that reporter from Halifax."

"Yes, it is true. I was hoping you would be willing to have a few words with me."

"Only if you will print that, once again, I am declaring my innocence! They have me trapped like a wild animal, and I definitely do not deserve this."

There was a wooden chair that was pushed in under a simple table. Benjamin pulled it out, sat down and faced Peter, who was sitting on the hard-plank bed. Peter put down the Bible he had been reading.

Benjamin noticed the Bible, and was surprised that Peter could read, and chose to read the Good Book. Maybe he was a Christian, after all.

"How long have you taken to reading the Bible?"

"Ever since I was able to read. I can read it in Latin, too!"

He then scooched forward to the edge of the bed, so his feet were firmly planted on the floor. As he repositioned, the chain around his ankle, attached to an iron ring in the middle of the floor, rattled.

He stared directly into Benjamin's eyes. "I must tell you again. I am not the guilty party. The law will deliver me out of this hole!"

Benjamin ignored the protests. "How are you feeling, Peter? How have you been treated?"

134

"These false accusations and prejudicial treatment must come to an end. I cannot see why they cannot see I am innocent."

Benjamin nodded. There was no doubt he was being treated like a chained animal. He wondered how many had attempted to actually get to know the man.

"When I was housed in the Digby jail, people were allowed to come in, hurl insults at me, and accuse me of being the murderer. This was all before I've even had a proper trial!"

"And what about the treatment you received from the jailhouse staff?"

"I must give credit where credit is due. They have treated me with the utmost respect and kindness. They have provided me with the most delicious home-cooked meals. I mean, look at me." Peter patted his stomach, "I would wager I have gained thirty pounds since I have been imprisoned!"

Peter laughed, and Benjamin could not but help join in.

"I have it under good authority that the sheriff here in Kentville, and the jailer, are also very kind to all who come through these doors."

Benjamin was not sure if that was the truth, but he needed to say something to lift the man's spirits. "Next week will be your preliminary trial for the Supreme Court. You should know more of your fate, then."

Peter nodded. "Pray for me."

10: Hang him now!

Benjamin was working hard at his desk when his assistant came in with a telegram in his hands. He quietly placed it on the desk before retreating.

Benjamin picked it up, expecting to find information about a new hot story worth pursuing. Instead, it was about more legal action in connection with the Annie Kempton murder case.

He knew he would never wrap his head around being a lawyer, and all inquisitions, petitions, affidavits and trials a case had to go through.

This telegram summarized the results of the latest preliminary trial, held at a Supreme Court session in Kentville. He was confused. Wasn't there already a preliminary trial?

First there was the coroner's inquest held in the Bear River hall in Annapolis County. There, they determined that Annie Kempton was indeed dead and by means of murder. Dr. Lovett took it beyond the traditional procedures and actually made an accusation and had Peter Wheeler arrested.

Then came the preliminary trial, held in Digby County at the Exhibition Hall. Here, they looked at the evidence to see who might be found guilty. Peter Wheeler was once again accused of murder.

This third trial, he supposed, was to determine if there was enough evidence against Peter Wheeler If so, they would then hold the actual Supreme Court trial.

When he mapped it out this way, it made a lot more sense. Since they had arrested Peter early, the process had not been as straightforward as with other cases.

With the timeline and trial schedule clear in his head, Benjamin picked up the telegraph to read the details.

On Tuesday, June 5, the preliminary trial of the Peter Wheeler case at the Kentville Supreme Court resulted in an indictment for the prisoner. A number of witnesses were examined before the grand jury, who on retiring, returned after some three hours, bringing in a true bill.

Benjamin could almost picture the witnesses testifying. He could probably recite their testimony by heart, as he had heard them so many times.
He continued reading.

Peter Wheeler will be tried by special court in Kentville on June 30. The witnesses, some 27 in number, returned to Digby and Bear River the next day.

On June 26, 1896, Benjamin walked out the main door of Kentville's Lyons Hotel and stood on the sidewalk. To his left, at the end of the street, he saw the majestic Aberdeen Hotel. He wondered what the rooms inside looked like, and wished the newspaper could afford to put him up there, even just for one night.

Behind the hotel was the train station. As one of the major hubs of the Annapolis Valley, Kentville was always bustling, but today was even busier. There was a steady stream of people coming off the train, crossing the tracks, and walking the block across town. Benjamin knew they were all heading to the same place, so he picked up his speed to make sure he was near the front of the line when the courtroom opened.

The Kentville Courthouse was next to the jailhouse where he had visited Peter Wheeler a month ago. It was a modest, two-storey wooden building, the main entrance to which faced away from the main road. The steps, which were at ground level, led to the arched wooden doorway, flanked by two Gothic windows.

After the original court building burnt to the ground, the new jail and courthouse buildings were constructed in less than a year, solely using the insurance money. Because of its quick build and lack of any significant design work, many considered this courthouse to be scandalously inefficient and an eyesore to the community.

Benjamin didn't care what it looked like, as long as he could get a seat and have a good view of the proceedings.

When Sheriff Belcher opened the door, Benjamin elbowed his way to the front. The size of the room certainly wasn't anything like the Bear River Exhibition Hall, that had easily accommodated the more than 800 spectators. He would be surprised if this room could even hold a quarter of that number.

He rushed forward and secured a spot on the bench right behind the railing. He tried to make himself as wide as possible, taking up two spaces, so he could finally repay the kindness to Simon from the *Digby Courier*.

As he waited, he surveyed the room. It was the first time for him to attend court here, and he didn't want to miss anything by not being prepared.

At the far end of the room was the judge's bench, in front of which was a table for the clerk, and two docks, one on each side: one for the witness, and the other for the prisoner.

Next to the prisoner's dock was an old wooden stove. Benjamin imagined that on cold, wintry days, it would have been someone's job to be stationed next to the stove, keeping it well stocked with wood to warm the building. On such a warm day in June, this room would instantly warm up, and there would definitely be no need. Officials must have been already anticipating this, as all the windows in the courthouse were open.

Facing the front were two tables, one for the prosecution and the other for the defence. Spanning the left side of the courthouse were two rows of six chairs each, obviously for the jury. Next to this was a raised stand for the sheriff.

As the crowd began filtering in, Benjamin kept looking over his shoulder, hoping to catch Simon's eye before he sat down. Just as he was about to give up, the man appeared.

Benjamin stood and waved him over.

"I cannot thank you enough! I could not get past the crowd leaving the station. It's a real log jam! I would say only a few more people, and the rest will be stuck listening from the grounds outside and through the open windows. I swear there are another hundred or so people out on the grounds. So, truly, I thank you."

"Don't mention it. Just repaying the favour. How is the community feeling about this trial happening in Kentville, and what are they saying about the outcome?"

Simon took off his hat and placed it on the floor beneath the bench. He took out his notepad and pencil, and in the cramped space, turned to face Benjamin.

"That's a great question. I know Digby County has been painted as barbarous, but I can assure you, the residents are nothing like this. There has only ever been a desire for justice. This is paramount to all other sentiments."

Benjamin nodded.

Simon continued, "Given the nature of this case, and because of its sensationalism and brutality, one cannot help but have a particularly strong opinion about it. Although people may have an opinion about the case doesn't mean they reached it prejudicially. To say so is offensive."

"I've written no such thing," said Benjamin, feeling defensive.

"Not you *per se*, but others in general. It is just so sad, and also a crime in itself, that our county has figured so prominently because of it. We have this to contend with, along with the heavy expenses that have incurred because of the prisoner and trial."

"The case has definitely drawn a readership and an interest from far and wide. Newspapers across the country have been picking up the story."

"I feel society today has grown to have such a horrible fascination with crime, murder, and now executions. It's not right," added Simon.

"We must admit that headlines such as these do help to sell papers," Benjamin said.

"This may be so. There is just something in particularly striking about this case. I feel it is one which will, with reason, be long remembered."

"I fear you may be right."

After a few more minutes of Simon giving his opinion on a variety of subjects, from the comfort of the train seats to the condition of the streets in Kentville, the door in the far-right corner opened. The room instantly went quiet.

A tall, thin man with a wiry moustache, wearing a long flowing black gown, appeared in the doorway. Justice Townshend made his way to the bench at the front of the room, sat down, straightened both his papers and his glasses, and looked up.

In the meantime, the lawyers filed out of a room next to the one from which Justice Townshend had appeared and took their places.

At the first table sat Albert Copp, who had been acting as the prosecutor for the entire trial thus far. For this trial, he would be aided by prominent Halifax lawyer, C. Sidney Harrington, a man in his mid-forties. Beside them was Harry Hamm Wickwire, a man in his twenties who was an up-and-coming lawyer in the town of Kentville. He also happened to be married to the sister of Dr. Lovett from Bear River, the coroner involved in the trial.

The three men made a formidable and intimidating wall.

Trailing behind them was Henry Ruggles, who had been acting for the defence from the beginning. Beside him was Mr. Robertson, a young lawyer from Kentville who had only been called to the bar. He was obviously there to shadow Ruggles and provide any needed legwork.

When the lawyers were finally seated, Justice Townshend nodded to Sheriff Belcher to bring in the jury members, who had been sequestered in another room.

John North entered first.

Benjamin had done his homework. As soon as the approved list of jury members had been announced, he began asking questions around town and to the officials, to find out who they were. They all, of course, were tax-paying, property-owning citizens of Kings County, which was why their names were on the list of potential jury members in the first place.

The chosen jury had elected John North as their foreman, and Benjamin could see why. He truly looked a gentleman in his pristine suit, slicked hair, thick moustache, and confident smile. It was no wonder, since North was the son of the wealthiest and most prominent shipbuilder in Hantsport, twenty miles away on the outskirts of the county.

The rest of the men who followed North ranged in age from their early thirties to late fifties. They were a mix of farmers and merchants, who owned property with a value of at least $500 and who had lived in the county for over a year.

The county clerk kept the names of such property owners in a large ledger. Benjamin had heard how much effort went into calling a jury.

First, the clerk had to make a secondary list of property owners who met the criteria for serving jury duty. Then he wrote the names of every potential juror from his book onto a ticket and then placed the folded ticket in the jury box. In an open court with witnesses, the clerk drew tickets, and those men received a letter informing them of their duty to appear at court.

Sometimes, a non-response meant traipsing through the county to find these gentlemen and serve them their jury duty summons. Failure to appear could result in a fine, whereas participation always resulted in a financial payment.

Word was that this jury had been relatively easy to assemble, and only a few potential members were challenged. Eventually, twelve men had been selected, and the trial was ready to proceed.

The other jury members looked fairly nondescript, with no one standing out. They all wore Sunday suit jackets and white shirts and filed quietly into their box.

When the jury was seated, Sheriff Belcher finally ushered the prisoner in to take a seat in the dock at the front of the room.

The crowd jumped to its feet, everyone trying to get a better look. Because Peter Wheeler was so short, those at the back of the room were forced to stand on the benches to catch a glimpse of him.

Several voices in the room shouted, "Murderer! Child killer! Guilty!"

Peter kept his head low.

When Peter was seated and Sheriff Belcher had returned to his seat next to the jury, Justice Townshend banged on his gavel and officially opened the court.

Before the proceedings began, Ruggles stood to make a request of the court. "Your Lordship, I would like to request that the witnesses be excluded from the court."

This was a fairly uncommon practice, having witnesses not present for the entire trial to hear each other's testimonies.

After some debate, Justice Townshend sided with Ruggles and asked for the over twenty witnesses to stand and be ushered into the rooms along the side of the courtroom with strict instructions not to discuss the case.

As those seats became vacant, those standing along the perimeter rushed to fill the seats, and a few more bystanders outside came to squeeze into a space along the walls.

With everyone finally in place, Justice Townshend motioned for Wickwire to rise and begin his opening address for the prosecution.

H. H. Wickwire, although fairly new to the profession, had already garnered a reputation for his strong elocution style and vivid recounting of details that transfixed those in the courtroom. For over an hour, he outlined the evidence that had been previously given at the preliminary trial and outlined why the trial had been moved from Digby to Kentville.

In conclusion, he said, "That is the outline of the information that has already been presented to the court. What you do not know, however, is that during this trial, the prosecution will be presenting some entirely new and damaging evidence."

People leaned forward in their seats, not wanting to miss any of the details, in hopes that this new information would be revealed immediately.

Benjamin looked over at Peter Wheeler who began nervously shifting in his seat. He could also detect the man's lips twitching.

Wickwire continued, "The Crown also has evidence to prove that Wheeler told a certain witness to alter his testimony and to change the timeline of events."

Several people gasped, while a few others tutted to show their contempt.

"Another point which has never been brought out before," continued Wickwire, "is to the effect that when the clothes were taken off Wheeler by Detective Power, there were some conversations about blood. Our expert witness is going to testify that the blood on his clothes is indeed human blood and that an unsuccessful effort had been made to wash the stains away."

A few angry cries went around the room, while others stomped their feet in protest.

When he had finished, and the crowd quieted, the prosecution called their first witness.

Omer Rice made his way to what he hoped was his last time to the witness stand.

"Do you know the prisoner, Peter Wheeler?" asked Wickwire, pointing to the dock.

"I have known the prisoner about ten or twelve years, as he has lived close to me ever since he came to Bear River."

"What do you remember about that morning, Tuesday, January 28th?"

"I remember that morning. I saw Peter Wheeler going into my house at about eight o'clock. I was in the barn. After he went into the house, he went down the hill towards the Comeau house, where he lives. Then my wife came out and informed me what he had told her. Then she and I went right up to the Kemptons' house. There was a well-trodden path down the hill through the snow, as several teams had gone that way, but above the Kemptons' house there was but a foot track."

"What did you do when you got there?"

"I went to the back door. It was not locked. I went into the kitchen and from that into the dining room. When I got into the dining room, I found a table in front of the door and standing on end with one leaf off it. It lay across my track."

"Where did you discover the body?"

"I first went to look at the body, which lay at the other end of the room. The head was facing towards the east window. It was lying on the left side, the chin drawn down towards the breast, with the feet towards the fireplace. It had a coat over it from the shoulders down over the hips. The coat did not cover her throat. The girl had a red wrapper on, like an entire garment or dress for wearing around the house. She also had on black stockings, but no boots. There was blood around it. The clothing was up around her hip some. Her underclothing was exposed. Her head was drawn down towards the left side. Her arms were on her breast."

"Did you notice any blood?"

"I noticed blood. There was blood around her neck and shoulders. There was quite a little pile of it. Her shoulder was in quite a pool of it, and it was clotted, and it was thick. Her shoulder laid in it. The blood was in her hair, so much so I thought her hair was loose, but it was just matted with blood. Beneath her body was one of those homemade rag rugs, which was on top of a carpet. The blood was spread all around this rug, but I don't think the spread was more than eighteen inches."

"And what wounds, if any, did you notice?"

"With regard to the wounds, as I looked at the body, all I could see was where something had hit her in the forehead. I could see no other wounds, like any to her throat, owing to the position in which she lay."

"Did you examine the body further?"

"Yes," said Omer. He scratched his head and closed his eyes, as if he was placing himself back at the scene, remembering every detail. "I took hold of her shoulder and rolled her over so that I could see the cut. When I rolled her, her body was cold and the whole body was stiff. Upon rolling her over, I found two cuts. One was cut into the left side of the throat and the other across the windpipe. Then, I let the body roll back again to its original position."

"So, in total, what wounds did you notice?"

"Besides the cuts on the throat, there was a wound on the forehead and another across her nose."

"And what about the state of the room? What else can you tell us about what you found?"

"In the room the lamp chimney was on the floor and there were two blood marks on it as though it had been taken by bloody fingers. I picked it up and put it on the lamp. On a stand near the body there was a spoon that had blood on it, resting in a cup that had tea grounds in the bottom. There were broken dishes on the floor."

"Did you see any clothes about the room?"

"Quite close to her head, there was a rocking chair, and piled on that were a pair of corsets and a fur cape. Right under the mantelpiece, close to the stove, there was a pair of women's overshoes with blood on one of them. It looked as if four or five drops of blood had dropped on the overshoes and had run down the side of them."

"Anything else you can tell us about the room?"

"On the mantel, there was also a lamp with no oil in it, and there were matches there on the mantelpiece."

"What about any possible weapons that might have made the cuts?"

Wickwire asked, leaning forward for dramatic effect.

"There were two knives."

Although most people had heard this story numerous times, it still brought shock and caused several people to gasp.

"What did you do with said knives?"

"I picked the knives off the floor and laid them on a chair. They were silver-plated knives with round points on them. One of them was quite sharp and the other quite dull. I tried the sharp one. It was as sharp as a good many jackknives are, and the other seemed almost too dull to cut anything with. They were about eight or nine inches in length. They were table knives. They had blood on them, but just on the blades. There was also a butcher knife that seemed to be under the mat; just the end of the handle was out. This really was a large knife; I suppose the family would have used it as a bread knife. It had a wooden handle, and the point was sharp."

"Are these the knives you found?" asked Wickwire. He returned to his table and from a wooden crate beneath it, drew out three knives and waved them dramatically in the air.

A few women in the crowd swooned or cried loudly into their handkerchiefs. A few had to be ushered outside, stepping over rows of people to get out.

Wickwire passed the knives to Omer, who carefully examined them.

"Yes, they do look to be the same. They have the same marks of blood on them."

As Omer said this, Wickwire logged the knives as evidence and laid them on a table before the judge.

"Any other possible weapons about?"

"We found a stick of stove wood on the floor of the dining room which had blood on it and was quite close to the body."

"Does this look like the piece of wood you found?" Wickwire to the crate and pulling out a small log.

"It looks like the same piece of wood. It had marks of blood on it when I picked it up."

Wickwire placed the piece of wood next to the knives on the table. He then produced the overshoes, chimney from the lantern and various other items. Omer confirmed that they all had been in the room, so they were then all added into evidence.

"Anything about the windows?" prompted Wickwire.

"There was a window near her head. This faces east, down the hill to-wards the power station. The window looked as though it had been raised, on account of the stuff that had fallen in between it and the storm window."

Benjamin grimaced, remembering how he had slid open the window on the day the body was found and taken from it a letter that Annie's mother had written her, that had fallen between the panes.

"The window was down when I saw it," continued Omer. "But there were marks of blood on the window casing."

Benjamin thought about this again. *Was that Annie or the murderer trying to get out who had left the bloody fingerprints?*

"I also saw some blood on the door leading to the kitchen, and then on the cellar door."

"Did you explore other parts of the house?"

"I looked in the bedroom and noticed the bed sheets were turned down over the foot board. I didn't really notice anything else, other than the carpet looked ruffled up as though there had been a scuffling."

By this point, Omer had already been on the stand for several hours and Justice Townshend called for an hour's recess.

When court resumed, it was Ruggles' turn for cross examination. He focused primarily on nailing down the timeline, questioning Omer as to how certain he was that everything had happened in the precisely the amount of time that he had indicated.

"Would you be able to distinguish between three quarters of an hour and an hour and a half?" he asked.

"Probably not," Omer admitted. "I was not thinking of the time then and was kind of excited."

Then Ruggles moved on to the footprints in the snow. "Can you be certain the larrigan tracks were made by Peter Wheeler?"

"Most people in the country wear larrigans in the wintertime, and one larrigan track looks just like another regarding shape and everything except size."

After another exhausting hour, Omer Rice was finally finished and was released from his seat in the witness box at the front. As he left, he kept his head low, avoiding eye contact with anyone, and especially with the prisoner.

Next to the stand was Dr. Ellison, who was questioned this time by Harrington.

"Did you know Annie Kempton?"

"I knew her by sight. She was a well-developed girl. Fleshy. She probably weighed between 130 to 140 pounds."

"When did you first see the body of the deceased?"

145

"I was summoned around half past nine on the morning of Tuesday, January 28. I did not make any official examination of the body, but I did ask for someone to remove the handkerchief that was covering her face, so I could have a better look. I stooped down to see where the blood had come from and could see no wounds except for the one on her forehead. I could see no wounds on the throat," Dr. Ellison said.

"What prevented you from seeing the throat wounds?"

"She was very fleshy, and her head was curled in, which hid the hole. She was lying upon her left side. I did notice a pool of blood around her neck and shoulders. There was quite the pool of clotted blood extending out some ten to fourteen inches right around from the shoulder, neck, and head."

"What can we learn from the blood?"

"It was coagulated. Both arterial and veinous blood will coagulate if exposed to the air. It would be an easy matter if I had seen the blood at first, to state whether it was arterial or not."

"Can you please describe the examination you conducted on the deceased?"

"I commenced the examination at approximately three o'clock that afternoon. By that time, the body was not in altogether the same position in which it was found. It had been moved several times. But I started by first turning the body to see where the hemorrhage was from and saw that her throat was cut."

"What else did you discover?" Harrington asked.

Dr. Ellison described once again the five distinct wounds he saw on the body, starting with the wound on the forehead that was made in a downward striking motion. He then confirmed that the stick of wood, which was previously logged into evidence, was the same one he had seen at the Kempton house that afternoon.

"That stick fit into the wound I referred to. The blow went clear through to the bone. From a wound such as that I would look for considerable blood. It would pour down over her face."

"What other wounds did you notice?"

"The next wound was just back of her ear and a little above on the right side. That wound was an inch and a half in length. I probed that. I probed all round with my finger to see if there was any indentation and I could find none. It was the result of another downward blow like the first one. I don't believe these wounds were enough to cause death, as the skull beneath was not broken."

Dr. Ellison then described in great detail the wounds he discovered across her throat. He also identified the knives which were shown earlier in court as being the ones he saw at the house that day and asserted that they could definitely have made the wounds.

At these graphic descriptions, several people shifted in their seats.

Harrington then moved on to discussing if a blow by the wooden stick would have rendered Annie unconscious or insensible. "Suppose insensibility had occurred, what effect would that have upon the bleeding of the arteries?"

"That would be according to the shock. If the heart was in a manner paralyzed, there would be no spouting and a vein would merely empty out. If the heart was not entirely paralyzed, according to the strength of the heart, there would be spouting. Ultimately, though, I don't think there would be much difference in the quantity of blood lost whether the person was insensible at the time her throat was cut or whether she was not insensible. The blood would all pretty much drain away."

Harrington nodded and gestured for the doctor to continue.

"All the tissues on the throat were cut, including the muscles and jugular. The jugular is one of the largest veins in the body and bleeds profusely but would not spout. The carotid artery, if cut with the heart in action, would spurt according to the strength of the heart. The energy of the spouting of the blood would depend entirely on the heart's action, whether stronger or weaker."

"Was the carotid artery severed?"

"Yes," Dr. Ellison confirmed, "both the internal and external branches of the carotid were severed. The wound was about two-and-a-half inches deep. The wounds were all jagged and cut with a dull instrument. For this reason, the wounds would not bleed as freely as if cut with a sharp instrument. The least twist, and the small arteries will be plugged. A small artery or vein can be twisted and plugged in that way. In fact, many surgeons do it with larger veins."

"Would she have died immediately?"

"The wound would have most certainly produced immediate death. A person with a severed carotid artery could only live a few moments. This would be the same as the jugular vein."

From the front of the room, Benjamin could hear Mrs. Kempton sobbing. It was a graphic and gruesome description that no mother should have to hear. Throughout the descriptions, Peter kept his head low, and never moved a muscle.

"And do we know how much blood was lost? And does the rate of blood loss affect the time it takes for the body to cool?"

"There is a rule regarding the amount of blood in the human body. This states that one-fifth of the weight of the body is supposed to be blood and one fourth of that one fifth is supposed to be arterial blood. The flow of blood in this case would not make very much difference in respect to the time in which the body would cool."

"In what order do you think the wounds were made?"

From his responses, Benjamin painted a gruesome picture in his mind of what had happened on that fateful night.

> Annie hears a noise or a knock on the door late at night and is disturbed from her bed. She throws off the bed sheets to go investigate. Either that, or she is sitting in the dining room, drinking tea, and eating preserves....

He interrupted his own thoughts. *There were remnants of a broken dish on the floor. No one had said what this was. Could it have been a second teacup? Was Annie entertaining a guest?*

The detective had not intimated this, so he dropped the theory and kept going.

> Annie is caught off guard when someone takes a piece of wood from the pile by the stove and strikes her on the back of the head. Perhaps she turns to face her attacker, and a great struggle occurs in which the table is knocked over, and dishes are smashed. Eventually, maybe as she falls to the ground, she is struck again, this time on the forehead. The attacker has to have been standing above her, as the wound is from a downwards motion.
>
> With her rendered unconscious or semi-insensible, the perpetrator can search for a weapon, find the knives, and end everything. Dead men don't tell tales.

But then, the bloody fingerprints on the lamp chimney, windows, and door casings—were they Annie's, as she tried to escape? Or were they the mad man's in his rush to leave? If there were only a way to find out! But would it make a difference? The result is the same. Poor Annie Kempton is dead.

No matter how he tossed it around in his head, the scene was gruesome and terrifying.

Benjamin looked over at Peter Wheeler. *Does he really have it in him to commit such a gruesome crime? Are there other possibilities that hadn't been explored?*

The community was so intent on getting justice, that perhaps any justice counted, he thought.

Harrington's voice asking the next question brought him back to the present moment. "What time do you estimate as the time of death?"

"From when I examined her body at three o'clock, I would say fifteen hours earlier, so around midnight."

Benjamin nodded. This is what Dr. Ellison had consistently been testifying since the beginning, that Annie was killed around midnight. It still didn't line up with the other evidence. But this kind of new-fangled scientific information was so far beyond most people's scope of understanding. Stories of circumstantial evidence and timelines were much easier to understand, so would probably be given more weight by both the jury and the gallery.

"Is it possible the wounds could have been self-inflicted?" asked Harrington, pre-empting such questions from the defence.

"No, I don't see how the wound at the back of the head especially could have been."

In his cross examination, Ruggles wanted to further explore the concept of time of death. "Is it possible for the body to have cooled faster than what you are suggesting?"

"There have been a number of cases in which bodies have been known to cool after nine or ten hours. No two bodies would cool alike. A fleshy person would not cool as quickly as a lean person. The extremities would be the first to cool and then the chest and abdomen are the last parts," Dr. Ellison explained.

"And how did you test the temperature of the body?"

"Only with my hand. The body was colder than my hand."

Ruggles then returned to the blood loss from the wounds. "You mentioned the ragged nature of the cuts twisting some of the arteries and veins. Would this also reduce the spurting of blood?"

"Yes, it would make quite a difference. When the jugular vein was severed, the blood would be apt to spurt at right angles if there was a square cut. Otherwise, it would depend upon the way it was cut. In this cut, the arteries and veins were torn, and you could not tell which direction the blood would go."

After all the discussion of blood spurting and wounds, Benjamin was ready for a break. There was to be no reprieve, however, for the prosecution next called Dr. Lovett to the stand.

As he approached the witness box, the doctor nodded in acknowledgement to his brother-in-law, H. H. Wickwire, the lawyer aiding the prosecution. Benjamin wondered if this was an advantageous connection for the Crown, but realized it was probably hard to find someone in the Valley not connected to another. Lovett also acknowledged a few others in the room, whom he probably knew from having grown up in Kentville.

The doctor explained that he was the coroner for Digby County. He described again how he arrived at the Kempton house and found the body lying on the left side with the only wound visible in that position the gash in the forehead. He did not notice the other wounds, like the one to the throat, until the body was moved and later examined during the inquest.

"Was there any heat in the body when you examined it?" Harrington asked for the prosecution.

"The body was quite stiff when I saw it. There was no heat about it that I recognized. There might have been some heat. I tested the body with my hand. I calculated that there was no heat whatever. There might have been a degree of heat in the body. To the touch, the body was cold when I got there between nine and ten o'clock."

Benjamin looked over at his fellow reporter with a raised eyebrow, but his colleague didn't seem to notice. The only thing the doctor was sure about was that he was unsure.

"After you gathered your jury and began your inquest, what was your first task?"

"I examined several witnesses. I started with Peter Wheeler, for he was the one who originally found the body. I swore him in and took his deposition down in a manuscript. This is the original deposition taken by me and signed by Peter Wheeler in my presence."

Dr. Lovett opened the leather satchel he had carried with him and dug through it until he found a few pieces of lined paper, which he pulled out and waved in the air. "This deposition was taken under oath and accurately represents all that was said by him during this examination, which took place in the house at the scene of the death of the girl. He made no objection to me examining him and or to giving his statement. The jury and I asked him questions and he did not refuse to give the answers."

"Will you please now read that deposition here in open court?" asked Harrington.

Ruggles jumped to his feet. "Objection!"

Harrington, caught off guard, glared at the defence lawyer.

"On what grounds?" Justice Townshend asked.

"Permission to question the witness, and my point will be made clear."

Harrington nodded, indicating he was finished, and returned to his seat.

Ruggles approached the witness box. "Did you sign this deposition?" Ruggles asked Dr. Lovett.

"No, only Peter Wheeler signed it. But I took it down. I signed the entire dossier of depositions at the very end on the last page, however."

"And in which county was the information collected?"

"The first part was in Digby County, where this deposition took place, and then I finished the inquest in Annapolis County."

"Prior to interrogating the accused, was he at all cautioned or told that the evidence could be used against him?"

"No, I did not caution him in any way before taking his evidence, nor did I tell him that his evidence might be used against him. I did read the deposition over to him, though, before he signed it."

"This is the grounds for our objection, your Lordship," Ruggles said, facing the judge. "We object the reception of the deposition on the ground that the prisoner should have been cautioned, and also on the ground that the coroner completed the work in the Annapolis County, outside his jurisdiction. This makes the depositions null and void. Additionally, the coroner should have signed each deposition."

Benjamin scratched his head. He wondered how many other communities had a county line go right through the middle of them. *How confusing it is for legal procedures. Besides, this doctor is so new it is evident he really hasn't much of an idea what he is doing.*

No one else had seemed to notice this, though.

"I would like to remind the court," Harrington said, standing, "that Peter Wheeler was not under arrest at the time his deposition was taken, and therefore was not required to be cautioned. Do you have his original deposition?" he said, turning to Dr. Lovett.

"These are my original notes. I swear that this statement is exactly what he said at that time."

"Objection overruled," said Justice Townshend.

Ruggles sat down, deflated.

"This deposition was taken at the Kemptons' house and Peter Wheeler stated as follows," said Dr. Lovett, beginning to read from his notes.

Peter

Peter was awoken by a sharp toe to his side. He'd fallen asleep on top of the quilts next to the stove.

Groggily, he opened his eyes to see Tilly looming over him.

"Up and at 'em," she said.

Peter attempted to roll over, but Tilly prodded him again with her toe.

"I need you to go up to the Kemptons' and fetch the milk. Take the kettle."

"Why can't the kids go?" he protested.

"They are getting ready for school, I'm getting ready for work, and besides, your feet are younger than mine."

Peter rubbed the sleep from his eyes, stood, took his coat and the kettle, and headed up the steep hill to the farm.

He knocked loudly on the front door.

Hearing no response, Peter entered the Kemptons' house through the back door. After having worked as a farmhand for the family for over a decade, he felt comfortable enough sticking his head inside to shout for Annie, who may not have heard his banging.

"What in tarnation?"

Peter pushed on the door, but something behind it was preventing the door from opening. He pushed harder, and knocked louder, causing a banging noise from the other side.

Once he opened the door, he realized a small stick had been placed up against the door, preventing it from opening.

"Annie?" he called out. "Tilly wanted me to come up and get some milk from you. Annie?"

Hearing no response, Peter walked through to the kitchen and could see through to the room where everything was topsy turvy.

"Annie?" he called, this time getting a bit more nervous.

His eyes frantically searched the room until he finally found her lying on the floor, on her hands and knees. "Oh, Annie! Thank heavens you have only fainted!"

He rushed over to her, knelt beside her, and gently put his hand on her forehead. His hand snapped back quickly, as if he had been burned; however, it was the opposite. Annie felt cold to the touch.

There was blood both on her and under her. He could see a cut on her neck. What barbaric act had happened here?

Seeing her in an awkward position on her hands and knees, Peter gently rocked Annie's body onto her left side. He quickly looked around, and spotted Mr. Kempton's coat in the front entrance way. He grabbed it and used the coat to cover Annie's body from the shoulders down.

Peter's mind started racing. What if someone was still in the house?

He rushed to the front door, only to find it still locked. He ran through every room in the house, covering everywhere from the upstairs to the cellar, but could find no one.

I need help, he thought. *Omer!* He was the nearest neighbour and would know exactly what to do.

Peter took one last look around, left through the front door, and began running down the hill, through the snow, towards the Rices' farm to tell them the news. Afterwards, he would continue home to tell Tilly.

The reporter

Although he had heard the account many times before, and was even there when Peter Wheeler originally gave it, this time Benjamin picked up on a few details he hadn't noticed before.

First, in his testimony, Peter mentions Annie being on her side, yet, he claims to have told several others that he found her on her hands and knees and rolled her onto her side. An important point, if true. Could a dead body actually freeze in position on its hands and knees?

Dr. Lovett continued reading. "I saw Annie yesterday afternoon about half-past four or five o'clock as she was coming to or returning from the bridge. I saw her in front of her house, but I did not speak to her. She did not speak to me."

Another point not mentioned in this deposition is the fact that he and Hardy Benson did in fact go back up to the house later that night. These details came out much later, so Peter is caught in yet another lie, having recounted the last time he saw her.

"I did know that Grace Morine was going to stop with her last night. Annie Kempton told me in the forenoon that Grace was going to top with her that night. I saw Annie in the front door as she came and called to me. I was passing up the road before noon. I went into the house and was there for about half an hour. No other person was around. She was at dinner and offered me some beans, but I declined. I was sitting down in the room, and she was making flowers."

Benjamin could picture these flowers perfectly, having seen her creations still on display at the Bear River Hotel. *So much beauty; gone too soon.*

"Annie asked me where Tilly was working, and I told her at the hotel. She wanted to know how long she was going to stay there at the hotel, and I said I didn't know exactly, but I told her I knew she had to work every day this week. So Annie told me that Tilly need not mind coming up to stay with her for she was going to get Grace Morine, for it would be just fun for Grace to come and stay all night. I do not know if Grace actually promised to come, but Annie said she would get her."

And this is the crux of the whole argument right here, thought Benjamin, the start of his downfall. *Did Peter make this up as an excuse to find Annie alone?*

"I did not go to the Kemptons' house often. I never attempted to frighten her at any time."

There were a few guffaws from the crowd, but Dr. Lovett kept on reading, without looking up.

"I used to see Hardy Benson coming home with her. He came from the bridge with me, and I know he did not go home with her that night."

Hardy Benson, thought Benjamin. There were too many unanswered questions about his movements. He made Benjamin uneasy.

"Annie told me, before noon, that she was going to the bridge later that day to get paper. I didn't see any other people going home with her. But what I did see was at twenty minutes of two this morning, three men went by the house talking. I don't know who they were, but I could give a general height and description. I know this, because I was cooking meat to go into the woods. I fell asleep laying on the quilts next to the stove. I was so cold, and the talk of these men roused me. I built the fire and let the meat cook and kept it going until morning."

Dr. Lovett kept reading, page after page, pausing to catch his breath and clear his throat.

"When Hardy Benson and I came from the bridge, and got to the corner, there was a man there that came out from under Clarke's mill. I did not know who he was, and I could not describe him. I am pretty certain that Benson saw him, too. He went down towards the hill leading to the Reserve, but was wearing a long overcoat, but he was not a tall man. I could not tell if he lived up on the Reserve or was a white man. I didn't look back at him."

After many other details the deposition returned once again to the murder scene.

"When I came in, I saw blood before I pressed my hand to her forehead. There was a piece of wood that was alongside the stove with blood on it. I never looked for knives or anything. I saw the cut without raising the head of the corpse. I had no idea she was dead, or her throat cut, and I wanted to see. Then I went to see Mrs. Rice and told her Annie was lying on the floor with her throat cut. I had gone up for milk but did not get any. I was just in the house long enough to go into two rooms and the cellar and run all the way home. I did not stop to look for tracks."

When he had finally finished reading Peter Wheeler's deposition, Dr. Lovett put the papers down and finally looked at the crowd.

"Sure sign he's guilty!" cried a man.

Benjamin turned to locate the voice. He wasn't sure if he was a man from Bear River or someone local who had come to take in the ordeal. It was just another middle-aged, white, upper-class man who looked the same as the rest.

"He certainly had the opportunity! Hang him now!" The more the crowd cheered, the more the man continued to shout.

Peter continued to stare straight ahead, without any reaction.

Harrington stood from where he had been leaning against his table, listening to the reading of the deposition. "At what stage of these proceedings did you put Wheeler under arrest?"

"It was a little time after he gave his evidence. On the same day I thought it was right to put him under arrest."

"Damn straight! Confess and repent! Your punishment is a lifetime in hell!" The same man continued shouting, egged on, Benjamin believed, by the crowd.

After a few more medical questions about the wounds, cooling of the body and the blood spurting, Ruggles finally had his chance to cross examine the witness.

"How much experience do you have conducting inquests such as this?" he asked, crossing his arms and leaning in.

"I have only conducted two coroner's inquests—two including this one. I think I got the statements down exactly as the witnesses said them. I read it over to each witness after I took it down and asked them if there was anything wrong in it, and if so, to tell me and I would have it changed."

"As to the position of the body and the wounds, is it not true that Wheeler demonstrated how he found the body?"

"Yes, I saw Wheeler get down on his hands and knees beside the body to show how he found her."

The fact that the body may have been in a different position was never considered by any of the doctors or to Detective Power, thought Benjamin.

Ruggles then focused on the deceased's body temperature so he could pinpoint the time of death. Benjamin recognized the tactic. Peter Wheeler had an alibi for after nine o'clock in the evening, and if the body was still warm, then the murder would have happened around midnight, and Peter would be innocent.

"You told us at the preliminary examination," Ruggles said, "and I quote, 'I noticed a degree of heat'. Is this not true?"

"I think I said there might be a degree of heat. I cannot say that I noticed a degree of heat. If I said that, I was mistaken. As I remember it, I think I said that there might be a degree of heat."

"Do you deny that you said that you noticed a degree of heat?"

"Insofar as I remember, I deny that I said it."

While he was talking, Benjamin noticed Ruggles' co-counsel at the table frantically leafing through sheafs of paper. He finally looked satisfied and sat back in his chair, arm outstretched with a single piece of paper.

Ruggles swooped it up and began to read. "I have the transcript here from the preliminary trial. In front of the magistrate for that trial, you were recorded as having said, 'She was almost cold.' Did you use that expression?"

"If I said that it was a mistake."

"You would naturally remember better about the condition of the body at that time than now, wouldn't you?"

Ruggles let the question linger in the air without expecting a response. Then, he sat back down and the witness was dismissed.

A few other witnesses were called to the stand to testify seeing Annie Kempton walking home from the shops in downtown Bear River around five o'clock. Following that, surveyor Bernard Parker, who helped trace the footprints in the snow, was called to the stand.

Under Harrington's examination, Bernard explained how, in the company of Omer Rice, he went out around the Kemptons' house and property looking for footprints in the snow and took measurements of them.

Bernard presented four maps he had drawn of the land and one of the layout of the Kempton house. Two were drawn to scale with measurements and chaining, while the other two were drawn by guess, using some sight and some pacing.

Benjamin knew what Bernard was talking about, for he had seen him out in the area doing some of these measurements. It involved dividing the area into a series of connected triangles, erecting poles and measuring the distance between them using chain link.

Bernard then repeated his story of going to the Kempton house and seeing the body for the first time. He could not see any wounds on An-nie's neck but did notice a large quantity of blood in the neck area.

When it was Ruggles' turn for cross examination, he returned to the point about the rabbit snares. Peter Wheeler had suggested he was in the area that day in question because he was checking on his rabbit snares. Bernard had said he had gone out specifically to look for them a few days later but found none.

"Why do you think you didn't find any rabbit snares?" Ruggles asked.

"If the snares had been set in that wood previous to the snow fall on Sunday, it would be difficult to find them if they were snowed over. It would be a matter of considerable difficulty going along through the woods to detect snares set in a brush fence unless you were looking par-ticularly for them. Rabbit snares are frequently set in brush fences."

By the time Bernard had finished, it was late in the day, so Justice Town-shend adjourned the court until the following morning.

11: I don't remember

Knowing how many people had tried to attend the proceedings the day before, Benjamin rose extra early and decided to camp out in front of the courthouse shortly after seven o'clock in the morning. The weather was warm and beautiful, and he enjoyed watching people passing on the sidewalks.

Men and women were both in their best outfits, including long tails, top hats, and bonnets. This was probably the event of the season, if not the year, and they wanted to tell their friends and children that they too had seen the murderous Peter Wheeler.

Benjamin wondered if they should be charging admission, if for no other reason than to pay for the jailhouse bills that his *Digby Courier* colleague kept complaining about.

When the doors finally opened, he secured a seat at the front. He was thankful he got there early, for there were more than double the people outside the courthouse who could not get in, than those inside.

Justice Townshend brought the proceedings to order and the first witness, Jeremy Louis, was sworn.

Harrington began the day's questioning asking the witness to describe the position of the body, as he was one of the first on the scene.

"She was lying there on her left side. Her head was turned towards the window. Her right arm was bent up towards her throat. Her head was kind of twisted down and her chin was on the floor. I could not see any cuts on her throat. I saw blood on the carpet right by her throat."

"After the fact, Wheeler actually told you that he found the body in a different position, isn't that so?"

"Yes, sir," he said. "I had a conversation about the body with Wheeler. He said the way she was laid was not the way they found her. He showed me the position that he said he saw her in when he found her that morning. He said that she was lying on her knees with her elbows and head on the floor. He actually got down on the floor and showed me the position.

He said he thought it was not right for people to go there and see her lying like that, so he moved her to her side and got the coat and covered her."

"So, what you are saying," said Harrington slowly, "is that the way Peter described the scene is categorically different than what you and the previous witnesses, who were some of the first on the scene, saw."

Harrington turned his back to the witness and strolled back to his seat. "No further questions."

But if he had moved the body, wouldn't that have made the murder scene different for the first few witnesses? Benjamin didn't understand.

Then, with a flick of a finger, Harrington signalled to someone at the back of the room, and the main courtroom doors were flung open. Standing in the entranceway was Detective Nicholas Power, who had just arrived on the train from Halifax.

With his large, looming shape, he blocked the sunlight, casting a shadow in the room. He stood there, hands on hips, surveying the room, before the crowd parted and allowed him to walk to the front, where Harrington guided him to the witness box.

The crowd went silent, knowing they were in the presence of someone important, although they might not have known who the man was.

As Detective Power positioned himself in the witness box, he shuffled, trying to get comfortable in the small space. He took off his hat and placed it on his knee. Once ready, he looked over at the prisoner and glared, then turned to Harrington and nodded.

"For the record, can you please state who you are and your connection with the case," said Harrington.

"I am Detective Nicholas Power, here from Halifax. I was first employed to act in this case on Wednesday, the 29th of January, the day after the body was discovered. I was sent down there by local government—the attorney general—to lead the investigation. When I arrived, I proceeded at once to the Kempton house."

"And what were some of the first activities you undertook upon your arrival?"

"At first, Mr. Bernard Park and I went to look at the footprints in the snow. I saw the ones behind the pig pen, around the barn, and on the road and in the field on the opposite side from the house. We examined those tracks and took notes."

"Then what?"

"I took the prisoner's clothes to examine for blood."

Detective Nicholas Power

"What would you like to do next, sir?"

Charles Dunn stood, hands on hips, looking at Nicholas Power. He had been following the detective around all morning, continually informing him as he conducted his investigation, reminding him of his connection to the American Detective Agency.

First, they measured the fields and area surrounding the Kempton farm, then they talked to a few of the witnesses. Dunn tried to soak up every morsel, trying to improve his detective skills with every step. Although it was cumbersome to have someone continually in his shadow, the detective did enjoy the flattery.

"I think it is time to go see our friend, Peter Wheeler."

"Yes, indeed. I was thinking just the same thing. The community is most certain that he is our murderer! I shall take you to him myself," said Dunn. "He's staying over in the jail cell in Constable Henshaw's house."

In small towns, where the most common infractions tended to be public drunkenness, illegal poaching, or riding horses too quickly through town, it was not uncommon for a jail cell to be found in a family's home, when a formal courthouse and prison were not close by. Like other local jailers, Constable Henshaw also worked elsewhere, as keeping the jail was not a full-time occupation. When not housing prisoners, he worked as house joiner.

Dunn guided Detective Power to the Henshaw home, not far from the Kemptons' and Tilly Comeau's houses.

Detective Power stood in front of the large, framed house that, from the outside, looked like any other house in the area. The only tell-tale sign was that there were iron bars across some of the windows.

"Thank you, Mr. Dunn. You have been most helpful," he said, slightly bowing his head.

"You are most welcome. It is my pleasure to bring you here."

"I mean, I can proceed from here on my own."

Dunn's face looked crestfallen. "Are you sure, sir? I don't mind at all. I could—"

"I am quite certain. I now have my bearings. You have been most kind and generous with your time."

Without giving him a chance to argue, the detective proceeded up the steps and knocked on the wooden door.

"Mrs. Henshaw, I presume?" he said, taking his hat off when a woman in an apron opened the door.

The young woman had obviously been baking, for the bottom corner of her apron had been hastily tucked into the waistband, creating a triangular shape hanging in front of her dress. He had seen his own domestic do this countless times when she answered the door, or greeted the family, wanting to hide the dirty part of the apron from guests.

"Yes?"

"I am Detective Power from Halifax, and I am here to speak with your prisoner, Peter Wheeler."

"Yes, sir. Right this way, sir," she said, stepping back and allowing him to enter.

"He's just down this corridor, last door on the left. You must excuse me; I have some soup on the stove and bread in the oven for his dinner and ours."

She turned and left the detective to fend for himself.

As he walked down the main hallway in the house, Power noticed how several of the rooms had been converted into jail cells. The cells were lined with metal on the ceilings, walls, and floors. The bars on the windows were probably made by the local blacksmith. In the centre of the house, there was a wood stove that was used to heat the cells. Besides having a door made of iron bars, each room also had an outer wooden door that could be closed to block out noise from rowdy prisoners.

When he reached the end of the hall, he found Peter perched on the bed in his cell, reading the Bible. He raised his head when he heard a noise at the door.

"I am here to investigate the case, my friend," the detective said by way of introduction. He took an iron ring of keys from a hook on the wall, unlocked the door, and entered.

"Thank you for coming, sir. I hope you will soon be able to clear up this vast misunderstanding."

"That is my intention. I will be heading the investigation from here. The first order of business is to take all the clothes you are wearing. That is to say, I need your coat, vest, shirt, pants, and larrigans."

"But what shall I put on instead?"

"That is not my concern."

Peter stood, turned his back, and slowly started to undress. As he took off each item, he folded it and placed it on the bed in a neat pile.

Taking pity on him, Detective Power called again for the mistress of the house and asked her to bring an extra set of clothes for the prisoner.

"I have a better pair of pants than these," Peter said, referring to several holes and places where the fabric was threadbare. "This is the only coat I have, though. It's the best thing I own."

Detective Power said nothing, but was inwardly revolted by the dirty, dark-blue sack coat. He would never have been caught wearing the likes, especially one in such a state.

"You might find blood there," said Peter pointing to the right side of his coat at the part that would hang around his hip, just below the pocket. As he took it off. "But if you find any blood there, it's from a dead rabbit."

"Is that so?"

"If you do find blood there, I can account for it because I carried a dead rabbit which I shot some time ago. I got blood on my coat when I carried it back home."

"Where?" the detective asked. "Show me."

Peter picked up the coat and began to examine it but was having difficulty. "I can't find it now."

Power swooped up the clothes Peter had been wearing for the last several days and tossed him new ones to put on. The detective held Peter's clothes at arm's length because of the smell and left as quickly as he had arrived, leaving the mistress to re-lock the cell.

The reporter

"Before he made these remarks about the clothing, did you use and inducement, threat, trick or device of any kind to induce him to say anything?" Attorney Harrington asked.

"Certainly not!" said Detective Power, highly offended. "I said nothing of the sort whatsoever."

"What he said was completely voluntary?"

"It most certainly was."

Not happy with the responses, Ruggles continued the line of questioning in his cross examination. "Did you make any statement to him whatsoever at that time?"

"I told Wheeler I was there to investigate this murder case. I think he understood that I was a detective on the case. I told him I wanted his clothing, and I got him others to put on. He took off his coat."

"Did you make any remarks as to his guilt or innocence of the crime?"

"No."

"Did you caution him in any way that what he said might be given in evidence against him?"

"No, I did not—nor did I interview him in any way."

"What else did you say to him before this conversation took place?" Ruggles asked.

"I had very little conversation with him. I told him who I was and what I was there for and asked him to take his clothes off. That is about all I said to him. I might have said something else."

"Do you remember saying anything to him about the attitude of the people of Bear River were taking in regard to him?"

"No."

"Are you positive on that point?" Ruggles asked, leaning in. He was not afraid to take on the big city detective.

"I don't remember that I did. I hardly had the opportunity of knowing that attitude myself. I was only there a few hours. It was about five o'clock when this investigation took place."

"You do not swear that you did not say anything such as that."

"I don't remember saying it."

"Will you swear positively that you did not say it?"

"No, I will not!" he said with great force. "I do not see where it would come in. It would have been completely uncalled for."

"Do you remember saying anything to the effect that you were his friend?"

"No."

"Will you swear positively that you did not say that?"

"I think so."

"But will you swear positively?"

"I feel confident that I did not. I do not think I did, but I will not swear positively that I did not say that to him."

Benjamin's head was going in circles. Ruggles was like a dog with a stick—not wanting to give up.

The defence lawyer then turned to the judge. "Your Lordship," he said, "I object to the admissibility of any statement made by the prisoner to the detective under the circumstances."

He then returned to his table where his co-counsel passed him a book with an underlined passage. "There is case precedence as cited in section 592 of the Code, and it refers to the case of the Queen versus Thompson in 1893."

Benjamin was still getting used to court cases referring to the criminal code. It had only existed here in Canada for less than five years, and lawyers and judges were still new to referencing it themselves.

Judge Townshend turned to the witness and asked a question. "Can

you undertake to say definitely whether you used these expressions together or not: 'The people of Bear River are down on you, but I am your
friend.' Can you definitely swear?"

"I am satisfied that I did not use these words together," said Detective
Power. Then with even more conviction, he continued, "I feel convinced I
did not use them."

"Then, all statements from the accused are admissible," the judge
ruled.

Exasperated, Ruggles sat back down, and Harrington readdressed the
prisoner.

"Did you indeed examine the coat for blood?"

"I did, but could find no signs of blood," he said.

Harrington moved on to the conversation that Detective Power had
with Peter when he was transporting him from Bear River to the Digby
jail.

"On that drive to Digby, did you prompt the accused to say anything to
you?"

"No," he said adamantly. "The driver of the sleigh was in the front and
he and I were in the back. We had driven fully a mile or more before he
or I ever opened our mouths. But after that, the prisoner began to talk
about the case. He complained to me about how he was being used or
suspected."

Detective Nicholas Power

When the sleigh and driver pulled up in front of Constable Henshaw's
house, Detective Power was waiting on the front steps. Peter Wheeler
stood beside him with an oversized coat, which obviously was not his
own, draped over his shoulders. His arms could not go through the holes,
for his wrists were still manacled. Detective Power held him strongly by
the elbow.

The detective half guided, half pushed Peter down the stairs towards
the open sleigh. The two climbed into the back seat while the driver sat,
facing forward the entire time, in the front.

With the cold chill in the air, Detective Power tucked a bearskin
blanket around Peter in preparation for the ten-mile journey to Digby,
which would take several hours. Although they could have gone by train,
this way they were assured privacy, and the prisoner would not be let
out of the detective's sight.

After they had left Bear River and were well on the way, Peter was the first to break the silence.

"I am completely innocent, you know! I have not done these things the community has said about me. Annie Kempton was my friend."

"Is that so?" asked Detective Power, who kept his gaze straight ahead.

"I have been used. They are trying to blame this entire tragedy on me, but I swear I had nothing to do with it."

"The evidence shows that you were the one who told Tilly Comeau not to go stay with Annie, for Grace Morine would be going instead."

"That Grace Morine girl is giving false testimony against me!"

"Peter," Detective Power said, turning to face him for the first time, "the Morine girl's evidence is corroborated because where she said she saw you going walking, we found foot marks that were supposed to be yours, and she corroborated that."

"Grace Morine?"

"Yes, the one who lives above the Kemptons' house."

"No, that's her cousin, Sadie."

"Sadie. Grace. Easy enough to get them all confused! It was Sadie Morine who said she saw you out walking in that area."

"Where was that?" asked Peter.

"Down through the Kempton barn, in back of the pig pen."

"I was never there! Even if I was there, what time was that?"

"Between five and six o'clock."

"Well, even if I was there at that time, Annie Kempton was alive then."

"How do you know that?"

"Because I saw her passing our door at seven o'clock that evening going home."

Peter tried to cross his arms under the blanket, while keeping the coat around his shoulders, all the while inhibited by the manacles. After a few more minutes of silence, he continued.

"Now, you also took away my clothing, and you took my shirt. If you happen to find blood on the front of my shirt, I can explain how that got there, too."

"And how would you explain it?"

"On Sunday night, Tilly Comeau was sick, and I came into contact with her."

"I did not see any blood right away on the shirt."

"Well, that's a relief. I can explain everything. You just need to give me a chance to show I am innocent!"

After a few more moments, he continued. "I also have something to say that will come out later, but it will help my case immensely."

"What is it?"

"I need to talk to my lawyer first."

"Why not tell me?" urged Detective Power.

Peter sat tight-lipped, refusing to talk.

After considerable silence, Detective Power said, "Well, you might as well tell me."

Reluctantly, Peter said, "I was at the Kemptons' house the night of the murder."

The reporter

"Is this when Peter Wheeler finally exposed that he and Hardy Benson went to see Annie Kempton later that night?" Harrington asked.

"Yes, right before we arrived at the Digby jail."

A few more shouts echoed in the room. "He's just admitted he is guilty! This case is a waste of time! Hang him now!"

Ruggles jumped to his feet. "Objection! This evidence should not be admitted."

"Sustained," said Justice Townshend.

"And what did you do with Peter Wheeler's clothes?" Harrington asked, changing his line of questioning.

"After looking at them myself in my office, I took the coat, vest, boots, and trousers to Halifax, under the orders of the Attorney General, to Dr. Jacques for further examination. Dr. Jacques has been a senior house surgeon and the medical superintendent at the hospital in Halifax."

"And when you were measuring the larrigans against the footprints in the snow, how was this done?"

"I first measured a larrigan, and it measured a strong ten inches. We then took the larrigan and measured it on the top and, doing it that way, it would not go in the track," the detective explained.

Benjamin did some quick math. If the prints were ten inches, that meant roughly a size 8 or 9 shoe. Peter claimed he wore between a size 4 and 6. This didn't quite add up. But then again, he made a living out of words, and not numbers.

"So, I took it as if a man were actually walking, put my hand inside the boot and set it down into the impression and it appeared to be a perfect fit. It fit perfectly in terms of length, breadth and shape. We did this again in the fresh snow, me using my hand to make a fresh print in the snow and measured it. Once again, it was the same as the footprints that were already found. I did this in several locations along the trail of prints."

Benjamin nodded. He now understood. He could never help himself being mesmerized by the detective's reasoning.

"Are you able to say whether or not the party that made the tracks in the field is the same party that made the tracks behind the pig pen?" Harrington asked.

"They were all alike. I should say very much alike. The track appeared similar all throughout. It was a perfect chain except the break at the road, which was only a foot path."

Justice Townshend noticed that one of the jury members had his hand up. When he motioned, the jury member stood and asked his question.

"Did you look for other tracks?"

"That was one of the first things I asked the men who were with me. Bernard Parker and I went around searching for other tracks and could find no other tracks in the vicinity other than the ones I have already spoken of. Because it was daylight, and I was there to make a careful investigation, I know we did not see any other tracks."

Benjamin thought about this for a moment. *Elmer Crabbe had been hunting in the area on the day in question. The day before Omer Rice and Bernard Parker had gone out looking for tracks. Were their tracks not all visible, too? How could there be no other tracks when Detective Power arrived on the scene? Or maybe he meant no other tracks that could not be accounted for.*

Where was the mention of the button and other new evidence that Detective Power had referred to in one of their recent interviews? Benjamin wondered if perhaps further experts would be called to testify. He would have to see what else unfolded.

Next to the witness box was 17-year-old lumberman, Elmer Crabbe. As before, he testified he had been hunting rabbits the day of the murder and, while out and about, had seen Peter Wheeler going over a hill near Omer Rice's pasture and watched him going near Kempton's old barn and towards the house. He recounted how he called out to Peter, who did not answer him.

In cross examination, Ruggles had Elmer point out how he had been wearing size 8 larrigans that day, as well, when he was out hunting, and wandering around the pastures.

Next up was Omer's wife, Susan, who said she saw Wheeler pass their house the night before the body was discovered, at quarter past five in the evening, but saw no more of him until the next morning. That was when he appeared at her house to tell her that Annie Kempton had been found dead with her throat cut.

Again, in his cross examination, Ruggles worked to raise doubt concerning the timeline. "How do you know it was a quarter past five when you saw Wheeler passing?"

"I did not look at the clock, but I thought it was about that time. I would not say exactly as to the time. I remember my husband going out to milk the cows, so I judge it on that," Susan Rice said.

A jury member raised his hand and, when recognized, asked if there was any blood on the victim's hands.

"There was definitely blood on the back of her hands, and on the back of her fingers, but there was no blood on her palms."

Benjamin let this soak in for a moment. If there was no blood on her hands, that means she probably didn't put up a fight against the knife wounds, for if she had, there should be marks on her palms. He wondered if she had been knocked out by the blow to the head first. No matter which way, it was not a pretty sight to imagine.

Following her, 11-year-old Sadie Morine, who lived above the Kempton farm, was sworn in and gave her evidence with the nervousness that one would expect of a child. She recounted seeing both Elmer Crabbe and, after him, Peter Wheeler on the road going towards the Kemptons' barn. Peter crossed the road ahead of her, she recalled, went over a fence and through the pasture and down behind the pig pen.

As Ruggles stood for his cross examination, there was an almighty bang as the chimney pipe on the stove next to Peter Wheeler came crashing to the floor, narrowly missing the prisoner's head. Several women screamed as the pipe hit the floor and rolled across the front of the room. A cloud of soot billowed throughout the area, leaving a dusting of black powder all over Peter and the lawyers.

Benjamin laughed thinking it looked like a scene from a minstrel show.

Peter jumped in his seat, having felt the brush of the pipe against his hair.

Sheriff Belcher ran to rescue the rogue pipe. He nestled it behind the stove, lest it try to roll away again.

"Good thing that wasn't lit and hot!" Sheriff Belcher said to Peter as he passed by, "You had a narrow escape!"

Peter looked at him and laughed at the absurdity of it all.

"I think this is an opportune time to take a break for dinner," Justice Townshend said. "The court will resume at two o'clock this afternoon."

A good idea. It would take awhile for Peter and the lawyers to get cleaned up.

Benjamin stood and stretched out his legs and his fingers. It had been a rather uneventful morning, with no new information to report. If it hadn't been for the stove pipe incident, he might have considered it even boring. There was definitely no new information that would help sell any papers.

He took a sandwich from his bag and ate it silently as he watched the building caretaker unsuccessfully mop away the soot. A fine dust had coated everything and washing it up mostly created a bigger mess than they had started with.

Benjamin heard the mutterings as people filed out.

"It's a sign from God!"

"It was God's way of showing us he is guilty!"

Benjamin waved to Simon, who was on the other side of the room. They had not managed to get seats together that morning, but just as well, as Benjamin was happy to sit and listen without having to offer his own thoughts.

When the court resumed, as Benjamin had expected, Peter came in wearing new clothes. He shuffled his way into the dock, his chains clanging and rattling as he went. Once seated, he lowered his head, and sat with his usual marked indifference.

The first witness of the afternoon was 15-year-old Alice Morine, whose sister Sadie had seen Peter Wheeler the afternoon of the murder. She, too, helped establish that Peter was seen near the Kemptons' barn and field around six o'clock that evening.

Then, Grace Morine, her 17-year-old cousin, was called to the stand. When she talked about her and Annie being great school friends, she started to cry and pulled a handkerchief from her waistband. Most importantly, Grace said that she had never stayed the night with Annie while Annie's parents were away.

Following her, another teenager was called to the stand. Herbert Comeau, the 16-year-old son of Tilly, with whom Peter resided, said that, on the day of the murder, he went to school, and later came home to cut wood. As he was doing so, he saw the prisoner coming from the direction of the Kempton house.

"Did he say where he had been?" Harrington asked.

"Yes, he said he had been up to Stanley Rice's place."

"Did he say anything more about this?"

"No, he just helped me pile wood on the sleigh."

"And what time was this?"

"It was just beginning to become dusk when Peter came along, so maybe six o'clock. I distinctly remember hearing the five o'clock bell ring when I was on my way to start cutting the wood."

"We understand that you had an encounter with the accused when he was in custody and was under the watch of the constable in an office downtown. Tell us about that," Harrington said.

Herbert

It had been a long day at school. Herbert hated being there, anyway, and didn't see much of a point, when all he wanted to do was be out logging in the woods and making some real money. Besides, since Annie's death only a few days earlier, there wasn't much learning happening at school. The girls kept crying, and the boys were distracted or acting out. It was hard to fathom how something like this could happen in their small village.

Even worse for him was the fact that Peter could be involved. He had known Peter since he arrived over twelve years ago and started boarding with his mother. Herbert was only four years old at the time, so didn't have any clear memories without Peter in them. He had always been a part of his family life, which made the whole situation particularly hard for him. Not like he would talk about it, though.

The inquest had been going on during the day, and Herbert had to miss school the day before to give his testimony. He decided not to go to the trial that day, as he knew he would get the highlights from everyone else that evening. It was just too stressful, not to mention long, to sit through the whole ordeal.

Herbert trudged down the hill from the Academy towards the bridge in the centre of the village. The tide was low and had left chunks of ice along the rocky banks which the rising tide would pick up again in a few hours.

As he neared the village centre, the door to one of the business offices opened and constable Henshaw stuck out his head. Herbert knew him from the community, but also his son, William, was his age and sometimes sat with him in school.

"Herbert! Herbert! Come here, lad," the constable called. He only poked his head through so as not to let the cold air into the rest of the building.

Herbert crossed over. When he got closer, Constable Henshaw said, "Peter is inside here. He saw you through his window, coming down the hill. He wants to talk with you."

"Is that allowed?" Herbert asked, looking around.

"I don't see a problem with it. He's under my custody here, as we wait to go back to the inquest this evening."

"What does he want?"

"He didn't say. He just asked me to call you over."

Reluctantly, Herbert opened the door and stepped inside. A wood stove kept the room warm, so if nothing else, it was a pleasant reprieve from the harsh cold air outside.

"He's in there," Constable Henshaw said, pointing to an adjoining room. There was an internal window so Peter could be watched, but a thick wooden door was locked from the outside, keeping him inside.

"Am I to go in?"

"No, if you go back outside to the side of the building, you can talk with him through the window. I can't open the door for you, or anyone."

Through the glass, Peter waved at Herbert, who reluctantly waved back. He wasn't sure how he was supposed to react, let alone feel.

Herbert trudged back outside and around to where Peter could see him.

"Herbert! It's so nice to see you, boy," Peter said, talking through a gap in the window.

"I'm not sure if I should be here, Peter."

"I know, I know. I just wanted to ask you if you had given your evidence at the inquest yet."

"Yes, I did yesterday."

Peter looked crestfallen. "What time did you tell them you saw me coming down the hill?"

"I said it was six o'clock."

"Oh, you have condemned me."

Herbert looked at him inquisitively. "How so?"

"The authorities are clocking my movements and show a gap of time between half-past five and six o'clock, claiming that I had time to murder poor Annie in that time. Herbert, you know me! You know I would never do a thing like that!"

Herbert just stared at him. He didn't know how to respond.

"The next time you go on the stand," Peter continued, "say it was between four and half-past four that you saw me."

"I don't want to tell a lie! Lying is a sin!"

"Please, Herbert! Will you say it?"

"I don't know."

"It would do you no harm to tell a little lie to get me out of this scrape."
Still, Herbert said nothing.

Peter sighed. "In any case, they've taken my shoes. Can you please run home and get me another pair of boots?"

"That I can do," said Herbert, turning to leave on his errand.

The reporter

Upon listening to the testimony, Benjamin could see Peter becoming increasingly agitated. Not only was he shifting uneasily in his seat, but Benjamin could also see his neck and face flushing, which he tried to hide from the view of the court.

In his cross examination of Herbert, Ruggles again tried to ascertain the timeline, determining how long it would take to get from one place to a next, to determine if he had indeed seen Peter at six o'clock. It was difficult to determine without a watch, and by just guessing how long it would take getting from here to there.

Ruggles then moved on to the dead rabbits.

"I know about Peter bringing home a rabbit and a partridge in the winter. He had been out shooting with a friend. I wasn't there when he came in but came in right afterwards. He had on the same coat that he always wore. I remember it because he came in with a partridge, too, and that was when there was a fine on for shooting partridge."

Benjamin smiled to himself. The lad was a little tattletale! However, it did show that if Peter was willing to break the hunting rules, what other laws was he able to break?

Ruggles then asked about the family routine.

"I was studying my lessons that night, and went to bed in a room off from where Peter sleeps. The door was open, and I did not hear Peter moving all night. He could not have gotten out without me hearing it."

"Did you notice any blood on him that night?"

"No, I was in the room with him all evening, and I did not see any blood on him. I did not see him washing his hands or coat."

"And what was he wearing?"

"He had been wearing the same coat as he always does and wore it the next morning."

At that point, another jury member raised their hand and was acknowledged by Justice Townshend. "Did Peter Wheeler often go up to the Kemptons' to collect the milk?"

"Not usually. But my mother asked him to go up there for milk, as I was going to school, and Peter had not yet left for the woods. No one in particular was in the habit of going for the milk. Any one of us could have gone on any day."

Another jury member waved his hand in the air to gain the attention of Justice Townshend. When acknowledged, he asked if Peter Wheeler carried a jackknife.

"Peter Wheeler had my little brother's jackknife and carried it with him. Peter first borrowed it from him over a year ago. Peter didn't carry or have a sheath knife, though."

When Herbert left the stand, Benjamin was surprised to hear a completely new name be called forward. Finally something new. He didn't think it could be half as interesting as the stove pipe incident.

He was right. The man merely testified that he had seen Herbert Comeau out cutting wood between five and six o'clock in the evening.

Then came the prosecution's star witness: fifteen-year-old Hardy Benson, who swaggered to the front of the room. He talked about having known Annie for the past four or five years. He said the last time he had seen Annie alive was around four o'clock the day before she died, as she was walking to the shops and he was walking home from school.

"Describe what happened in the evening before the body was discovered," Harrington said.

"I met Peter on the bridge that evening. It was a still, moonlit night with snow on the ground—good for sleighing. It was not very cold, nor was it blustery. I walked along with Peter towards his house, with the intention of only going that far. I thought I might have met Annie there. We had been keeping company for awhile, and I thought she might be there."

"What conversations did you have with the prisoner at that time?"

"Peter said that the Morine girl was going to stop with Annie that night and that Tilly wasn't going to be going up after all. I asked Peter if Annie was up there and gone home yet. He said he didn't know but suggested that we go up there to find out. I said I would go with him, but only go as far as the gate, and not go all the way to her house. I did not make a habit of calling upon her when she was alone."

Harrington motioned for Hardy to continue.

"When we got to the crest of the hill, and could start to see the Kemptons' house, we could see a light in the window. That's when Peter turned to me and said, 'The Satan is home! Come on!' and he took off running to her house, but I stayed put."

Upon hearing this, Peter, who had been extremely self-contained throughout the entire proceedings, gave a loud guffaw. Noticing he had done so, he quickly covered his mouth.

Both Harrington and Hardy turned to glare at Peter in the dock. As Hardy continued, Peter became more engaged, leaning forward to catch every word.

"I walked on slow behind him," Hardy continued. "When I got up to the gate, he was going around the corner of the house. He kept saying 'The Satan is home!' and went ahead."

Peter laughed out loud again, this time looking up and over at the jury members, eyebrows raised, as if to dare to say, Can you believe him?

It's a risky manoeuvre, thought Benjamin. It was the first time he showed any emotion, and laughing at the star witness, a respectable lad from the town, would not win him any friends.

"During the time I stayed at the gate, waiting for Peter to come out of Annie's house, I did not see any light at all anywhere," Hardy said. "I heard no noise. I was there about fifteen minutes, and at the end of the fifteen minutes, Wheeler came out the same way he went in."

"More like two minutes!" Peter cried out, not able to contain himself any longer.

Justice Townshend looked at Peter admonishingly. Peter nodded, getting the hint.

"Did Peter tell you to do anything when you got up to the gate and he was going into the house?" Harrington asked, ignoring Peter's comments.

"No, I stopped of my own accord at the gate."

"What happened when he came out?"

"When he came out, he was kind of running, and when he got near me, he gave a jump and threw his arms around me. I don't know why he did that. He'd never done that before. He threw both arms around me. I asked him if Grace Morine was there, and he told me no. Then, he turned to me and said, 'Don't let Tilly know that you and I were up here!' That's when I figured Annie was alone."

Peter let out a huge sigh, but Hardy kept talking over him, more determined to get out his tale.

"Knowing that she was alone, I asked Peter if he thought I should go back and stay with her awhile, and he said yes, he thought I should. But I didn't go. I had never been in the habit of stopping with her when she was alone. I did not intend to go back. I just said it as a joke. I think he understood me to have been joking."

Peter shook his head, and Benjamin could see his lips moving as if he were muttering, but he could not make out any of the words.

"Halfway down the hill," Hardy went on, "I looked back and could still see the lamp burning in the window. At that point, Peter stopped and made water, and then continued walking down the hill."

At that, the courtroom erupted in laughter to the reference to Peter urinating at the side of the road. Hardy smiled.

"Nothing more was said about any of this," Hardy said. "Nothing else of importance occurred."

"What happened after that?" Harrington asked.

"We went back to Tilly's house and were chatting there for a while. He said to me again that it was too hard for Tilly to be traipsing up and down the hill to Annie's house to sleep there, and then to come back and get her breakfast and then go to work. He said the Morine girl would be staying there instead. It was the third time he said it to me. He said it be-fore we went up to Annie's, on the way back down from there, and then when we got to Tilly's house."

Anger erupted from the crowd, and several people stomped their feet in protest. "He set up the perfect alibi!"

Benjamin was sure it was the same man who was shouting earlier.

"After that, it was about nine o'clock, and I left for home," Hardy said.

"And how about when you saw Peter Wheeler the next morning? Did you have any further conversations with him then?"

"I saw him when I was on my way going up to the Kemptons' house after I heard about the murder. He was on his way back down from there and said to me, 'Hardy, for God's sake, don't let on that you and I were up here! You know that there were two knives up there on the floor and they will say that you and I done it.' So I said I wouldn't say anything."

"Did he show any sort of emotion?"

"Not when he first saw me, but when we saw another neighbour, he started to whine and bawl, and really pour it on when he was telling her."

Ruggles was quick to his feet to start his line of questioning. "I want to circle back to something you just said, Mr. Benson," he said, and read from his notepad. "You just said that when you met Peter the morning of the murder, he wasn't crying when he said that poor Annie was dead. But, when I look at the transcript from the inquest, you said then that he was indeed crying. Are you adjusting your story?"

"I think I said at the coroner's inquest that when Peter met me that morning he said Annie was dead and that he was sorry and he com-menced to cry. That is correct," said Hardy.

"You forgot to tell us that a minute ago when you said he had not been crying before," said Ruggles, scolding the boy as if he had been one of his own children.

"I was confused. I thought you were talking about when we met the other neighbour. He was not crying when he met me, just when he met the neighbour."

"Why do you describe it as whining and bawling? Do you think he was putting it on, then?"

"I don't know if he was putting it on or not. He seemed to feel pretty badly over it."

"And what time was it when you got home, Mr. Benson?" Ruggles asked, again in his fatherly tone.

"It was nine or a few minutes afterwards. I looked at the clock. I will not say for sure. I didn't walk very fast when I left Tilly Comeau's house."

Then the questions came in rapid fire.

"Did you see any blood on Peter when he came out of the house?"

"No, there was no sign of blood."

"When Peter Wheeler put his arms around you, you got no blood on your clothes?"

"That is correct."

"Do you know of any other Morine girls who may have stayed with Annie?"

"I do know of another Morine girl who stopped with Annie a few nights. Her name is Etta Morine. She is Grace's sister, but lives with their grandparents. Etta stopped with Annie last winter, but I'm not sure exactly when."

"You used the expression 'Morine girl' in your testimony. Is that the expression Wheeler used?"

"No, he said Grace Morine."

"So, when, in Wheeler's presence, Tilly Comeau asked if she had better go up to Annie's place, are you saying that he then said that the Morine girl was going to stop with her?"

"Yes," Hardy admitted.

Benjamin could understand this point. Morine was one of the most common names in Bear River, and all the girls seemed to be roughly the same age. He wasn't sure how anyone kept the sisters and cousins straight.

"Why would you think that Annie might be out walking around late in the evening?"

"I had seen Annie at the Salvation Army sometimes. That meeting gets over about half past nine or ten o'clock, and I had been in the habit of walking out with her sometimes. I thought she might have been there that night, too."

Benjamin sighed. Something didn't sit right with Hardy's testimony. He had the strong feeling the boy was holding back some pertinent information. But looking around the room, Benjamin realized he was alone in his thinking. Everyone else seemed to think of Hardy as the village's golden boy.

After Hardy was dismissed, the teenaged son of Constable Henshaw again testified how, when in custody, Peter asked him to deliver a message to Hardy Benson saying that they had only walked as far as the electric light station, and that they had seen a light moving in the Kemptons' window, like someone was walking back and forth in front of it. Although Peter had whispered the message to him, his father had still heard. The lad had not delivered the message.

Stanley Rice was the next witness. He employed Peter Wheeler at his logging camp. On the stand, Stanley talked about having had a conversation with the prisoner about Annie Kempton, claiming that Peter spoke frequently about what he would do with her if he got a chance.

"Peter said something about Annie at different times. Lots of times. He said he was going to screw her the first time he got the chance and all that he was waiting for was a good chance. That conversation took place while he was working for me this past December and January. He often spoke about her and it seemed to be in his mind a good part of the time," said Stanley.

"Objection, your Lordship!" Ruggles shouted. "How can this witness know what is on someone's mind?"

"Sustained."

Stanley tried a new direction. "I remember he once spoke of it in the camp, and I told him he ought to be ashamed of himself to talk about a girl that way. He then said, 'Oh my God! She must have a big leg and fat belly and I am going to do it.' I cannot fix any date for this conversation, but it was in December 1895 or January 1896."

Ruggles rubbed his hands together, itching to get at the witness. "These are rather crude expressions, Mr. Rice. Were you shocked to hear them? Or are they expressions you yourself would typically use?"

"I was very much shocked at these expressions. I don't remember using such expressions myself."

"Have you ever used such expressions?"

"I—I—I don't remember."

"Do you swear you never use them?"

"I don't remember. I never used any such expressions such as he used."

"Did you ever use the expression, referring to any girl, that you would like to screw her?"

A few women in the room gasped, while others tutted at the vulgarity of the line of questioning, calling it completely uncalled for.

"I don't remember."

"Will you swear that you never used such an expression as that?"

"No, I can't swear it because I don't remember it!"

"Did you use this type of language before the Magistrate? 'I have seen a girl going along the street and said I would like to screw that girl'?'"

"It was not a decent girl!"

"Did you use these words before Mr. Purdy the Magistrate?"

"I might have said that about an indecent girl. I never used this expression about a decent girl!"

More women gasped at his vulgarity. The fans they had been using to ward off the heat were used with greater intensity as if trying to erase the words from the air.

"Have you heard other people use such expressions like the one you have used?"

"I have heard Peter use such expressions. I cannot swear that I have heard others. I don't remember."

Ruggles repeated himself, not willing to give up on the topic. "Did you use these words before the Magistrate: I may possibly have spoken of some girl in this way?'"

"Yes," Stanley finally admitted.

"How many times in all did you hear Peter Wheeler speak that way?"

"It seemed to be on his mind all the time—a good part of the time. I have certainly heard him use the expression a dozen time and it might be over that. I was there alone when I heard him say this but there were others who heard him say that he would like to do it to Annie Kempton. I only remember him saying this once in the presence of others besides myself. I might have talked about some woman, and I probably have to Wheeler."

"These men are all vile!" whispered a woman sitting beside Benjamin. "They all need to get to church!"

"So, what you are saying is you and he would have conversations about women," Ruggles pressed.

"He would most always start it."

"Answer my question: yes, or no?" Ruggles stepped inches away from the witness and stared at him in the eyes.

"Yes."

"I understand there is a warrant out for your arrest for you using obscene language in the Salvation Barracks at Bear River."

"I don't know anything about that."

"Do you deny using such language?"

"I don't remember."

Apparently, thought Benjamin, *he doesn't remember much.*

"But will you swear it? What about a conversation you had with Peter Wheeler about Inez Rice?"

Benjamin looked up, startled. Stanley Rice talking about a Miss Rice?

The church woman next to him saw his reaction and leaned over to whisper, "Not his sister."

If people in Bear River weren't named Morine, they had the last name Rice. Even if it wasn't his sister, Benjamin was sure it must have been a cousin. He couldn't keep all these relationships straight, and apparently, they couldn't either.

Ruggles took off his glasses, walked up to Stanley and looked at him directly in the eyes. "I need you to be very careful here," he said sternly. "Be very careful of how you answer and think long and hard before you do. You need to remember that Wheeler's life might depend upon your testimony."

Stanley looked down at his feet, avoiding the lawyer's gaze.

"I cannot swear that I did not because I don't remember. I swear I never spoke to Wheeler about Inez Rice, using any bad language about her. I never asked him how he would like to do this to Annie Kempton. I did not tell this before the Magistrate using the expression about the legs and belly. I thought of it only now."

"I understand that you and Peter Wheeler had your differences."

"Yes, that is right. Wheeler and I had a disagreement about money matters. I owed him a balance of two dollars for his work in the woods and he jumped the gun and sued me. He did not get his money until after he was arrested. He sued me before the girl was killed."

Enough about the language, thought Benjamin. He had seen how Stanley Rice had backed himself into a corner, and he could understand Ruggles' tactics.

Peter Wheeler sued Stanley Rice. He humiliated him, he called into practice his ethics and business practices. Stanley was angry with Peter, and now Stanley was making accusations about Peter's ethics with women.

It seemed fishy to him, but from the looks of it, Benjamin was the only one who thought so. He looked up at the jury to scan their reactions to the testimony. All he could decipher were looks of disgust, probably from the vulgar language.

Finally, Stanley was released from the stand, only to be replaced by young Charlie Parker, who had worked at the logging camp with Peter and Stanley. Charlie repeated the story of how Peter had made sexual references about Annie Kempton. Although Ruggles showed that Charlie's pride had been wounded by Peter's teasing about his lack of sexual prowess, the damage had already been done to Wheeler's character. Both Stanley and Charlie had planted the idea that Peter was a sexual predator with designs on Annie.

Following these witnesses, Charles and Estelle Rice, father and sister of Stanley Rice, were called and testified that Stanley was in the woods at the time of the murder, and that they did not see Peter Wheeler that day. Peter had intimated to Herbert Comeau that he had gone to Stanley's house to collect money owed. These family members disproved this.

When these witnesses were released from the stand, the night sky was starting to close in. Sheriff Belcher rose from his seat and lit the kerosene lanterns that hung on hooks around the inside of the courtroom. A warm yellow glow filled the room.

"We shall proceed with one final witness this evening before we lose all our light," Justice Townshend said as he moved the lamp on his desk closer to his papers.

Benjamin watched nervously as the lanterns swung above the heads and shoulders of the spectators in the crowded courtroom. One big bump, and a lantern could come smashing to the floor. He had covered too many stories about barn fires from lanterns blowing over, catching haybales on fire, sending the entire building up in flames in seconds. This courthouse had already burnt down once, it didn't need another catastrophe. Besides, the way this trial had already been going, with the stove pipe crashing down, it would be just the luck for the lanterns to break, too.

He did, however, enjoy watching the shadows dance across the walls and the floor of the courthouse, and was thankful they could continue these evening sessions, just to get this trial over faster. He also realized that it was thanks to Abraham Gesner, who grew up not two miles from the courthouse and who invented kerosene fuel for lanterns, that they could be here still operating a trial in the evening.

"The Crown calls Isaac Kempton to the stand."

Slowly, the door to the room along the side of the courtroom opened, and Benjamin watched as the victim's father limped to the front of the room. The courtroom was silent, and the sound of his wooden leg thumping against the hardwood floors reverberated throughout the room.

He slowly situated himself and looked up. Benjamin was surprised to see the man had aged dramatically over the past few months.

On the stand, Isaac Kempton confirmed that he did ask Tilly Comeau to stay with Annie, as he had previously, while he was away logging in the woods. On the times Tilly couldn't stay, he always made arrangements for someone else to stay.

Upon cross examination, Ruggles asked, "Did a Miss Morine ever go to stay with Annie when you were away?"

"Yes, there was a Miss Morine who stopped for two nights once with my daughter. Etta."

"Did Peter ever go up to your house to get milk?"

"I know for certain he went up to our place for milk about two weeks prior to the incident. But that is the only time I know of for sure. I don't know who came up for the milk when I was away."

A jury member raised his hand, and, when recognized, asked, "Do the knives in evidence belong to your house?"

"Yes, they do," Isaac answered.

At the end of this testimony, as promised, Justice Townshend adjourned the court until Monday morning.

Benjamin looked at his pocket watch. If he hurried, he would have time to just board the train and head back to Halifax for the rest of the weekend. He could certainly use the break and change of scenery, and it would give him some time to gather his thoughts for his next story.

12: Anything is possible with God

Feeling refreshed, Benjamin stepped down onto the platform at the Kentville railway station. He was becoming well familiar with the town and was starting to recognize some faces.

Although it was early in the morning, the crowds were starting to gather, so Benjamin knew he had to act quickly if there was any hope of getting a seat. He grabbed his hat and satchel and weaved and wended through the crowd towards the courthouse.

When he arrived, the sidewalk and adjacent lawn were already over-flowing with people.

"Benjamin!" It was Simon.

Benjamin traced his voice and found the other reporter standing near the front of the line, stationed and ready to charge in when the doors opened. He beckoned for Benjamin to join him.

Although he received a few glares and comments from those further back in the line, Benjamin ignored them and went to join his friend at the front.

"Is it just me, or does it seem like there are a lot more people here today than there were last week?"

"Oh, there are definitely more people here," said Simon. "I think their walking advertisement yesterday, helped."

"What are you talking about? I went home Saturday night and missed everything, I guess."

"Yesterday morning, the jury members filed out of the Aberdeen Hotel and marched down the street in a row to church for the Sunday morning service. After the service, all twelve of them then marched around town for their afternoon constitutional. If people didn't know there was a trial happening in town, they certainly did after that!"

"That would do it, alright! Thank you for securing us a place at the front."

"My pleasure. I've been camped out here for hours. I hear Wheeler's landlady, that French lady, Tilly Comeau is up first. We can't miss that."

At half-past eight, Sheriff VanBlarcom unlocked the doors, and the crowd flowed in, scrambling for any seat before they doors were once again shut, leaving those on the other side to listen through the windows or rely on information flowing out, like in a game of whispers.

At nine o'clock sharp, the sheriff brought in the prisoner amidst a barrage of angry shouts.

"Repent and save your soul!"

"Hang him!"

"Murderer!"

Both the sheriff and Peter ignored the crowd and took their seats.

As predicted, first on the stand was Tilly Comeau.

"My name is Matilda Comeau, and Peter Wheeler has lived with me for eleven years, and I have known Annie Kempton since she was a baby."

Tilly described how she would sometimes stay with Annie when her father was out in the woods and her mother was away. She confirmed Mr. Kempton's testimony by saying she would have stayed with Annie on that fateful night had Peter not told her otherwise.

"Did Peter Wheeler have any connection with you on that Sunday night, the night of the murder?" Harrington asked.

Benjamin stopped taking notes and looked up. *Where is this question coming from?*

He could hear the tittering in the room. Tilly Comeau was a single woman, with obvious loose morals, and Peter, a nubile, young man, but he wasn't sure what this had to do with anything.

Apparently, Ruggles didn't either. "Objection!" he cried. "This line of questioning is completely irrelevant and merely is an attempt to degrade the witness!"

"Sustained."

On cross examination, Tilly mentioned that it wasn't unusual for her not to stay with Annie.

"In the past, when Etta Morine was to stay with her, she would tell Peter, who would then tell me, and I would not go up. Once, Annie even told us about having stayed all alone in the house. She did not tell me if it was this winter or last, but I know she has done it before. She likes to feel grown up."

Tilly then said all the doors of her house were fastened on the night of the murder, and it would have been impossible for Peter to have gone out without her hearing him. This was especially true as she had had a bad cough for two years that prevents her from sleeping much.

"Did you see any blood on Peter that night? You mentioned he was wearing a white flannel undershirt with another shirt and collar over top, along with a bluish coat and vest and pair of gray overalls over his pants."

"Yes, that's right," Tilly confirmed. "He had on those clothes on Monday, went to bed in them, and was wearing the same clothes on Tuesday when the body was discovered. I never saw any blood on him. And I never saw him washing his hands, nor did I see any marks on him. If there was anything wrong with anybody's clothing that night, I suppose I would have noticed it."

"Did you ever hear Peter speaking negatively about Annie?" Ruggles asked.

"Never," she said. "I never heard Peter saying anything against Annie. He always spoke kindly of her."

"Was Annie in the habit of taking off her corsets and shoes before retiring for the evening?"

"Yes, she was. She used to take off her day clothes and put on her red wrapper to go milking. It was like an old dressing gown. I have also seen her sitting in her stocking feet in the winter. Actually, she and I both have sat together that way and warmed our feet before going to bed."

"And would she go early to bed?"

"No, sometimes she liked to stay up to midnight. Especially if she was working on her music lessons. She had her sights on becoming a music teacher, you know. Other times, she would go to the Salvation Army meetings and they get out late, and sometimes to the Baptist meetings, and they always get out early."

John Brooks was sworn in and explained how he lived on the Bear River Reserve, across the river from the Kemptons' house. As he worked there as a farmhand, he would often get there by going across the river and going in front of the Kempton house to strike the road there. He said lots of people used that path, including his sons, who also worked at the farm.

He then talked about seeing a clear, steady light in the Kempton house on the night of the murder. It was dark and the light was burning brightly up to ten o'clock at night. At two o'clock in the morning, he saw the light there, and about daylight, it was becoming dim.

Again, a jury member put up his hand. "Are you just guessing at the time?"

"Well, we had a clock in the house, but it didn't work, and the time wasn't correct. I was judging by my own time. My window wasn't frosty that night, so I could clearly see."

Benjamin scratched his head. He wondered how this testimony could be used to establish a timeline. It could, however, prove that the lamp was burning late into the night and that many people travelled the path near the Kemptons' house and barn.

The morning was moving so slowly, and Benjamin was beginning to regret having taken the journey back to the Valley. Nothing new, and nothing of consequence, was coming out in this trial. If this was the case, he wondered why there was a need for so many trials. He started to nod off, when he heard a new name called as a witness.

The prosecution called Myrtle Godfrey to the stand.

Benjamin turned to see a young girl with long braids, dressed in a Sunday white dress, walk nervously to the front of the room. Her eyes darted around the room. Benjamin couldn't tell if she was deathly scared, or mildly excited about being in the witness stand.

From what he could gather from the gossip around him, Myrtle was the granddaughter of freed slaves who had been brought to Nova Scotia. Her family stood out as being the only family of colour in the community.

"My name is Myrtle Godfrey, and I am the 13-year-old daughter of Richard Godfrey. We live on the Annapolis side of Bear River. I knew Annie Kempton from school."

"I understand you had an encounter with Peter Wheeler. Can you please tell the court about this?"

Myrtle took a deep breath and began. "I was at Tilly Comeau's house last fall. I'm not exactly sure when it was. We already had our first snow fall, but I don't know when that was. Peter Wheeler was there at the time."

"What happened as it relates to this trial?" Harrington asked.

"Annie Kempton went by the house when I was there, and when she did, Peter said, 'I wish I could get that girl alone, and when I was done with her, she would be no good to herself or anybody else.' I then asked him why, and he said it was for him to know and me to find out!"

Benjamin looked up and saw that Peter kept his head down but was shaking it slightly.

When Myrtle had finished her tale, Ruggles stood and approached the witness. He looked sternly at her, square in the eyes. Myrtle squirmed in her seat, but the lawyer did not look away.

"Did you tell anyone about this conversation at the time?" Ruggles asked.

"I told my mother about this at that time, after she came home that night. I never told my father, though."

"And when did your father finally hear about this?"

"I told him after the murder."

"Did your mother or father say anything about this after you told them?"

"When I told my mother, she said nothing. She might have said something, actually, but I don't know what it was. My father just asked me to repeat what Peter had said. That was all."

"Before this, did your father think that Peter was a bad man, or was he on bad terms with him?"

"I don't know. He never said anything against Peter."

"And what were your feelings towards Annie? Word is that you two didn't get along and you didn't like her very much."

"I certainly did not hate Annie!" said Myrtle, who instantly covered her mouth, realizing how loudly she had answered.

"Were you eager to come here to give evidence?"

"Mr. Copp asked me to come give evidence," she said, referring to the crown attorney from the previous trial.

"Did you repeat these words to many people before you came here? Your story presents a bit like lines you have rehearsed for a school play," Ruggles said, taking off his glasses and staring more intently at the young girl.

"I have not repeated these words at all! I only told my mother and father and nobody else! And I didn't go over this as if studying for a lesson or anything!"

Unshaken, Myrtle left the stand and took a seat.

Benjamin took a moment to let what had just happened to percolate. *Had this young girl actually heard Peter say these words? Or was she a young girl having a jealous spat with a friend?*

Most likely, thought Benjamin, *young Myrtle wants some attention. This entire trial is primarily based upon the testimony of teenagers. Did she make this up so she, too, could gain notoriety? Things just aren't adding up.*

Benjamin's attention was brought back to the room when another new name was called as a witness. The side door opened and in strode a distinguished gentleman. As he walked, the tails of his coat floated in his wake.

Benjamin sat up, knowing he was in the presence of someone important.

"My name is Dr. Hartley Jacques, and I live in Halifax and practice medicine there. In the course of my studies, especially for the last three

186

or four years, I directed special attention to microscopical analytical works."

"And how did you become connected with this case?" Harrington asked.

"I received from Detective Power some clothing, which I now have in my possession here in court. This included trousers, overhauls, a vest, and coat. He handed them to me to make an examination and determine the presence of blood. They have not been out of my custody since that time."

"How do you test for the presence of blood?"

"I started out using a hand glass to look for suspected spots. I could find no spots on the inside of the coat. Then, I applied more rigorous tests. There are four or more standard tests for confirming the presence of blood. The first test employs the microscope. We take a small section of the suspected portion of the clothes and tease it out by putting it into a chemical solution to separate these bodies known as corpuscles from the serum. We then put the solution on a glass slide and place in under the microscope. If there is blood present, you can see these corpuscles."

"How reliable is this test?"

"That test is absolutely infallible so far as blood is concerned."

"Did you perform any other tests when looking for blood?"

"Yes, I performed two other tests that involved a series of chemicals and the microscope."

Benjamin tuned out as he went into the scientific explanation of these tests. Whatever they were, they definitely sounded complex. He could also see those around him starting to lose interest. These tests were relatively new and, as a result, people, including Benjamin, didn't quite know what to think about them, or whether to trust the results.

"And what did you find?" Harrington asked.

At this point, Benjamin noticed Peter perk up. He shifted in his seat and leaned forward to listen attentively.

"I first examined the pair of pants and did not find any blood evidence from them. There were also no suspected spots of blood on the vest."

"What about the coat?" Harrington asked. The lawyer walked to the evidence table and picked up the dirty, dark-blue woollen sack coat. He held it high in the air, revealing several holes near the shoulder where patches of fibres had been cut out.

"I cut out a number of pieces of fabric from the coat and applied them to the microscope. The microscope revealed two spots of blood. They were very small clots about the size of a pin head. Chemical tests also revealed the presence of blood."

"Did you find blood anywhere else on the coat?"

"I examined ten other spots which seemed like suspected portions, first with the microscope, but I could not obtain anything definite. All I have to say is that I can positively swear to two spots of blood, and a few other areas were simply consistent with the presence of blood."

Benjamin noticed Peter shifting uncomfortably, and at the mention of finding the blood spots, his face flushed. He bowed his head and placed his forehead on his hands, hiding his face. Benjamin could only imagine what the man was thinking, and none of it good.

"Is there a test to differentiate between human and animal blood?" Harrington asked, anticipating a question for the defence.

"When testing for blood, there is no difference that can be told between human blood and the blood of other mammals, like dogs, rabbits, or oxen. All chemists would refuse to swear to the difference," said Dr. Jacques defiantly.

When Harrington had returned to his seat, Ruggles picked up his notepad and approached the witness.

"Are there other substances besides blood which, under chemical tests, will give the same results?"

"There might be."

"Over what time period have you been conducting these tests?"

"I received the clothes on February 14 and have been doing tests at various intervals since then. I found two spots of blood on March 31," said Dr. Jacques.

"At this point, any blood would have been well dried. Is it more difficult to conduct an analysis when the blood is dried and more difficult to distinguish the type of mammal?"

"I would not undertake to distinguish the difference between blood types in fresh blood, and I would be utterly at sea looking at blood that had dried. It would be very unsafe to try and distinguish between any kind of corpuscles after they had dried. You would not be certain that they would retain their original shape. It is the plasma, or the water in the cell, where the corpuscles float, and this would not be present in dried blood."

"Returning to the differentiation of blood," Ruggles continued, "I would like to ask you again: Is there any way to distinguish if the blood on the coat was from a human or a rabbit?"

Dr. Jacques ran his hand through his thick sandy-blond hair, then down across his face and moustache, letting his fingers rest on his chin.

He finally answered, "It is almost impossible to distinguish the difference between the two, even in fresh blood."

Ruggles returned to his desk, where his co-counsel passed him an open book.

"I assume you are familiar with Taylor's *Medical Jurisprudence*, the latest edition being published in 1893," he said, tapping the book.

Ruggles waited for the doctor's affirmative response before he continued. "In this tome, seen as the ultimate reference in courts of law for forensic pathology, it speaks a great deal about blood. It says, 'The diameter of the blood corpuscle of a rabbit is about the same as that of a human being. The blood of a rabbit would be one of the most difficult to distinguish from human blood.' Do you disagree?"

"No, I agree with that statement."

Ruggles smiled, closed the book and dismissed the witness from the stand.

After the long technical testimony, Benjamin was exhausted. His hand hurt from writing so quickly, and his head was starting to throb. The heat from the mass of bodies inside the courtroom was becoming overwhelming and he craved some fresh air.

The prosecution had other ideas and, instead of a break, called Digby's Officer Bowles. He was present when Wheeler first arrived at the Digby jail and claimed that Peter had confessed to him.

"What were your duties as it related to the prisoner?" Harrington asked.

"When the prisoner first arrived, Sheriff VanBlarcom asked me to go into the jail cell with the purpose of keeping him safe, or, rather, watching him so he didn't take any desperate means."

"What would you do when you went into his cell?"

"Sometimes, I would go in for a few minutes and sometimes for a quarter or half an hour. On one of these occasions, I had a conversation with him. And eventually he confessed something to me."

Harris Bowles

"Officer Bowles!" Sheriff VanBlarcom's voice echoed through the empty corridors.

Bowles jumped to his feet and straightened his jacket. As far as he could tell, the sheriff was probably double his forty years, or at least it seemed so. Regardless, the man demanded respect, and if the sheriff called for you, you responded immediately.

"Yes, sir?" he said, coming to join the sheriff in the main entrance of the Digby prison.

"I am off on official duties and need you to stand guard over prisoner Wheeler."

"I can assure you the door is well locked, and his chain is fastened around his ankle to the bolt in the floor. It's quite secure."

"He is not a security risk. Or not in that sense of the word. With this being such a tragic case, and things looking quite bleak and hopeless for him, many are worried that Wheeler may attempt to take his own life, rather than having to go to trial and letting justice provide the punishment."

"Oh, we certainly can't allow that to happen. God views every life as precious—even that of the sinner. I shall pray for his soul," Bowles said.

"I need you to do more than just pray. I need you to go down there and watch him, and make sure he doesn't do anything harmful."

Bowles did as he was asked, walked down the corridor and stood in front of Peter Wheeler's cell. He took his wooden baton that was hanging at his side and ran it against the metal bars. The clanging reverberated throughout the prison.

Peter, who had been sitting reading on his bed, merely glanced up from his page.

Bowles grabbed a nearby stool and sat in the hallway, staring in at Peter. He sat with his arms crossed, not saying a word. Peter went back to his reading and ignored him completely.

Eventually, the silence got to him, so Bowles asked, "What are you reading?"

Peter didn't answer, but raised the plain, leather-bound book in the air for Bowles to see. Even from that distance, Bowles recognized the simple gold font. His demeanour softened.

"It makes my heart happy to see you reading the Good Book. If you had only one book, that is the book to have."

"It has certainly provided me with a lot of comfort in these dark times," Peter said, closing the book and looking up. "'Yea, though I walk through the valley of the shadow of death, I will fear no evil, for Thou art with me. And I will dwell in the house of the Lord forever more.'"

"Psalm 23 has always been a favourite of mine, too," Bowles said. "Are you a God-fearing man, then, Mr. Wheeler?"

"I am, indeed. My mother raised me well, during the short time she was with us."

Bowles let that comment slide, not wanting to get too intimate with the prisoner. "You attend church, then?"

"I do when I am able, sir. That is, if I'm not out to sea or working at the logging camp. And if I can't get there, I still have my trusty Bible."

"I'm a strong and faithful member of the Salvation Army here in Digby. Through that, we preach the word of God in a powerful way in the surrounding areas."

"Yes, we have an outpost down in Bear River. I go to the meetings sometimes."

Bowles smiled. "This makes me very happy, Peter! Then, you will know that it was our first parents, Adam and Eve, who first disobeyed God by eating from the forbidden fruit in the garden of Eden, thus causing all men to become sinners. We are all then justly deserving of His wrath."

Peter nodded.

"We are all sinners, Peter, and some of us more than others. You know what is written about murder. Thou shalt not kill."

"I am well aware of the Ten Commandments."

"The good news is, however, that, no matter our sins, no matter our crimes, God will forgive us. Repentance toward God, and faith in our Lord Jesus Christ are both important and necessary to our salvation. If we truly repent, we can be made whole again through Jesus Christ."

"I would definitely rather be in prison, than be cast out of heaven," said Peter, lowering his head.

"Then think about it, Peter. Do you not think it is better to confess your sins if you have committed them, and to receive God's grace? If you committed the murder, it is better for you to confess. We can learn a lot from Second Chronicles: If my people will humble themselves and pray and turn from their wicked ways, then I will forgive their sin."

"I shall reflect heartily upon your words," Peter said. He began rubbing at his ear and tapping it with his finger.

"Your ear bothering you?" Bowles asked, leaning forward.

"Yes, I've been having a dull ache for the past few days. I think from the damp weather and travelling back and forth between here and Bear River by sleigh in the cold wind."

"It is actually more apt to be this inner turmoil and conflict that you are dealing with. Remember the Bible story about Jesus who meets the invalid man? Jesus tells him it was because of his sinful ways that he was afflicted. He heals him, and tells him to sin no more, lest a worse thing happen to him."

Peter nodded, remembering the story.

"This is what is happening to you, Peter. I have prayed that you would become afflicted so that you could see what your sin was doing to you. This earache of yours is the first sign of that. This is a sign that my prayers for you have been answered."

Peter sighed, and slowly bowed his head, as if taking the officer's words into his heart.

"You should confess your crimes for our own good and it would be best to do so when you are under my charge; someone who understands God's enduring power of forgiveness."

"I see what you are saying," Peter said.

"A confession, Peter, will go a long way. Not only would God see fit to forgive you, but so might the justice system."

"What do you mean by that?" Peter slid to the edge of the bed, so his feet hit the floor. As he moved, his chains rattled. He leaned over to rub his ankle, where the chains had begun to wear his skin raw. "Are you saying that if I make a confession, I could petition the officials of the court for a pardon?"

"Anything is possible with God, Peter."

Peter bowed his head as if he was saying a prayer or thinking about the officer's words.

Bowles then reached into his pocket and pulled out a lead pencil. He stood and reached through the bars of the cell and wrote the day's date on the wall. "After you are convicted, and come back to this cell, I want you to look upon this mark and remember this date of your confession and remember our conversation and the salvation of your soul."

The reporter

Ruggles, in his cross-examination stood in front of the court with his hands on his hips. "So, you had been urging Peter Wheeler to confess. When did this happen?"

"Yes, I had been telling him how confession would benefit him. But I don't know upon which date I urged him to confess."

Benjamin wondered why the man did not merely go back to the cell and look at the mark upon the wall!

Ruggles then turned to Justice Townshend. "Your Lordship. I object to the admission of any evidence in relation to any alleged confession brought out by Officer Bowles."

Interjecting, Harrington stood to ask Bowles another question. "Were you speaking of his spiritual or temporal welfare when you urged his confession?"

"Spiritual," Bowles said.

Regardless of the man's religious fervour, Benjamin did believe the officer did have Peter's eternal soul at heart and wasn't merely trying to find evidence for the trial.

The two lawyers battled out whether Peter's confession to Bowles would be admissible. Finally, Harrington conceded and decided to no longer question the witness. The judge dismissed the officer from the stand.

Benjamin sighed, feeling deflated. He had been sitting on the edge of his seat, waiting to hear this confession. Maybe he had been wrong all along, doubting Peter's guilt. If the man was about to confess, perhaps Peter was truly guilty.

Etta Morine next testified that she had once stayed at the Kemptons' house for a week. The night of the murder, however, he had made no arrangement to stay with Annie.

Benjamin recognized the next witness to the stand. It was yet another youth from Bear River. This witness was Denny Brooks, the young son of John Brooks, whose house was on the Reserve, across the river from the Kempton house.

"My name is Denny Brooks, and I think I am 13 years of age. Sometimes I attend the cattle up at Mr. Kempton's house. I was last there on that Monday morning and night."

Benjamin couldn't help notice that the young boy looked terrified on the stand. His eyes darted around the room, and he constantly wrung the cap that was resting on his knees. His voice wobbled each time he spoke.

"Did you go across the river, and along in front of Mr. Kempton's house after the snow fell on that weekend?" Harrington asked.

"I was across there quite a lot of times after snow came. It was a sort of short cut across."

Interesting question, Benjamin thought. He wasn't sure why the prosecution was drawing attention to someone else making footprints in the snow. This is perhaps why they moved quickly to the next question about his whereabouts the night of the murder.

"I was coasting around nine o'clock in the evening on the hill that is in sight of Mr. Kempton's house. I could see his windows from where I was, and I noticed a light on. It was a bright light, and it was going out and lighting again—likely somebody going between the window and the light. That's what attracted my attention. When I got home around half-past nine, I noticed the same movement in the window twice from there, too."

Ruggles picked up on the footprints in his line of questioning. He asked if other people also used that shortcut across the river. Denny confirmed they did.

A jury member raised his hand to ask if Denny saw anyone in the area around the house that night.

"I could see the house plainly, but I could not see the road. I didn't see anyone around the house, but I don't think I could have seen any person in the road or front of the house before the gate."

The next witness was Albert Copp who had acted as the crown attorney for the preliminary trial. He first described how he had been to the home of John and Denny Brooks shortly after the murder to examine their clock. He determined it was running 45 minutes fast. That being the case, it made their timeline unreliable.

Then, he talked about who was in charge of the evidence at various points in time between the trials. Most recently, the items were in the hands of John Coleman, the jailer in Kentville.

Soon afterwards, Coleman testified and confirmed that the pieces of evidence were indeed in his custody and remained in a sealed crate until the first day of the trial, when he brought the crate to the court and it was opened.

At this point, a few of the jury members had some questions for previous witnesses, so several were recalled.

First, John Brooks confirmed that the clock he showed Copp was indeed the one he was referring to on the night of the murder.

Then, Hardy Benson was brought back to the stand. The teenager looked around, wide-eyed, as if wondering what he would be asked next.

A jury member stood to ask his question. "Mr. Benson, could you please illustrate to us the position in which Wheeler had shown the body to be in?"

"You want me to show you?" Hardy asked.

"Yes," Ruggles said. "Show us."

"I'm not sure I can do it just as he showed me."

"Try." Ruggles pointed to the floor in front of the witness box.

Hardy came around in front of the box. He got down on his hands and knees.

Benjamin stood slightly to catch a glimpse over all the heads in front of him. Unfortunately, so too did those in front of him.

From what he could see, Benjamin noticed Hardy fidgeting around on the floor, shifting from one position to the next.

"And?" Ruggles asked, getting impatient with the display.

Hardy ended up on his hands and knees, with his forehead resting on the floor, and his head cocked to the side. "I am about in the position now. I'm sure of it!"

Ruggles allowed the lad to remain in that position for a few seconds longer before he said that was enough. The judge dismissed him.

It was well after lunch when Harrington addressed the court. "Your Lordship. I only have three more witnesses I wish to examine for the Crown. However, they cannot be produced before five o'clock, as they are on the express train bound for Kentville as we speak. I can assure the court they will only occupy half an hour of the court's attention once they arrive."

Justice Townshend turned to Ruggles and his defence team. "And will you start calling your witnesses this evening?".

"No, your honour. The defence does not intend to call any witnesses."

At the mention of this, the crowd erupted. Several men from behind Benjamin began shouting.

"See! Not a friend in the world!"

"No one to stand by you, you murderous fiend!"

"You should have never come here in the first place!"

"We already know he's guilty!"

All the while, Peter sat motionless, staring into his lap.

Justice Townshend banged his gavel a few times to restore order in the room. He took out his pocket watch and noted the time. "Court shall resume three hours hence, at five o'clock sharp, upon the arrival of the next witnesses."

Benjamin sighed with relief and pulled at his shirt collar. With so many bodies in the room, the air was suffocating. His hand was cramped and his back hurt.

Simon noticed his struggles and said, "Why don't we go in shifts? You go and get some air and something to eat, and I'll stay here to save our seats, and then we can swap."

Before he could change his mind, Benjamin nodded, took his hat and satchel, and headed for the door.

He decided to stretch his legs and walk around Kentville. He carefully crossed the street, dodging between carriages and stepping over piles of horse deposits, to peer in the windows of the dry goods shops on the opposite side of the road. He thought about buying something to remember his time in Kentville, but figured the trial memories would be forever etched in his mind.

He carried on towards the train station, where he heard a whistle blow, indicating the arrival of what he guessed was the express train. He decided to get some food from the train station restaurant so he could catch a glimpse of who was disembarking.

~

When court was back in session, the first witness sworn was Joseph Pictou from the Bear River Reserve. Benjamin remembered his story well. He had gained considerable notoriety as the man who had travelled early to Yarmouth, and whom everyone thought knew something about the murder.

According to Harrington's explanation, the prosecution had sent to Bear River and got him to appear as a witness. Benjamin couldn't see that there was any real importance attached to his testimony, other than to eliminate him as a suspect and to satisfy the jury as to his where-abouts the night of the murder, and his reasons for leaving the village so early the next morning.

"That morning, I walked to the railway station, leaving around half-past five, and took the train to Yarmouth. As I was walking to the station, I saw a light in the direction of where the Kempton house is, but I didn't really take a close, particular notice of it. It was dark and blustery cold."

The second of the three newly-arrived witnesses was John McEwan. He too, lived on the Reserve, about 700 yards across the river from the Kempton house. He testified to seeing a man near the Kempton house that night, walking from the upper barn towards the lower barn, then he lost sight of him. He also saw a girl on the road above the barn. "I knew it was not Mr. Kempton, because he walks lame, and this man I saw did not walk lame," McEwan explained.

This confirmed the testimony of young Sadie Morine. Everything was adding up to establish a timeline as to Peter's whereabouts on the day of the murder.

Although he had no watch when he was out chopping wood and saw these two people, McEwan reckoned it was around five o'clock.

The final witness was Constable Henshaw of Bear River, who was called to the stand to identify the carving knife which was found on the floor about three feet from the body. He also confirmed that Tilly's son,

Herbert, did indeed have a conversation with Peter Wheeler while Peter was in custody in Bear River.

"Wheeler wanted him to go and get a pair of shoes for him. I did not hear what took place between them as they were talking through the window and were whispering there for five or ten minutes. I couldn't hear what they said, just that they were whispering."

After a few more questions and, as promised, in less than half-an-hour, Harrington stood up to address the court.

"The Crown now rests. We will call no further witnesses, your Lordship."

Justice Townshend looked over to the defence table. Ruggles stood.

"As previously stated, your Honour, the defence will call no witnesses."

With no further witnesses, Justice Townshend turned to the jury box, instructing the jurors to ask any questions that were on their minds. As a result, a few witnesses were recalled clarifying various points.

By the end of the evening, Benjamin's head was spinning with all the details. He had taken copious notes, while most of the jury members had just sat there listening, relying on copies of the court transcripts from the clerk.

Once so certain the facts presented left a shadow of doubt, now Benjamin wasn't so sure. Hearing all the facts laid out together, there was no denying the circumstantial evidence was strong, as Detective Power had intimated.

And there was still the matter of the confession. *Was Peter really about to confess to the officer about the murder?*

Benjamin churned the ideas over and over again in his mind, never satisfied with the results.

What boggled his mind even more was the lengthy argument that ensued about who should present last to the jury in closing arguments the next morning.

Ruggles argued heartily, referring to the Criminal Code of Canada that if the defence presents no evidence or witnesses, they should then get to speak last to the jury. Benjamin figured it was important to be the last person the jury heard before deliberating, and it also gave the lawyer a chance to refute anything the other side had said in their arguments.

Eventually, Justice Townshend sided with Ruggles and announced that court would adjourn until the following morning at half-past eight, when the Crown would present its closing arguments first.

13: The hardest thing to do

The next morning, Benjamin ensured he was at the courthouse bright and early. He was not going to miss his opportunity to be inside the court room, when potentially the final judgment in the case would be made. All that was left to hear were the closing arguments from both sides and the judge's charge, and then the waiting would happen as the jury deliberated.

The sun beat down on his face and, in the distance behind the courtroom, he could hear a mixture of bird sounds coming from the area along the riverbank, mixed in with the sounds of trains arriving. As time ticked on, the noise of increasing traffic drowned out the sounds of nature.

As he had suspected, hoards of people arrived either by train, carriage, or by foot, for what might be the final day of what could be classified as the biggest trial of the century.

"Benjamin!"

Benjamin whipped his head around to catch a glimpse of Simon running along the sidewalk. His satchel bounced with each step.

"I overslept this morning! This case has been keeping me up all night." He caught his breath after joining Benjamin in the line that had been growing in front of the courthouse. "Besides, I lay awake all night, thinking wondering if Peter Wheeler would actually still be here today."

"What do you mean?"

"Didn't you hear the big news? I have it on good authority that the officials found a bottle of poison in Wheeler's cell last night!"

How is Simon always privy to the inside information?

Benjamin said, "That certainly would corroborate what one of those witnesses said about Wheeler bragging that he would never hang for the crime. Guess he meant he would take things into his own hands well before any hanging."

Benjamin pondered this rumour for a moment, then asked, "What is your prediction for today? You think we'll see a verdict?"

"Absolutely. Not much to get through this morning, and I think it will be a quick decision for the jury."

"You think so?" Benjamin asked.

"Well, the evidence is pretty clearly stacked against Wheeler. I don't see any other possibilities or ways this could end. If I were a betting man, I'd say we will know our answer by sundown. What do you think?"

Benjamin sighed. There was so much swirling around in his head, and his opinions had been going up and down like a pump cart. How could he explain all this to his competitor-turned-friend in only a few words?

At first, like the rest of the community, Benjamin had been convinced of Peter's guilt. Detective Power laid out such a clear path of circumstantial evidence, it was difficult to conceive of anything else. But then, after getting a chance to speak with Peter and hearing all the evidence again, that niggling feeling had come back that something wasn't right.

All the pieces of the jigsaw puzzle did not fit completely together. It was more that they were being forced together. The examination seemed more set on proving Peter Wheeler's guilt rather than looking for evidence in any other quarter.

But as Simon said, he too, didn't see any alternative explanations.

"Hard to say," was all Benjamin could muster.

He was saved from having to elaborate, for the courthouse doors were opened wide and the throng of people pushed in, taking whichever seat they could before the sheriff announced the room full to its utmost capacity.

Once everyone was seated, Justice Townshend opened the day's session.

Benjamin looked over at Peter, who was moving about more than he had throughout the trial. He figured Wheeler must realize this was his last hope, and the reality of that was sinking in.

Harrington addressed the court first, summarizing the key pieces of evidence, followed by Ruggles, who did the same for the defence.

In his remarks, Ruggles agreed that Peter may have been seen in the vicinity of the house and was around the pigpen, but no one actually saw him go into the house at that time. He discussed how medical evidence indicated the murder actually happened after midnight. Ruggles also argued that Peter had had many opportunities to get Annie alone, had he wanted to, so no credence should be put into that piece of information.

"No marks were found on the prisoner, and it would have been near impossible to have gone through such a struggle as the room presented without receiving some marks."

After covering a few more points, Ruggles finished off by leaving the jury with something to think about. "Please consider well the evidence and, if a possibility of a doubt exists in your mind, give the prisoner the benefit of the same and return a verdict of not guilty."

By the time the closing remarks had been made, several hours had passed. Benjamin could feel himself drifting off, not only from the heat that was building up in the room, but also from sheer boredom. He had heard these arguments so many times that he was certain, if given the chance, he could do a half-decent job making the remarks himself.

Upon Ruggles' completion, Justice Townshend called for a lunch break, after which he would make his charge to the jury.

~

When court resumed, Justice Townshend took a few moments to look over the crowd. Benjamin couldn't help but think how regal the gentle-man looked, up on his bench, looking down at everyone. It was easy to see he was a refined man, and all his features were small, thin, and poin-ted, like him. His voice was clear and strong.

"Gentlemen of the jury," he began, "you are empanelled to try the pris-oner for the crime of murder. He is charged with having murdered Annie Kempton in the month of January last at Bear River in the County of Digby. It will be for you to say whether he is innocent or guilty of that crime."

He then very slowly said, making each work important, "It is hardly necessary for me to impress upon you the solemn and responsible duty you are to perform, as it does involve the life of a fellow man. While all would agree that, if guilty of this abominable crime, he should de-servedly suffer the extreme penalty of the law, yet, on the other hand, to doom to death an innocent man would be shocking to our common hu-manity."

He paused and then continued, "You must be guided solely by the evidence produced at the trial and avoid founding your conclusions on mere suspicion or hastily-drawn inferences from suspicious circum-stances. You must use well-established facts that irresistibly point to the prisoner's guilt before you find him guilty. The crown must find him guilty. The prisoner, under British law, does not need to say one word."

Justice Townshend paused to take a drink of water.

"Counsel have done great work in presenting the facts as they pertain to the prisoner's innocence or guilt. I trust you will carefully weigh the evidence and give such a verdict as will commend itself to your consciences."

A few jury members nodded in agreement.

"Now, I will briefly go over the salient facts. Both sides concede that a murder happened between half-past five in the evening and seven o'clock the next morning."

The judge spent a few minutes reviewing the evidence, especially that of Omer Rice, who had described perfectly the condition of both the room and body when he arrived at the scene. Justice Townshend spoke of how the blows to Annie's head would have made her insensible, but not killed her.

"Now comes the question. Did the murderer cut her throat then, or did he return later and, finding her alone and still breathing and knowing if she recovered his liberty, if not his life, was in danger, complete his diabolical work by cutting her throat? I offer no opinion on that."

He then reviewed the Crown's theory that the initial assault was indisputably committed around half-past five.

"The evidence shows that, as far as the rest of the night is concerned, after nine o'clock, Peter Wheeler was not out of the Comeau house, so, if he were the guilty party, he committed the crime between half past five and nine o'clock."

Benjamin could hear Simon muttering, "Yes! Yes!" as he madly took notes beside him.

"And remember, the cow had not been milked. This is of great importance because it was one of the victim's duties to do so, and she certainly would have done that by seven o'clock or earlier in the evening. Additionally, she had dressed in her wrapper, which she did before milking the cow."

Benjamin found himself being swept up with every word the judge was saying.

"We have a good deal of evidence from the doctors as to the time in which the body would become cool. I do not place a great deal of confidence in that testimony in assisting us in determining the exact time. The doctors may have some mode of determining the precise time which we laymen do not understand."

A few jury members nodded. Benjamin could understand how they felt, having no medical background either.

"The medical testimony puts the time of cooling from fifteen to twenty hours, and if we say twenty hours, this would be around seven o'clock in the evening. Fixing the time of the murder is important. The defence counsel says the victim must have been killed after ten o'clock that night. However, that is against the theory of the Crown, as the victim was not in bed."

For the next twenty minutes or so, Justice Townshend talked about circumstantial evidence, providing examples to the jury, then followed that with a discussion on reasonable doubt. Benjamin started to tune out as the judge droned on and on.

"We have no direct or positive evidence in this case. The evidence is merely circumstantial. We can draw certain conclusions, though, from the facts, for example, the accused being seen in the vicinity of the house by different parties that evening."

Following the lecture, Justice Townshend began commenting on the evidence of the witnesses and referred especially to some of the testimony which, in his opinion, was extremely strong against Peter. Benjamin followed along and couldn't help being swayed in that direction once again.

At the time of the murder, which was established to be around half-past five, Peter was seen in the vicinity of the Kempton house, although not in the house itself. Three reputable witnesses testified to this and the fact was further corroborated by the footprints in the snow which were made by the prisoner almost to the door of the house.

"I cannot help speaking of the very correct way in which these men at Bear River took hold of this matter and worked up the evidence, securing such traces as would lead to the discovery of the murderer. Everything was done promptly and with care, and I think it is most creditable to the authorities in that vicinity."

A few people in the crowd clapped and cheered. The judge paused, smiled, and nodded.

He then discussed how Hardy and Peter had gone to the Kempton house later that night in search of Annie. In speaking of Peter, Justice Townshend asked what he was doing in the house during the fifteen minutes while Hardy waited at the gate.

"Hardy Benson's conduct is extraordinary here. He is young and perhaps a bashful man, and he remained outside the house when Peter Wheeler went inside. Certainly, Annie Kempton was in the house then. Was she alive? If the defendant was the murderer, did he cut her throat then or had he done it before?"

There are so many questions, thought Benjamin, *with so few answers and so many possibilities.*

Justice Townshend then referred to the conversation between Peter and Hardy when Peter had just come out, and how the defence counsel had emphasized this point. He reminded the jury that Hardy had asked Peter if he should go up and stay with Annie, and Peter had agreed that he should, since she was alone.

"That was an extraordinary statement for Wheeler to make after this visit. If he were indeed the murderer, and it had already taken place, then why should he make this remark to Hardy Benson?" he asked.

The jury looked confused, as if they were thinking deeply about this very point.

The judge continued, "This point puzzled me too, until I heard the statement from Hardy Benson that it was said in the way of a joke. It is otherwise inexplicable."

The jury nodded.

"Counsel drew your attention to the period when the accused started lying," said Justice Townshend. "He started lying even before he was accused of the crime, or when no one knew a crime had been committed. This was when he told young Herbert Comeau that he had been up to Stanley Rice's house to collect money, which has been proved beyond a doubt as a lie. If he lies about something this simple, what else does he lie about?"

Justice Townshend then outlined several inconsistencies and lies in Peter's explanations. First was his denial of having been at the scene of the murder, and his description of the position of the body of the girl when he claimed to have discovered it were inconsistent, which opened him to the gravest suspicion.

"Peter Wheeler first declared that he found the girl with her throat cut, but when it subsequently appeared that it was impossible to tell from the position of the body and the concealed wounds in the neck that her throat was cut, he altered his statement, saying that he moved the body. This was evidently false, inasmuch as it was clear from the medical testimony that rigidity of the body would not be affected by any attempt to move it. It therefore seems that the accused found it necessary to abandon his original statements regarding the position of the corpse when he found it, and his whole statement seemed to be based on falsehood and deceit."

There were a few "Hear! Hear!" cries from the crowded courtroom.

"Furthermore, the fact that Wheeler adopted an unusual path in approaching the Kempton house on the night of the murder, and his eccentric behaviour about that time, are facts that reasonable men would draw an inference from as to his guilt."

As Justice Townshend listed off each of these points against Peter, the prisoner shifted in his seat. From where he was sitting, Benjamin could see him start to flush. Still, Peter refused to look up.

"In cases like this," the judge continued, "it is usual to look for motive. This type of crime is hardly conceivable in a Christian land. I must say, however, it is not necessary for the Crown to prove any malice or malicious intent. The laws presume malice when a life is taken. If a person, however, would like to have the crime reduced to manslaughter, malice must be disproven. The motive in this case was plainly and palpably lust. He went there to violate her."

A hiss went through the crowd. "Devil! You are going to hell!" yelled a man behind Benjamin.

As he had through the entire charge to the jury, Peter remained calm, showing little emotion or anxiety.

Benjamin continued to ponder the comment about the Christian land. From what he could tell, Justice Townshend was alluding to the fact that Peter Wheeler was from some foreign country where such Christian values were not adhered to.

From there, the judge went through the credibility of several of the witnesses.

"There were a few witnesses who gave evidence as to motive. I do not put any trust into the words of the little Black girl, Myrtle Godfrey, but that decision is entirely in your hands. Then, there are Stanley Rice and Charlie Parker. You must remember that many young men are in the habit of engaging in filthy talk about girls, and they don't have any actual intent."

Benjamin looked up from writing with a questioning look. *Is the judge saying that it is permissible for young men to talk about women in such a manner? Maybe the man has missed a few Sunday School classes.*

No one else seemed bothered by these statements, so Benjamin carried on with his notes.

"Then there is the testimony of that boy from the Reserve who saw the light in the window. I think this is important; however, we shouldn't pay much attention to his idea of time. We all know that these people are rather indifferent to such matters of time."

Benjamin sat forward, wondering who was going to be insulted next.

"All I can say is that the time that boy from the Reserve saw the light in the window corresponds to when Peter Wheeler was at the Kempton house for the second time, while Hardy Benson was at the gate. Was he the man whose shadow the boy saw?"

Benjamin leaned back once again, wondering when this supposedly brief charge to the jury was going to end. He just wanted to skip ahead to the verdict, as did everyone else in the crowded room.

"We also need to talk about the blood. Dr. Jacques said he could only find two spots of blood on the coat. The learned defence counsel said, however, that if her carotid artery was severed, blood should spurt and cover the clothing of the murderer. Remember, however, that, according to the evidence of the doctors, if the girl was rendered insensible, her heart would be so paralyzed by these blows that the blood would not rush forth. But, if it spouted, wouldn't it too go all over the room? We didn't have an indication that that happened."

Benjamin cringed at the gruesome details.

"There is one piece of evidence, however, that has me boggled. I cannot figure out why there are bloody finger marks on the chimney of the lamp and on the spoon. Did the murderer have a cup of tea after the murder? It is impossible for me to form a satisfactory theory. Happily, it is not necessary to know precisely what happened at this point."

When he had finally finished, Justice Townshend put down his papers from which he had been reading and looked up over his glasses at the jury. "Gentlemen, now that I have concluded my comments, are there any parts of the evidence you wish to have read back to you?"

Foreman David North conferred with the other jury members. He then announced that they did not wish to hear anything again.

Justice Townshend then reminded the jury that, should they want any part of the evidence read, they merely had to ask the sheriff.

"From this point on, it is for you and only you to draw a conclusion and to give a verdict of guilt or innocence. I may have made suggestions, but they are only intended to help you and not to bind you. From me, you are only bound to take the law. All else is left to your judgment."

Peter Wheeler looked up imploringly at the jury. He said nothing, and made no gesture, but to Benjamin, the message was clear.

"The accused has had a fair and impartial trial. The place of the trial was removed from a county where it was thought prejudice against the prisoner might exist, to a county where there is none. The prisoner has not been hastily tried and every consideration was shown by the Crown. It is not for you to think that, because the prisoner is a stranger, he is to be judged leniently if guilty."

Then the judge ended his more than an hour-long diatribe with his final thoughts. "You must not forget that justice demands his punishment if he is guilty and that no argument should lead you to acquit him if you, in your hearts and consciences, believe he really did the deed."

He banged his gavel, gathered his papers and made a motion to arise.

"Your honour!" For the first time over the past few days, Peter Wheeler, who had remained motionless and quiet, called out.

The courtroom fell silent, shocked by the sudden cry from the prisoner.

"Your Lordship, will you allow me to speak a word?"

Peter began to stand and turned to face the jury. The shock of this unprecedented move kept everyone still.

Eventually, the judge responded. "Yes, but through your counsel."

Ruggles, looking equally as puzzled as the rest of the courtroom, quickly approached the prisoner. From where he was sitting, Benjamin could hear nothing of what was said, and the conversation took place behind the cover of the lawyer's notepad, so that no lips could be read.

"Your Honour, we apologize for this sudden outburst, but the accused has decided not to make a statement after all."

Peter nodded somewhat begrudgingly. Ruggles returned to his seat at the table.

With that, Justice Townshend instructed the jury to rise, and Sheriff Belcher ushered the twelve men across the front of the courtroom to the room on the opposite side of the great hall. Peter Wheeler was then ushered out the back door of the courtroom to another room to await his fate.

As he went, the crowd erupted in jeers, throwing anything from newspapers to garbage at the man.

Exhausted, Benjamin leaned back in his seat. "I wonder what he was going to say. Do you think he was going to confess? Or maybe tell his side of the story? We are never going to know, now! I can't take much more of this."

"What do you mean?" Simon asked. "There can be little doubt in your mind as to his guilt. The evidence so clearly points to him."

"I think it does," Benjamin agreed. "But there is a part of me that has doubts."

"This is no time to be a Doubting Thomas! Justice Townshend clearly laid out the evidence against him. And listen to those around us. You would be hard-pressed to find anyone in this room who believed the man innocent, or who was willing to admit it. It is apparent that a guilty verdict is going to be rendered."

"I don't think I can leave the courtroom. I'd be too worried I would miss something. I think I'm just going to stay here and wait it out."

"Could be 30 minutes, or it could be all evening. It's three o'clock now. We shall start the timer!"

Benjamin stood and stretched in place, careful not to bump into anyone who was packed in tightly around him. He took a few deep breaths, then sat back down and started drafting his next article.

~

Benjamin had just nodded off to sleep when he heard a commotion on the far side of the room. He looked at his watch. Only two hours had passed since the jury left.

Crowds of people had attempted to put their ears to the door to try to hear the deliberations inside, only to be shooed away by a constable. Likewise, those who remained outside tried to peer in through the windows to catch a glimpse as the jury at work, or to hear any snippets of conversation. Becoming wise to their ways, a second constable was sent to patrol the perimeter of the building.

"They are back! They have a verdict!" cried someone seated on the far side of the room. "I can hear them moving around inside."

People hurried back to their seats and cleared the area in front of the heavy wooden door just before it swung open, and Sheriff Belcher appeared in the doorway. He quickly closed the door behind him and knocked before entering the judge's chambers in the adjacent room.

The sheriff reappeared, this time with Justice Townshend close behind. As the judge approached the bench, the crowd stood.

Then, the door to the jury room reopened and the twelve men were ushered back into their box on the opposite side of the room.

Benjamin searched their faces for any kind of clue but could find none. His heartbeat quickened, and his breathing rate increased. He could not take much more of this.

When the jury was finally seated, the judge asked, "Have you agreed upon a verdict?"

David North, the foreman of the jury, stood. He turned to look at each member one last time, and they nodded their agreement. Then he turned back to face the clerk. "Yes."

"What is that verdict?"

Benjamin looked down and saw that he was clutching his knees. Beside him, Simon seemed relaxed and at ease.

David North cleared his throat and, in a loud voice that echoed throughout the silent room, said, "Guilty."

At first, there was a death-like stillness as people weighed the enormity of what had just happened. Then, as if on cue, the room erupted with cheers. Men stomped on the floor, while others shouted, "Praise God!" "Justice at last!"

With so much noise and commotion, Benjamin quickly looked towards the stovepipe, and noticed it had since been tied securely in place. He wondered what else could fall from the walls.

Throughout it all, Peter sat stoically, never moving or flinching. The only reaction Benjamin could see was his skin turning pale. In fact, Peter may have been the only calm-looking man in the court.

Simon looked over at him and smiled. "See! There was no other conclusion possible."

Harrington stood up and, as he turned to address the court, the room quietened. He still spoke loudly to ensure his voice was heard. "I move for sentencing."

"Hang him! Hang him! Give him what he deserves!" The same chorus of men echoed each other at the back of the courtroom.

Before the judge offered his sentence, he turned to the condemned man. "Do you have anything to say as to why this sentence of death should not be passed against you?"

Peter stood slowly and looked, wide-eyed, at the men who had sealed his fate. "I don't understand you! It is not because I am ignorant, but because I truly don't understand!"

There were angry cries throughout the room. No one from the jury responded, nor could they entirely look Peter in the eyes.

Ruggles approached Peter and, after a few moments of conversation, Peter sat back down, deciding to say nothing further.

Once he had regained control of the room, Justice Townshend spoke again. Benjamin hoped this speech would not last for hours, like the last one.

He turned and spoke directly to Peter "I hope you will now pay great attention to what I have to say to you. The jury has convicted you of the murder of Annie Kempton, and in their finding, I concur. Your offence was of such an atrocious nature, you cannot hold out any hope that there will be any modification of the sentence. You have had a fair trial and every effort has been made on your behalf to establish your innocence, and a patient jury has given it the fullest investigation. The jury was not from the place where the crime was committed, and consequently, were not prejudiced and have fairly brought this awful sentence against you."

He paused a moment before continuing.

"Probably the hardest thing to do is for one man to pass the sentence of death upon another. I cannot help thinking of the cruel way the poor girl was murdered."

Then the judge moved to matters of heavenly judgment.

"There is but one thing now for someone in your position, and that is to endeavour to fully realize the serious nature of the crime you have committed and to become truly penitent. I will give you ample time to re-pent for the crime of which you have been found guilty. I hope and pray that you may devote the remaining few weeks in preparation for the fu-ture world. I do not know your religious views, but I do sincerely hope you will be repentant."

Peter closed his eyes tightly and bowed his head.

Although still facing Peter, Justice Townshend directed his comments to all in the courtroom. "I hereby direct that you be taken hence to the jail in Kentville and from there to the jail in Digby and be detained there till the 8th day of September 1896, and that on that day you be hanged by the neck until dead."

Benjamin gasped, the gravity of what just happened, finally sinking in. Around him people cheered. He could hear people already making plans to attend the big event.

No longer able to keep his stoic manner, Peter exclaimed, "Well, your worship, all I have to say is that I hope that, by that time, the man who did the deed will be found out!"

There was an eruption of boos and hisses from the crowd, admonish-ing Peter for attempting to evade his just punishment.

Justice Townshend turned back to the jury. "Gentlemen, I would like to thank you for your patience and intelligence in this matter. This county is fortunate to have such men as yourselves living here."

He then turned to the sheriff, "Sheriff Belcher, remove this prisoner from the courthouse."

As Peter shuffled along behind the sheriff, his manacles rattled and clanged. The noise was soon drowned out by the cries, first of those in the courtroom, followed by those waiting outside, who watched as the prisoner was marched across the lawn to the jailhouse.

Benjamin closed his eyes, feeling as if he had just watched an import-ant piece of history being made.

~

After the announcement of the verdict, the courtroom emptied quickly, with people rushing off to fill in friends and neighbours on the moment-ous news.

"Are you coming?" Simon asked as he grabbed his things. He evidently had hopes of seeing Peter Wheeler one more time as he crossed the courtyard.

"No. I think I am going to linger for a few moments."

Benjamin wanted to sit and fully absorb what he had experienced over the past few days. As the room emptied, the comparative quietness filled him.

He wasn't sure what he thought about the trial, let alone the final ver-dict. Peter had seemed so sincere in his plea for innocence, yet there was no denying the evidence stacked against him.

As he was about to leave, the main doors of the courthouse swung open and Detective Power strode in. His footsteps echoed in the empty room.

"I am available now for your interviews," he said, but stopped short when he realized he was speaking to an empty room. "Where did every-one go?"

"I'm still here, sir," said Benjamin, which caused the detective to jump as he hadn't noticed him sitting on the bench. "I would be honoured to interview you."

Detective Power paused and Benjamin knew the man was contem-plating honouring the request for such a meagre audience.

Eventually, the detective conceded and sat down on the bench oppos-ite where Benjamin was seated. Benjamin pulled out a fresh notepad and a sharpened pencil and began with his questioning.

"How do you feel the trial went?"

Benjamin wasn't sure how well the detective could answer, for he had only made an appearance for his own testimony and spent the rest of the time making his presence known through town.

"Wheeler had an impartial trial. In my opinion, the man is un-doubtedly guilty. The chain of evidence was a most complete one. These claims cannot be argued."

Detective Power puffed up his chest and wiped away imagined dust from his shoulders.

"How do you feel the Crown did in presenting their case? And what about the defence?"

"I believe that Mr. Harrington outlined the case in a clear and convin-cing manner. All the points were well brought out. The case for the prisoner was well-handled by Mr. Ruggles. Did you know he did not receive a cent for his services?"

"I had heard such rumours."

"Yes, Ruggles knew that Wheeler was without friends or money. He spent considerable money in working up his case. The prisoner had nothing to pay him with. When he was arrested, he had a mere 35 cents in his possession."

"In his closing remarks, the judge put an awfully strong emphasis on confession. Do you think Peter Wheeler will confess?"

"Yes, I think he will. I have it on good authority that he told the jailer here in Kentville that, on his arrival in Digby, he would like to see a clergyman."

"Any other comments you would like to make about the case?" Benjamin asked..

"The only issue I have is with newspapers, such as your own. The newspaper reports did not convey the exact value of the chain of evidence that brought the conviction. This was not clearly stated enough in your reports."

Benjamin looked up from his notebook, not sure what to say.

Detective Power tapped the notepad a few times and said, "I trust you are getting these words down correctly this time."

14: A conversion for both of us

Benjamin stepped down onto the platform at the Digby station. He took a deep breath. The air was a mix of the salt air from the Bay of Fundy and the coal-fired steam coming from the train. The sun was shining, and Benjamin felt good.

He had spent the last few days at home in Halifax and even participated in some of the Dominion Day activities happening around the city. After the few days of rest, he was refreshed, and ready to dive back into the Peter Wheeler case.

Although the verdict had already been rendered, readers were still anxious for more information about the case. What was Peter Wheeler thinking and feeling now? Would he confess to the murder to save his soul, although his body could not be saved?

Benjamin had to admit he wanted to know, too, and was about to attempt to find out.

He trudged up the hill to the large, two-storied, wooden courthouse overlooking the harbour and the rest of the town.

Officer Bowles greeted him. Benjamin remembered him as the staunch Salvation Army member who had ardently tried to convince Wheeler to confess. He was not about to tell the man the nature of his own visit, lest the officer insist on being present or trying to help him.

"I take it you are another person here to see the prisoner. You had better have your ten cents ready."

Benjamin looked confused, so the officer explained, "Wheeler is offering interviews but is charging ten cents a session. Claims the money is all going to be left to his landlord, Tilly Comeau. I reckon it should have gone to that defence lawyer of his, but who am I to persuade him otherwise?"

Benjamin chuckled at Peter's enterprising nature. He shoved his hand in his pocket and came out with a dime, displaying it in his palm.

"Proceed!" said Bowles, pointing down a long corridor. "You can't miss him. He's in the same cell where David Robbins stayed after he murdered his wife and before he was hanged. Rather fitting, if you ask me."

I didn't ask you, thought Benjamin, but he refrained from saying it out loud. He turned and walked down the corridor in search of the condemned man.

When he found him, Peter was writing madly at the small desk in his room. Papers were strewn about the floor and were all over the table.

Benjamin cleared his throat, but Peter was so lost in his own thoughts he did not hear he had a visitor.

Benjamin tried to get his attention again, this time calling out, "Good morning, Peter!"

Peter startled and looked up. When he saw Benjamin sitting there, he turned around in his seat and smiled. "You were just the person I was hoping to see."

"I am? I was?"

"Yes, I need your help."

Benjamin was a little taken aback. He had never had a convicted murderer ask him for help before.

"I came here to find out how you were making out, and what your feelings were with regard to the recent verdict."

"I have been in deep contemplation since then. I know there is no hope for my earthly body, but I know there is much I can do for my heavenly one."

Benjamin couldn't help but like the man. "So, you have been taking the judge's words to heart? Everyone has been wondering when and if you would be making a confession."

"That is what I have been working on," Peter said, pointing to the pile of papers before him.

"You have?" Benjamin was again surprised that the confession had taken so little time to come forth, especially from a man who had so adamantly proclaimed his innocence up until the last moments of the trial. There was also a part of him that was taken aback. He had felt for so long that Peter might have been innocent that for him to suddenly say there was a confession was a bit of a shock.

"I have written out my entire confession, and I want to offer it to you to print in the *Halifax Herald* so the whole world may know what happened. Perhaps it will make people more lenient."

Benjamin stared, open-mouthed. This truly was a gift from God. Although he should be happy about this manna from heaven, though, Benjamin felt somewhat resentful. *Why had Peter held out this long? Why had he let him be roped into believing there was a chance of his innocence?*

"You know what they say, guilt and shame have no place in heaven once you have confessed or repented. There is only love and light that awaits you," Benjamin managed.

"I am hoping for God's grace, indeed."

Peter pushed back his chair and stood. He gathered the papers, tapped them on the table to straighten them, and walked towards the cell door. The chain around his ankle rattled as he moved. He passed the papers through the bars to Benjamin's open hand.

It took all of Benjamin's strength not to rip the papers from his hand. He couldn't wait to devour them yet felt fearful about what he was about to read.

"I want you to sit and read them right now, right here, in case you have any questions."

"Okay," Benjamin stammered.

He found a stool in the hallway, sat down in front of the cell, and began to read.

> Now dear friends, men and brethren, hear ye all my defence concerning the guilt of which I am accused of before the ears of the public and all through the Dominion. Gentlemen and friends, the idea of me doing this is simply to try and turn the hard feelings in your hearts from against a poor mean sinner like me. I pray that you will all pray that you will all take careful and particular notice of what I am going to explain to you all.

Benjamin turned the page.

"Read it back to me," Peter directed.

Benjamin cleared his throat and began to read the rest out loud.

Peter

Peter looked around the small cottage. He had laid his few items of clothes on the floor in front of the stove. He went through the mental checklist of what he needed to bring out to the logging camp for the week. He had gone so many times, he could now pack for the trip in his sleep.

A strong wind rattled the house and Peter could hear the whistling through the windows. He looked down at the empty wood box beside the stove and decided to fetch some firewood for Tilly to use while he was gone. She had been so good to him over the decade he had lived with her, treating him as one of her own, that it was the least he could do.

He pulled on his overhauls and woollen jacket and stepped outside. Judging by the way the sun cast his shadow, he reckoned it was pretty handy to noon.

He picked up Herbert's axe, which was resting next to the side of the house, slung it over his shoulder, and trudged up the hill through the snow.

"Peter! Peter! Come here!"

It was Annie Kempton calling from her open front door.

Peter sighed, hating to be distracted from his task in the little time he had to get ready to head to camp.

"Peter! Do you know where Tilly and Hattie are? Are they both at home?"

"No, they are to work up at the hotel."

"Are they going to be there all the week?"

"I don't know. But I do know they have work for the week somewhere, for they are going to be away all week."

Annie wrapped her shawl tightly around her; she wasn't properly dressed for the winter air.

"Tell Tilly she need not mind coming up here nights after she comes from her work, for it will be too much for her to have to be away all day to work and come home and see after the children and walk up here every night and go back every morning and look after the children and to do her work. I will try and get Etta Morine, for it's just fun for her to come here nights and stay with me."

"That's very kind of you, Annie, to be always thinking of others like that."

The reporter

"Wait! Stop there," Peter interrupted.

Benjamin placed his finger on the page to mark his place. "What is it?"

"Forgive me, but I wanted to point something out. That's where I made the first mistake."

"What mistake?"

"Annie told me she was going to ask Etta Morine to come up to stay with her. Not Grace. I got the two sisters mixed up, and in my original statement, I said the wrong sister. Etta not Grace!"

Peter slapped himself on the forehead.

"Anything else?"

"Yes, you need to remember at this point Annie only said that she was going to go ask Etta to stay with her. She hadn't actually gone yet."

Benjamin nodded, then raised his eyebrow, to ask if Peter was finished.

"Pray, continue."

Peter

Annie looked as if she was about to retreat in the house when another thought came upon her. "Peter, while I have you here, I have another question. Tomorrow, I know there is going to be a big crowd coming from Digby and I'm making some flowers to sell up at the hotel. Do you happen to know if the party is in the morning or afternoon?"

Peter stamped his feet to stay warm. "I know it's tomorrow but I'm not sure of the time."

"Well, you're a great help! In that case, I had better get to work and make all the flowers I can before tomorrow," She laughed.

"Do you have any made yet?"

"I have one bunch already. Do you want to see?" Annie opened the door wider. "Silly me! It's freezing out here, and I should have invited you in earlier, but I guess we didn't know I was going to talk your ear off, now did we?"

She laughed again as Peter followed her into the house.

"See, this bunch is nearly finished."

Peter picked up the paper flowers and twirled them around in his fingers, admiring the beauty.

"I'm almost out of paper, so I'm going to have to go down to the bridge to the shop to buy some more."

"You are?" Peter thumbed through her stash of paper. "There is a stack of ten cut paper here already! You need more?"

"Yes, silly. That's not nearly enough for what I want to make. I want to have a dozen bunches!" She hit him on the arm.

"Shows what I know!"

"I'm just in the process of fixing some beans for my dinner. Can I offer you any? I have plenty."

"No, thanks, Annie. I'm just out getting some firewood for Tilly. Trying to get ready to go out to camp tomorrow."

The reporter

"Stop! Stop!" Peter directed.

"What is it this time?" Benjamin asked.

"I want you to pay attention to this detail. I remind you I was there at about noon and when I was there, she only had the one bunch of flowers finished. After she finished her dinner, she went back down to the shops in town to buy more paper. There are witnesses who said they saw her there at the shops, and then go back home around fifteen minutes past five."

"Yes, this has been established."

"So, tell me, if she is just coming home from the shop at this time, how can I have supposedly knocked her down at half-past five or six o'clock? And, then cut her throat at eight o'clock when I was there with Benson. So, how did she end up having time to make seven bunches of flowers? Please do tell me."

"Peter, we know what the evidence says for the timeline. This, too has been established."

"But how could she have made six more bunches of flowers if she didn't have the supplies?" Peter pressed.

"I thought this was supposed to be your confession."

"Keep reading."

"Why don't you just tell me what really happened."

Peter nodded. "I had just finished gathering wood for Tilly earlier than I had expected, so I decided to do a few other odd jobs I had been putting off. The first was checking the rabbit snares I'd set up along the fence lines of some of the fields up the hill. Then, I figured, if I had time, I'd stop in to see if Stanley Rice was home, as the useless scoundrel owed me two dollars.

"I figured that if I walked towards the Rices' place while checking my snares, and happened to see Stanley through the window, I would stop in and demand payment. It would be nice to give Tilly her rent before I headed to the woods.

"I went towards Omer Rice's house and cut through to the road in be-hind the house. Then I walked up through the fields, along the verges, re-membering where I had hidden all my snares. When I got to the top of the hill, I cut across the road to the Kemptons' old barn.

"While I was standing there, lost in thought, an idea suddenly struck me. I walked straight to the Kemptons' new barn—the one next to the house. I went around the back of it and through an opening in the foundation, crawled in under the barn, with the hopes of sneaking up and stealing some eggs.

While lying in hiding under the barn, I lit a match to help me find the eggs, but I was worried because surely the light would draw attention to me and expose my presence. So, I crawled back out and ran over to hide amongst the nearby grapevines.

"As I stood there, wondering what to do next, I watched Annie come out of the house and go to the barn, carrying a ceramic bowl. She was still wearing the same clothes I had seen her earlier that day. She then walked back into the house, this time with the bowl full of milk."

"Wait a minute," Benjamin said. "Witnesses said she didn't milk the cow. The cow gave extra milk in the morning, so couldn't have been milked that night."

"I'm just telling you what I saw. Go back to reading."

Benjamin picked up the letter again and continued reading aloud Peter's words.

> Once Annie was back inside, I felt it was safe to leave my hiding place, so I continued across the yard in behind the well house, back down the road, through the gate and back towards home. That's when I ran into Herbert who was there cutting wood. I stopped to help him load the last pieces onto the sleigh before we both walked back down the hill towards home.
>
> We weren't home long when Tilly and Hattie soon arrived and we all left to walk to the bridge downtown. Then, I met up with Hardy, and together, we walked back to Tilly's house. That's when he started urging us to go up to see if Annie was home.
>
> As we neared the house, Hardy was trying to get me to go in, but I kept telling him it was his idea, and if nothing else, we should both go in. He kept saying he only had on his old clothes so didn't want to go in. Eventually, I gave in and went in myself.
>
> He wanted me to find out if she was going to the Salvation Army meeting that night. She soon figured out that Hardy was waiting outside. She even peeked out the window and saw him pacing there by the gate. When she saw him, she smiled, and said she would go get ready and meet us later.
>
> When I returned to Hardy, he asked if she were alone, and I said, yes, and no, I didn't tell her that she was waiting for him. I asked him if he wanted to go in and wait for her, but he said he didn't and not to tell Tilly that we were up there that night. He

didn't want anyone to know that he went up there nights when Annie was alone. I assured him that I would never tell on him. After that, we just went back to my place.

As we walked down the hill, I remember looking over my shoulder and could see the light was still burning bright in Annie's window.

Annie never showed up, so eventually, Hardy had enough of waiting and decided to leave. Left on my own, I started cooking the meat Tilly had brought me, so I would have something to eat while away at camp.

"Peter," said Benjamin looking up from the papers, "I still don't understand. You told me this was a confession, and I don't see any sort of confession at all here. It's just another version of what happened."

"I'm just writing to the best of my abilities, everything I know that happened that night."

"But, according to your account here, it's already eleven o'clock in the evening, Tilly has gone to bed, and the murder still hasn't taken place. It doesn't fit the timeline laid out by the prosecution."

"Keep reading," insisted Peter. "I'll get there eventually."

Benjamin raised his eyebrow, doubt all over his face. Nothing was making sense anymore. So far, this matched what Benjamin already believed to be true.

"The Crown said the murder took place between five and eight o'clock in the evening. This does not line up with the evidence. What am I missing?"

Peter leaning forward in his chair. He pointed at Benjamin. "Keep reading. I want you to fully understand what happened. You are happy because you can print this in your paper, and I am happy because God knows I have repented."

Benjamin sighed and picked up the papers once again and kept reading. He could tell Peter had been well educated. His handwriting was neat and legible, and despite a few grammatical errors, it was a coherent piece. Everything he knew, or thought he knew, was being put to the test.

Peter pointed again to the papers, and Benjamin picked up reading from where he left off.

After my meat got cooking, I decided to get some rest and laid down on top of the quilts behind the wood stove. But I couldn't get the thought of Annie out of my mind. Her laugh, her smile, her joy was so infectious. She was so young and innocent, I just wanted to reach out and touch her, and feel her soft skin. I could smell her hair and imagine what it would be like to kiss her rosy lips.

My eyes bolted open with the sudden realization that she was alone in the house. If I didn't take advantage of the moment and tell her how I felt then, I might never have the chance again.

I lay there for a few more minutes listening intently, making sure I could hear everyone breathing deeply. Then, I stood and made my way to the broken window. As Herbert had showed me, I removed the panes and silently made my way through the window. I then replaced the panes and took a few moments to scan the area. Seeing no one, I walked up the hill, the Kempton house acting as a beacon.

When I got there, I tapped gently on the door. Behind it, I could hear Annie shuffling. I then saw her perfect face peer through the side window and watched as she covered herself with a red wrapper. Eventually, she opened the door a crack. When she saw it was me, she undid the latch and opened the door wide for me to come in.

The room was dark. She must have come from her bed as no lamps were lit. She was cold, so she asked me to come into her bedroom to talk to her there. She crawled in under the quilts and pulled them up under her chin. She patted the bed beside her, motioning for me to sit.

I suggested that I could crawl into bed with her to keep her warm, but she shook her head. I suggested a few things we could do other than talk, but again, she shook her head. Every time I tried to make an advance, she refused my proposals. I could feel the anger and frustration building inside me. With no one home, it was the perfect opportunity to finally be together. I could feel myself becoming excited, and lust taking over.

I leaned over and tried to kiss Annie, but she thrashed about, trying to avoid my lips. So, I grabbed her wrists and pinned her to the bed. She screamed for me to stop and asked what I was doing.

With her strength and being almost the same size as me, she eventually broke free, and tore off running towards the dining room. I jumped up and began to chase her. The more she resisted, the more I knew I had to have her. She tried to escape by going behind the table, but I threw it aside, dishes falling to the floor, smashing in the process.

Seeing a stick of wood beside the stove, I grabbed it and began shaking it in the air, keeping up the chase. Eventually, I over-powered her and struck her several times in the forehead and back of the head. Annie fell to her hands and knees.

I dropped the wood and readied to mount her. But she cried out again, "Peter! No! I can't be dishonoured like this! Kill me now! Put me out of the way. I'd rather die than have you do this to me!"

Then I asked her if she was sure she wanted to die, and she said, "Yes, kill me right now!"

I looked up, and on the small table beside me was a jackknife. Doing what she asked, I quickly used it to cut her throat several times while she remained still on her hands and knees, waiting for the deed to be finished. Being used to bleeding out animals, I knew to stand out of the way to avoid any blood spatter.

When the deed was finished, I brushed off my hands and left Annie still bleeding, exited the Kempton house and made my way back down to Tilly's house. I carefully slipped the broken panes of glass back out and crawled through the window. I stood for a few minutes to make sure everyone in the house was still asleep, before going back to my position on the quilts behind the stove. I didn't wake again until Tilly awoke me in the morning, asking me to go for milk.

"Wait a minute!" Benjamin interrupted. "I don't fully understand. There are some points here that don't quite line up."

"What do you mean?" Peter asked. "I'm telling you it exactly as it happened."

"Let's start with the blows to the head. Did you hit her in the front or the back of the head first?"

"I can't remember."

"At the murder scene there was a sheath knife. Did she use it in the tussle?"

"I'm sure that she did. She must have grabbed it and threatened to use it against me when I was chasing her."

"Wasn't there a second knife found at the scene? A big knife of some sort."

Peter scratched his head. He paused, remembering back. "I don't re-member seeing the big knife. All I know is that I took the case knife from the table."

There is an awful lot that Peter can't remember.

"You just said that you cut her throat while she was on her hands and knees and left her body that way when you went for home. What about you moving the body? How does that all fit in?"

Peter paused before answering in a calm and steady voice. "When I found they were on to me about my saying her throat was cut, I invented it that I moved the body. I think I blocked out everything else from my memory."

Benjamin nodded. That seemed to make more sense. *But if that now makes sense, what does that mean about this confession?*

"Peter, you mentioned the room was dark when you got there, but witnesses saw a light burning all night. And the chimney was found off the lamp with a bloody fingerprint on it. How did that come about?"

"I must have gone to the pantry and got the matches and must have left blood on the match paper."

"You mean chimney."

"Yes, chimney."

Benjamin rubbed his eyes and his temples. What was supposed to be a straightforward confession was giving him a headache. There were more questions than answers, and he hadn't finished asking about everything that was in his head.

"Whose blood was on the windowsill and door?"

"Must have been Annie's."

Benjamin imagined Annie with the knife in her hand, trying to defend herself, and then cutting herself, and getting blood on the door frame. But witnesses said there were no wounds on her hands or fingers. Maybe she had cut Peter and wiped his blood.

"Did you try to wash off any of the blood after you killed her?"

"No."

"Did she make any noise after you cut her throat?"

"No."

"What happened when you went up to the house the next morning for milk? You already knew what you were going to encounter."

"I did go up there, but when I arrived, I didn't touch anything. I didn't go through the house like I initially said I did."

The questions were coming rapid fire and Peter was answering just as quickly, naturally, in a coolness that Benjamin realized was even more cavalier and villainous than he had first imagined if Wheeler were guilty. The answers were almost methodical, like he was moving down a checklist, or agreeing to a contract about going to sea. There was no way Peter could have made up these details to this extent, had he not actually been there.

He could feel the bile in his stomach start to rise, and he tightly clenched the papers. Benjamin felt duped. His emotions had gone through the wringer, from thinking Wheeler was guilty, to being innocent, and now with this confession, he had to be guilty. He felt used, and he was angry.

"You—you—you—" he stammered, "You murderous fiend! You poor excuse for a human being. You are the true work of the devil."

Benjamin stood. His body started to shake. He was disgusted at having to listen to this foul description again, but even more so, he was angry at himself for having, even just for a moment, believed the man to be innocent.

Peter looked at Benjamin and laughed.

"And you think this is funny? You think murdering an innocent girl in cold blood is funny?" Benjamin spat the words out, spittle flying through the air.

Peter stopped laughing and sat up straight in his chair. Suddenly, he grew sober and looked and Benjamin straight in the eyes. "If you ask me, the murder can actually be seen as a conversion for both me and Annie, and is truly the only way we could both get to heaven."

"What could you possibly mean by that, you heathen?"

"Just that two or three nights before the murder, I dreamed someone was cutting my throat. It's the same type of dream that Annie had. She used to have dreams that Hardy Benson had met with the same fate of having his throat cut. It was another tie that bound us together."

"You disgust me."

"I now realize the gravity of my actions and I am fully ready to die for taking this young girl's life. I hope God will forgive me for I have been infatuated with Annie for quite some time now. She was at first happy to receive my attention, but after awhile she became tired of me and soon repulsed all my advances. As you heard, I had made several threats against her in the past."

"I think I am going to be sick," said Benjamin, trying to slow his breathing. "You killed her merely to prevent yourself from getting into trouble!"

"The only person I truly feel sorry for is my defence lawyer, Mr. Ruggles, who always worked so hard to protest my innocence."

Benjamin felt like balling the papers up and tossing them back in

Peter's face, but knowing he had a golden story prevented him. Instead, he stuffed the papers into his satchel and leaned forward.

"I hope you burn in hell, Peter Wheeler."

~

It was a hot, sunny day, and Benjamin was in his office, catching up on some of the latest news stories, trying to get his mind off Peter Wheeler. It had already been a week since his encounter with the murderer, but the scene still burned in his brain.

He opened the window in hopes of getting some fresh air, but figured it was only making the office more stifling. He enjoyed, however, listening to the busy city life outside his window. He could never get used to the inescapable silence of the countryside, and much preferred the gentle hum of the noisy city.

He had just finished writing an article when the telephone in his office rang. It was such an infrequent occurrence that it made him jump.

Figuring it must be an important news tip, he answered and introduced himself to the caller.

"Do you miss me?"

It took Benjamin a few seconds to place the voice.

"Simon!" he finally said.

"It's been over a week, so I thought you must miss me for sure," the Digby reporter chided him.

"What do I owe the pleasure of a phone call?"

"I just wanted to congratulate you on snaring the confession interview with our friend, Peter Wheeler. You certainly made the rest of us jealous!"

"Well, I'm not sure how lucky I felt, having to sit there and listen to all the sordid details again. I am more disappointed with myself for letting him play me during the whole case. One day I thought he was innocent, and the next day that he was guilty. It wreaked havoc on my head, not to mention my digestive system!"

"Where does your mind rest now?"

"There is definitely no doubt in my mind as to his guilt. That confession came so naturally to him, like it was pent up. There is no way not to believe him."

"I'm not so sure, now," said Simon.

"Whatever do you mean?"

"I have been talking with a people around town. At first, they were ex-

224

cited to read the confession, as it was a long-awaited moment. However, once the sensational element of it wore away, the general consensus was that the entire confession was nothing more than a story. A mere fabrication."

Benjamin couldn't believe his ears. He had thought of little else since returning from Digby. He had played the scene over and over in his mind. Although questions still remained, he was utterly convinced that what Peter had written and told him was the truth.

Simon continued, "Many believe the story could not possibly be a true statement of the facts. For, if it were true, the theory of the Crown was partly wrong. The evidence proved clearly in several points that Wheeler is now lying in this confession. Remember, the Crown proved that Annie Kempton was killed early in the evening."

"That is true," Benjamin said.

"I've gone to see him, you know."

"Wheeler?"

"You're not the only one who can visit him! I told him that people were saying that his entire confession was a lie. He seemed really surprised to hear that. He thought people would be happy to hear a confession. I said they would be happy to hear a real one."

"What did he say to that?"

"He said, fine, that he had a new confession to make!"

"He's going to change his story again?"

"It turns out he has a different confession for nearly every visitor. Officer Bowles was telling me that he now lies in his cell, apparently in good spirits, when there is a crowd there."

"He was charging admission!"

"Bowles also said, however, that, when he is alone, and the crowds are all gone, Wheeler breaks down and becomes completely unmanned. It's like he's beginning to realize something of his position."

"Is he actually going to change his confession?" Benjamin asked.

"Apparently, he wishes to withdraw his first confession, which he claims was in error, and says he has given the real facts to Officer Bowles."

Benjamin was taken aback, feeling used and exploited. *But what can you expect from a convicted murderer?* "Who is going to get the rights to print that confession?"

"Apparently, Wheeler told Bowles he would only give him the confession on the condition it is not printed until after his execution. Probably too worried about what people will say about this version, or he doesn't want to live up to the public outcry when the truth does come out."

"I guess time will tell," Benjamin said.

"However much Wheeler's multi-confessions may vary from person to person, the fact is that he is now confessing, and we know for a fact he is the guilty of murder. Only guilty people confess."

"You have done a good job of uncovering all of this, Simon," Benjamin said. "What else were you able to find?"

"Well, the paper received a letter from Hardy Benson once you printed the first confession, and we are printing a synopsis."

"What did that lad have to say for himself? Do you think he wrote it himself?"

"Here, let me read it to you."

The line went quiet for a few moments. Benjamin could hear Simon riffling through some papers before he picked up the receiver again. "Hot off the press. It's going to print later today, so you can't steal this one from me."

"Never would I ever!" Benjamin said. He knew the name of the game. Reporters reprinted each others' words constantly. It made reporting both easier and faster. This time, out of respect, he would stay true to his word.

"Benson says, 'Peter Wheeler has stated things untrue of me in his confession. I did not insist upon going to the Kempton house that night. It was Peter's idea. I was only going to go so far, but Peter said for me to go up further. Then he went ahead faster than me, and he rounded the back of the house even before I got to the gate. I waited until he came out and then we returned to Tilly's. It is useless for Peter to lie now about me, after he got me to accompany him up to the Kempton house. Peter also made many untruthful statements about our conversation. It is also a fact that there were no tracks found back of Tilly's house. If he got out of the window in the snow, his tracks would have been found during the search.'"

"That is a good point about the footprints in the snow," Benjamin said. Then he stopped himself, reminding himself not to be swayed yet again.

"Benson is a fine, outstanding lad from a good family whose blood has been in Bear River for generations. He is honourable, with no reason to lie."

"I will repeat myself," Benjamin said. "You have done a great job re-porting this murder, and now you have given me a lot more to digest."

"Criminal reporting is not in our usual line of stories but thank you. And one last comment. I hate to kick a man when he is down, as it is not in our practice, but the most lenient and sympathetic of men cannot but recognize how Wheeler is a human who has sunk to the lowest level. We said long ago that he was either a martyr or a hypocrite," said Simon. "He is the latter and worse."

Figure 4: Annie Kempton. Image from the Tripod website.

15: A sense of curiosity

It had almost been a month since Benjamin had last taken the 150-mile train journey from Halifax to Digby to see Peter Wheeler to get an update. To be honest, he had kind of forgotten about the man, as he was tucked so far away. He was literally out of sight, out of mind.

Besides, he did not have Detective Power continually knocking on his door looking for an interview, or at least not about that case.

In the weeks that had followed Peter's trial and sentencing, the American ship, the *Herbert Fuller*, arrived at the Halifax port, trailing a small boat that held three murdered corpses. Someone had taken an axe to the captain, his wife and the second mate.

Detective Power was fully entrenched in the investigation and, almost immediately after the ship arrived in port, had determined the guilty party to be the first mate, who hailed from St. Kitts in the Caribbean and, like Wheeler, was a foreigner, maybe of Portuguese or Spanish descent.

Peter Wheeler had been all but forgotten.

Benjamin walked through the main doors of the Digby jailhouse and in the lobby found Officer Bowles standing guard.

Recognizing him, Bowles said, "Did you hear you printed the wrong confession?"

Benjamin lowered his eyes but said nothing.

"I have managed to secure the only truthful confession of Peter Wheeler. He has entrusted me with the details. It's quite voluminous, I'll have you know."

"I would be happy to hear all about it."

"Not this time, you won't, I'm afraid. There are certain conditions this time around. This time, the confession is only to be printed in the *Digby Courier* and no other paper."

Benjamin was shocked. He wasn't sure why Simon had failed to mention this.

"On the morning of the big day, the *Courier* has already planned to print several thousand copies of an extra edition of the paper. Apparently, it's going to include photographic engravings of all the main people who feature in the tragedy, including yours truly, along with a complete history of the affair, the complete confession, and an account of the execution. They are already taking orders for copies!"

Benjamin nodded. He wondered why Simon hadn't called to tell him the news himself. But, then again, perhaps he did not want to appear a braggart.

If the information was that forthcoming from Peter, Benjamin would go see what he could find out himself.

He left Officer Bowles sitting smugly at the main desk and sauntered down the hall in search of Peter. He had not seen the prisoner since their last encounter over the confession, which, at the time, had been the one true one.

As he approached the cell, he noticed a sign tacked to the wall beside it. He read, "Peter Wheeler charges 10 cents for an interview."

Benjamin chuckled. *So, the rumours are true.*

"Are you going to charge me 10 cents to talk with you?" he asked, smiling through the bars at the prisoner.

"What does the sign say?"

Benjamin fished in his pocket for a dime and tossed it to Peter, who reached out and caught it with two hands.

"You lied to me, Peter."

Peter lowered his head. "I'm sorry," he mumbled. "It was the truth as I knew it at the time. I have prayed more fervently this time."

"You made me look unprofessional and like a fool. I took you at your word."

"I know you did."

Benjamin looked at the small man cowering in the middle of the room, chained to the floor like a wild bear in the circus. He could feel himself being swayed again. It was one thing to think the man a villainous monster capable of murder when he was away, but one look at the timid foreigner, and he started to doubt.

His tone softened. "Care to read me your new and improved confession?"

Peter laughed. "Not after what happened the last time. Everyone is still angry with me."

"It's because you didn't tell the truth."

"I gave them the confession they wanted. They should be happy. This time, my words will only be printed by the *Courier*."

"So I've heard."

"What have you come here for?"

"Just to chat. I wanted to see if you would be willing to give me a hint of what your new confession will contain."

"No, and besides, I am still writing it out. But I have told it to Officer Bowles, who is under the strictest of confidences."

Benjamin nodded. "Officer Bowles has been helping you write it, has he?"

"Yes, he has been most kind and generous. He's making sure I don't leave out any details this time."

Benjamin decided not to press the issue any further.

He took a moment to look around Peter's small cell. The man was still wearing the same clothes as he had been months ago. His face was haggard, and he looked as if he had hardly slept at all the last few weeks. His short-cropped hair was starting to grow back in, and a beard was growing around his moustache.

"Are they taking good care of you, Peter?" Benjamin asked with genuine concern.

"My life is literally in their hands."

~

Benjamin was buried amongst a pile of papers on his desk. Since the murdered bodies had come to shore on the ship only a few weeks prior, the subject dominated every headline. As with the Annie Kempton murder scene, people flocked to Halifax to see the mutilated bodies, which were on display at the local morgue.

The influx of people downtown made it difficult to navigate the streets, so Benjamin decided to stay in his office as much as he could, working on producing new stories to keep his readers engaged.

"Uncle?"

There was a knock at the door and Benjamin looked up. Normally, he would have admonished the person who had interrupted him, but hearing the nine-year-old's voice made him pause before he spoke.

"Is it important, Russell?" he asked.

As of late, Russell Shaw had become intently interested in the newspaper business, begging his uncle to let him come in on evenings and weekends, or during the summer holidays, to help in whatever way he could.

Truth be told, Benjamin loved his company and often told the young boy that, if he kept up his hard work and enthusiasm, one day this newspaper business could all be his. Russell beamed and was determined to work even harder.

"A letter has just arrived for you."

"About the murder aboard the ships, I presume?"

"No, this one seems to be about the Peter Wheeler case in Digby."

"Oh," said Benjamin, taken aback. "I had forgotten about one! Hand it over."

Russell dropped the letter on the pile of papers in front of his uncle. He stood hovering over the table.

"Yes?"

"I was just curious as to what it says."

"Your sense of curiosity will do you well in this business, my boy. Sit, and we shall digest it together."

Russell didn't have to be asked twice and pulled up a chair opposite the desk.

"Comes from Sheriff VanBlarcom down in Digby. He says Wheeler's new confession disproves the theory the Crown set out in the trial. It allegedly aligns with the popular rumours and theories as to what happened."

"What do you mean?"

"Peter Wheeler still insists the killing was done after midnight. He says Annie admitted him into the house, and that the tussle between the two of them, which resulted in the room being upended, lasted about twenty minutes. He says he would have given up for, as strong as he was, Annie was fighting for more than just her life."

Russell leaned forward, planting his elbows on the desk and rested his chin in his hands. "Do you believe him this time?"

Benjamin paused before answering. He went over all the ups and downs of the past few months, and how he swung like a pendulum to thinking Peter was guilty then innocent. Some things just didn't add up, but he also didn't see how there could be an alternative answer.

"Sheriff VanBlarcom says he doesn't put any weight into the story. He says that Wheeler's word is not to be relied upon in the slightest."

"If he's confessed, will he go to heaven?" the boy asked, wide-eyed.

"That's more of a question for the minister, Russell, but what the sheriff does say is that Wheeler spends his time reading the Bible, writing biographies of his own life, and talking aloud to himself."

Benjamin read further and laughed out loud. "VanBlarcom says Wheeler writes with a fine, lady-like penmanship and has a signature that many a businessman would envy, in that it never varies. But then, listen to this! Two weeks ago, Wheeler decided to give up tobacco be-cause a lady wrote to him from Halifax saying he could never get into heaven if he did not give up the fragrant weed!"

Russell chuckled. "I know a lot of people, then, who might not make it to heaven if this were the case!"

Benjamin grinned and reached across to tousle the boy's hair. He then kept reading.

"VanBlarcom says they had to build a blind, or a wall, in front of the east window of the cell, which also blocks the view of the Digby Basin. Apparently, many undesirable visitors were hanging about and trying to talk to the prisoner through his window."

Benjamin pictured the crowds of people who must be continuing to swarm the jailhouse. He hoped that even those outside had paid their ten cents to speak with Wheeler!

"It says that a great many are leaving feeling confused, for the pris-oner is nothing like they had been told. The general opinion was that the man was brutal and ghoulish in his conversation, particularly when it came to the topic of the murder. But they soon realize he is not at all like this."

"Did you find the same?"

"I did indeed, Russell," Benjamin admitted. "I had the feeling that, un-der different circumstances, he would be considered a respectable and hardworking man."

"Is it just the men who are going to see Wheeler?"

The boy had a lot to learn. "No, it's everyone! Men and women and of all ages. What VanBlarcom says is most surprising is the number of fine ladies who are going there to shake hands with Wheeler. He says that when you consider that they are exchanging the salute customary among friends with a murderer, it is bad enough, but to look deeper and see them actually clasp the very hand that was smeared with the blood of his victim is horrible beyond measure!"

"Did you see that happen when you were there visiting him?" Russell asked.

"I certainly did. And I have to agree that it was very off-putting. Once I saw a rather daintily-dressed American woman do just this. She reached in and heartily shook Wheeler's hand. I asked her why she was shaking his hand. Do you know what she said?"

Russell leaned forward, shaking his head.

"She said that Peter Wheeler had made himself notorious and, in their country, that entitled him to all the hand shaking he can stand."

Russell laughed.

"There is concern that, at the time of the execution, there may be an-other scene like there was when Robbins was hanged some twenty years ago. He murdered his wife and terrorized the community. The night be-fore his hanging, the officials had to call in the militia, for they were afraid that the angry crowd that had gathered outside, thirsting for blood, would storm the gallows and take matters into their own hands."

Russell stared, open-mouthed. Benjamin pursed his lips. He some-times forgot his audience and went beyond what a young boy should hear.

"It's really not appropriate, all that I have been telling you. Best not mention this conversation to your mother. She would forbid us spending time together."

Russell shook his head emphatically.

"Well," Benjamin continued, "Even during Wheeler's preliminary ex-amination in Bear River, feelings ran very strongly against him, and many a hardy lumberman who had known and respected Annie Kempton ex-pressed a strong desire to take part in the execution. Should they come to Digby this time, as is expected, there will need to be a plan in place. And Wheeler will probably not be able to maintain his bold composure as he has done to this point."

"Uncle, you have told me what the sheriff says about the situation, but what do *you* think?"

Benjamin smiled. The boy had a natural ability to press the right ques-tions. This skill would serve him well in the future. "I think he is still mis-leading the public."

16: The only thing left now

The fact that it was a slow news day, combined with the beautiful August weather outside, convinced Benjamin to take yet another a trip to Digby. He wanted to try again to tease out of Peter Wheeler information about his newest confession. Besides, it was merely two weeks from the scheduled hanging, and he wanted to find out how Peter was faring.

When he disembarked the train in Digby, Benjamin realized he wasn't the only one who had had the idea of trying to see Peter Wheeler one last time. Swarms of people were making their way up the hill towards the jailhouse. People lined up out front to get in, while others were attempting to circumvent the barrier that had been placed around the window.

Benjamin elbowed his way to the front, much to the annoyance of those who had been there ahead of him. He confidently walked to the door, on which was a notice that no visitors were to be admitted except for the condemned man's relatives, his spiritual advisor, and officials of the law, and pounded on it.

Sheriff VanBlarcom opened the door, prepared to yell at whomever was not obeying the sign. When he recognized Benjamin, he grinned and immediately ushered him inside.

"Thank you, sir," Benjamin said. "Quite the crowd out there!"

"Indeed. It's been like that for the last week, and I expect it will be for the next two until the hanging is done. Doesn't matter if the sign says no visitors."

"Anything you can tell me about the plans for the execution?"

"All I can say is that we have viewed the grounds and selected a place for the scaffold, but the details and arrangements are still to be discussed. It will be erected in the back garden, with a strong barricade built around the area to prevent people pressing in on the scaffold."

"I can imagine, having heard about Robbins' hanging and the crowds and riots that came about."

"The other issue," VanBlarcom continued, "that close behind the jail property there is a hill from which any number of people can view the interior of the jail yard where the scaffold will be and will even be close enough to hear the prisoner's voice. This makes things difficult, and so we still have much to discuss."

"Will you be looking after the hanging itself?"

"I will personally oversee the hanging, along with a few aides. We could have had John Radclive, the nation's official hangman, come, but I opted to look after the affair myself. Saves us $50 in the process. I will personally ensure that every minute detail is taken care of to ensure a smooth execution of the solemn sentence of the law."

"I have no doubt."

"Our hotels and inns are booking up, and people will be coming from far and wide to witness the event. We have been working closely with town officials to prepare."

"And what time will it take place?"

The sheriff tapped the side of his nose. "Never you mind," he said with a grin. "We plan to outwit the public as to the exact hour of the execution. We think people will start arriving very early Tuesday morning to gratify their curiosity in seeing a man hanged. For this reason, we are not going to announce the time."

"Any way you will let me see Wheeler?" Benjamin asked.

"It clearly says no visitors."

Benjamin smiled but said nothing.

"Unfortunately, he's with his spiritual advisors right now. They are having a Salvation Army meeting. He does not like to be disturbed."

"Can I go down and listen? Just not interrupt them?"

The sheriff paused for a moment, pursing his lips as if he was having an internal debate. Eventually, he said, "Just don't say a word."

Benjamin saluted the man and crept down the hallway. He leaned his back against the wall, out of the view of the men inside, and slid down till he was sitting on the floor. He took out his notepad to record what he could hear.

He could definitely pick out Wheeler's voice, and he was sure Officer Bowles, the staunch Salvation Army member, was also inside. There was another voice he assumed was that of Captain Allen, leader of the same church.

"All humans are infinitely valuable and deserving of care because of their immortal souls," Captain Allen was saying. "Through God, we can ensure salvation from sins and create a purity of life. We believe in the immortality of the soul, in the resurrection of the body, in the general judgment at the end of the world, in the eternal happiness of the right-eous, and in the endless punishment of the wicked."

"Amen!" a voice responded.

"I would like to say a few words of thanks to you all for showing me the way to everlasting life," Peter said. "You have instilled this in my heart over the past six weeks, and for that I am eternally grateful. I am pre-pared to meet my God, who has cleansed me from all sin. I feel happy over my deliverance from Satan and, because of that, am sure I am the happiest lad in Digby! I hope we shall all meet again one day in heaven."

Then, on command, the entire party burst into song, with Peter's voice being loudest of them all. Strains of *O Boundless Salvation* rang out from the cell.

When they were done, Captain Allen said, "You still look troubled. What is bothering you, Brother Peter?"

"The one thing that bothers me is the thought of my companions from my olden days. I feel they are rushing headlong to their doom and may not have had a chance to be fully saved. I wish I could go to preach to them and let them see the error of their ways."

"That is very noble of you to be thinking of their salvation. But how are you feeling about yours and the days to come?"

"I have no bitter words to say about my trial or my sentence. Overall, I am satisfied I received a fair trial, although there were some parts the Crown had rather incorrect. But that shall be revealed in time with my confession, which will be printed following my death."

"And your feelings about your impending death?"

"I have no fear. I truly do not."

"You aren't planning on doing any harm to yourself prior to that, I hope."

"No, I have no thoughts of cheating the law by poisoning myself or us-ing any other suicidal agent, even if I had the chance. I will walk to the scaffold calmly and I hope the Lord will have mercy on my soul."

"Your mortal body looks well and healthy. This reflects a healthy soul."

Peter laughed, "All this sitting around for the past few months, has certainly stacked on the weight! But soon, I suppose that will not matter where I am going. I have been treated so well while staying here in Digby. Both Sheriff VanBlarcom and his wife have been more than kind to me."

"We are glad to hear of this."

"I have also thought a great deal about my burial and what I would like."

"Pray, do tell us. We cannot make any promises, though, Peter."

"I do realize that, but I was thinking about a particular spot in Digby where I would like to be interred. It's a lovely place with a great view of the ocean. I'll draw you a map."

"After speaking with you over the course of these last few weeks, we can see that you truly are a repentant man."

"Amen!" said another voice.

"I am ready to die and will walk to the scaffold bravely. But I do wish I had ten lives, I would give them all for the life I have taken," Peter said.

Benjamin closed his notebook. He realized it might be the last time for him to hear Peter Wheeler's voice.

~

The days of Peter Wheeler on this planet are few. He only has three more days to live. Next Tuesday morning, between the hours of 4am and 8am, the lifeless body of the murderer will be seen dangling in the air.

Benjamin wrote these words for his next column. Seeing them on the paper before him, he noticed his heart was racing, and he felt a pit growing inside his stomach.

There were some—actually, more than some—who had been counting down the days, awaiting their pound of flesh. In their minds, in three days hence, justice would be served, and Annie Kempton's murder would be avenged.

Regardless, Peter Wheeler was still a man, and he was going to die in three days at the hands of other men, justified or not. Benjamin had grown fond of the little man, his calm and collected manner, and how earnestly he wanted to save his immortal soul.

Unable to write more, Benjamin leaned back in his chair, his hands behind his head, and thought about the latest update from Sheriff VanBlarcom.

Figure 5: Peter Wheeler in the Digby Jail (Admiral Digby Museum)

Peter

"Sheriff! Sheriff!"

Peter's voice echoed frantically down the hall.

VanBlarcom, who had not heard Peter call out so urgently before, hoisted his aged bones from his chair and moved as quickly as he was able down the hallway.

He could hear his wife's voice echoing in his ear that this was a job for a much younger man. He wanted to see this case through to the end, and then maybe he would consider retiring. Or, maybe next year, when he turned 75.

When he arrived at the cell, he found Peter highly agitated.

"We are going to have to charge you for wearing a path right through the floor, with all that pacing."

When Peter did not laugh at the joke, as he normally would, the sheriff knew something was wrong. For these past few months, Peter had been calm and collected, resigned to his future. Over the past few days, that solid veneer had eroded away, and a scared man was exposed.

"Three days! It's happening in three days. I have not accomplished everything I had wished to do. I thought I was ready to meet my maker, but now, the reality is sinking in."

As Peter paced the floor, the words came tumbling out.

"Deep breath, there, Wheeler," VanBlarcom said.

"I'm going to need something. Can you please send for the doctor? Have him prescribe me something like a little morphine or opium to help me calm my nerves. Especially the night before it all ends."

"I'll see what we can do, but that isn't customary, Wheeler. You know you must live with your deeds."

"I need something, please! My nerves can't take this!"

Peter approached the cell door and grabbed the rails in front of the sheriff. He stood on his toes to try to look the officer in the eyes.

Sheriff VanBlarcom gently patted his hand, and Peter resumed his pacing.

"Are they coming?"

"Are who coming?"

"You mean you haven't even asked them? I'm running out of time!"

"Peter! Calm down! Are who coming?"

"Mr. and Mrs. Kempton. I asked you to bring them here so I may speak with them."

"Yes, of course. They should be here any minute now. I'm sorry, I have been tied up dealing with the press. Someone had reported that you had tried to escape."

"But that's ridiculous! I'm right here."

"We both know that, and now the press knows that. I assured them the rumours were completely unfounded. People are just on high alert, feeling anxious and stressed."

"*They* are feeling anxious and stressed? There are many times I wish I hadn't given up smoking!"

Peter jumped at the sound of a sudden banging coming from the back of the house.

"That should be the Kemptons, now. I told them to come through the back of the house, to try to avoid the crowds."

As the sheriff left to bring in the victim's parents, Peter fell to the edge of his bed and fervently began praying.

Soon there was a cough behind him. He jumped to his feet and spun around to see Sheriff VanBlarcom, with the two Kemptons behind him.

"I shall leave you to it," said VanBlarcom. He went back down the hall to the front desk.

Isaac and Mary Kempton stood staring. Isaac's hands were folded across his breast, and he glared in at Peter. Mary wrung the handkerchief in her hands, tears streaming down her face.

For what felt like eternity, no one spoke.

Peter shuffled his weight from one foot to another, as if trying to find the right words. Eventually, he broke the silence. "Thank you for coming here today. I wasn't sure if you would come." Peter bowed his head, having trouble making eye contact.

The Kemptons said nothing.

"I wanted to let you both know how much you have meant to me over the years. You were always kind to me and offered me work when I arrived at a young age—younger than what Annie lived to be."

At the mention of her daughter's name, Mary's lip quivered, and she sniffed back tears.

"You entrusted your farm to me, and I broke that trust. For that I am truly sorry. I took from you what mattered the most. I will have to live with that knowledge the rest of my days—which at this point, isn't much longer."

Isaac harrumphed.

"I have prayed night and day, not only for your family, but also for poor Annie's soul. I have come to terms with my judgment and have asked the Lord for his forgiveness. I know God is good and will always welcome that lost sheep back into his fold. He forgives those who are truly repentant, and I assure you that I am."

Mary gripped her handkerchief tighter, and unsuccessfully wiped away her tears.

"I have made peace with myself, and I have made peace with God," continued Peter, stepping closer to the bars that blocked the cell's door. "The only thing left now is for me to humbly ask you to forgive me."

With this, Peter got on both knees and put his hands into prayer position. He bowed so his forehead rested on the bars.

Isaac opened and closed his mouth, as if he were contemplating what to say. His wife tightly gripped her husband's elbow, awaiting his response.

When he got no immediate response, Peter continued, "I am truly sorry."

Isaac uncrossed his arms and reached his hand out, as is to touch Peter on the head in an act of forgiveness.

With his head down, and not seeing this slight movement, Peter kept talking. "You will be glad to know that she died quickly. Her last words to me were that she wished to die then and there, rather than be assaulted or violated. She was a noble girl who was killed maintaining her honour."

With their mind's eye being drawn back to the lifeless body of their murdered daughter, a sudden shift came over Isaac. The palm that was outstretched in affectionate manner suddenly became a fist.

Through the bars, Isaac attempted to punch Peter, and then to grab him by the shirt collar to strangle him. The bars, however, blocked his range of motion, and Peter fell backwards, and slid himself back across the floor towards the bed. He huddled into a ball.

"Get back over here, you good-for-nothing murderer! I am not finished with you! You are a terrible hypocrite! Always pretending to read your Bible, but only when people are looking—there is nothing real about you! The world will be better off without you in it, and the hastier your removal, the better!"

Isaac banged his fists on the bars, and continued shouting. Mary, who could not contain herself any longer, began sobbing.

Sheriff VanBlarcom came tearing down the hallway and tried to usher the Kemptons back outside.

Isaac flailed his arms, angry at the attempt to stop him. "Open the doors now!" he demanded. "I am going to kill him myself!"

The sheriff used his body to steer the couple away, while looking over his shoulder and glaring at Peter.

Peter closed his eyes and sighed, as if to ask if there was anything he could do right.

17: Can I have ten more minutes?

Benjamin felt like he now knew every tree, field and station between Halifax and Digby. He had made the journey so often in the past nine months, he could almost describe it with his eyes closed. He had also witnessed every season, from the harsh, cold winter to the beautiful spring of blossoms, to now, when the red was beginning to pop on the apple trees.

When this case was truly done and done, he would miss the ride. Perhaps he would find a way to come back, but for a far less gruesome and morbid reason the next time.

Benjamin was happy that he had secured a good seat by the window, for, at every station, more people crowded on. By the time the train pulled into the Digby station, there was standing room only. People filled the aisles and were crowded in the vestibules that joined the carriages.

All he could hear was talk about the impending hanging.

"We've brought enough food to last us all day. We are planning to camp out on the hill above the jail so we can secure a place with a good view."

"I heard there are men coming who plan to storm the barricade and take the prisoner from the officials and lynch him themselves!"

"I heard that, too! They better not ruin the experience for the rest of us. Apparently, the town has sworn in a special squad of officers to patrol the area all day and night."

"I heard it on good authority that they weren't even going to use a constructed gallows outside, but rather hang him in the basement of the jailhouse, out of sight of everyone."

"That's ridiculous! They wouldn't do that. It's a public event!"

As the train came to a stop, the carriage lurched forward, causing the throng of people to nearly topple. Benjamin's seatmate was hit in the face with a large carpet bag. He nearly yelled at the woman, but the noise of all the people disembarking would have drowned him out.

As he had brought no luggage he had to collect, when Benjamin hopped down from the train steps onto the platform, he could head straight to the jailhouse.

Already there were crowds gathered around the building, many sitting on blankets in the surrounding gardens and the nearby church courtyard. Although the hanging wasn't scheduled until between four and eight o'clock the following morning, no one wanted to miss the almost-festive environment, nor any changes to the timeline.

Benjamin worked his way through the crowd and quietly made his way around to the back of the building, to the residential entrance for the sheriff and his family. Through the window in their door, he could see Mrs. VanBlarcom, with her back to the door. He knocked gently.

She started and spun around with an angry look on her face, then recognized Benjamin's face in the window. She went over to unlock the door for him.

"Mr. Shaw!" she said affectionately. "You wouldn't believe my day, or maybe you would. It has been non-stop, with people hounding us and the crowds are so thick, I hardly wish to venture outside."

As she spoke, she packed items from the kitchen into a basket.

"People asking me to sneak them in to see the prisoner or wanting to know if I have any further details about the execution. When my husband became sheriff, I did not expect that this came with it," she said, gesturing outside her window.

"I'm an old woman," she continued. "My nerves can't take this. I can handle a lot. I mean, I've had nine children! But I cannot handle this. Today."

"Looks like you are packing up to leave," Benjamin said.

"Yes, I'm taking the family, and we are moving out of the premises until all this is over. There are far too many rumours about people storming the jailhouse and causing riots. I do not feel safe here. If the mob breaks in, we cannot help it, but at least my family and I will be out of harm's way."

"Probably for the best," Benjamin said as he took a cake tin off the top shelf for Mrs. VanBlarcom. He was rewarded with a piece of the contents.

As he sat eating his cake at the kitchen table, the sound of the crowd swarming like bees outside the window, Sheriff VanBlarcom came through the door.

Benjamin stood to shake his hand. "How is Wheeler holding up?"

"I would say he's showing considerable nerve in view of the fact this is his last day on earth. He can hear the crowds shouting to him outside his window. Some insults, but many are just trying to get a glimpse of the condemned man."

"Does it seem to be bothering him?"

"No, I feel he craves some human connection. He's trying to see out the window, but of course, there is a closure around the window of the cell. But so great is his desire to see the visitors that he has placed a box upon a chair and stood on it in effort to see out!"

Benjamin chuckled at the thought. The man was both determined and short.

"Despite his brave face, he is feeling anxious. When I took him his breakfast this morning, he declined to receive it, remarking he wasn't feeling hungry."

"What are the details of the hanging? I'm hearing so many rumours, I thought best to come right to the source."

"Not you, too!" the sheriff scolded. But he pulled up a chair beside Benjamin at the table to enjoy a piece of his wife's cake.

"It's going to be a very private event."

"How private?"

"Only myself, my assistants, the medical man, the coroner and my jury are allowed to be present."

"And the press."

"No, I am refusing permission to representatives of the press to witness the execution."

A look of horror crossed Benjamin's face. "But you can't! This is completely unheard of, not allowing the press!"

"These are extraordinary times, my boy. We need the utmost secrecy to ensure things go smoothly and safely."

"But no press?" Benjamin had not travelled on this nine-month journey only to be denied entrance at the final moments.

"Well, we might make exceptions for a few newspaper men, but no others will be admitted."

Benjamin sighed with relief and picked up his fork to continue eating.

~

The grandfather clock in the living room had just chimed eleven times. Benjamin knew because he had been counting each chime for the past few hours. He was feeling jittery and was hardly able to sit still.

He had lost count of the cups of tea he had ingested after the eighth one. It was the only thing keeping him going—the pressure on his bladder, and the numerous trips to the bathroom.

Outside the VanBlarcoms' living room, he could see crowds of people still gathered. Bonfires flared in metal barrels, and the noise of the people escalated each hour. To fit the mood, a dark shroud of fog covered the town.

The sheriff came in and beckoned to Benjamin. "Follow me."

Benjamin looked confused. He had been prepared to stay camped out in the man's living room until the hour of the execution and had even dreamed about taking a nap.

"Things are getting underway."

"What do you mean? The execution is not supposed to happen for another five hours or so."

VanBlarcom walked towards the door that led to a large waiting room that was used for official business of the jail. When he opened it, Simon Sabean from the *Digby Courier*, who had been sitting there, jumped to his feet and rushed to shake his colleague's hand.

"Can you believe they moved the time of the hanging? No one knows except for the few who are involved!"

Benjamin looked incredulously at his friend. He wasn't sure if he had heard correctly, or if the lack of sleep and excess of hot tea were playing tricks on his mind.

Sensing his confusion, Simon continued, "It will be at two o'clock this morning, rather than at four o'clock. This way, there will be no damage the mob outside can inflict. Brilliant, if you ask me."

Benjamin was shocked at the news but nodded. *How did Simon always have the inside scoop?*

Just then, two men entered the room behind them.

Simon continued his explanation. "They can't have all the jury members showing up at once, as that would cause suspicion, so instead they have summoned them at staggered times throughout the night and are sneaking them in the back."

Now that he was caught up, Benjamin looked around the room and recognized a few faces. Huddled in conversation in the corner were the prison doctor, the coroner, and a famous local physician by the name of Fred Kinsman. Benjamin only recognized him because he was also a well-known cricket player in the area.

The room was eerily silent, save for the arrival, every half hour, of two more men who had carefully eased their way through the crowd to get there. Between those moments, nary a word was spoken. The men sat around the perimeter of the room, staring at each other. A few whispered conversations happened but most were too tense to speak.

The light burned only dimly so that the crowd assembled outside could not get any hint that preparations were already going forward.

Below the parlour were the jail cells, including the one in which Peter Wheeler was spending his final hours. Every so often the sound of almighty wailing came through the floor. The men said nothing but gripped their hands on their knees until the whites of their knuckles showed.

When Sheriff VanBlarcom came to check on the waiting men, Simon begged him for an update on Wheeler's condition. Benjamin smiled grimly to himself, knowing that Simon's interest in further news was only a cover to set his mind at ease, as he had to listen to the lamentations from below. Benjamin admitted to himself that he felt the same way.

"Wheeler is in good company. Officer Bowles and Captain Allen are with him now and doing their utmost to comfort and console him. Wheeler assures everyone that he is confident of pardon and salvation."

"He doesn't actually believe there will be a last-minute pardon?" a jury member asked.

"No, he knows there is no earthly hope. He is thinking more of a heavenly pardon."

There was another knock at the door. Behind Sheriff VanBlarcom appeared a young officer who had been stationed out front. He carried with him a wicker basket covered in a white linen cloth. "It's a basket of baked goods and flask of hot tea for the prisoner. Sent from Mrs. Bowles and Mrs. Allen."

The sheriff lifted the corner of the cloth and smiled. "Very kind, indeed, and I would have expected no less Christian charity from them. I shall take this to him forthwith. His appetite has not been good today; not surprising, given his circumstances, but I know he will appreciate the gesture."

"I've also gone and announced to the crowd that the hanging would take place at 7 in the morning, as you had suggested," the officer said. "And, as you predicted, most everyone left, intending to come back in the morning. Clever thinking!"

The sheriff smiled again. He then took the basket from the officer and attempted to balance it in his arms along with a few other items he had to take downstairs to the prisoner.

"Here, let me help you," Benjamin said, jumping to his feet. He took the basket from the older man and, without giving him a chance to disagree, headed toward the stairs that lead down to the cells.

"You shouldn't be down here."

"I know. I won't go near him, and I won't say anything."

As he walked along the hallway, Benjamin could hear Officer Bowles instructing Wheeler. "It is time to exchange your old clothes for these ones."

As soon as Sheriff VanBlarcom entered the cell, Benjamin sneaked closer so he could observe what was happening.

He saw Officer Bowles take from the sheriff a stack of neatly-folded clothes and hand them to Peter. Over the next few minutes, with the utmost care, Peter changed into the black pants, white shirt, suspenders, and patent leather shoes. He smoothed out any wrinkles, tightened his laces, and stood back to examine himself in the looking glass on the far wall. He adjusted his clothes again, smoothed his hair and reached out to touch his reflection.

"You look mighty fine, Peter," Captain Allen said.

Peter stepped away from the glass, and silently walked around the room, running his fingers over his meagre possessions. He ensured the clothes he had removed were neatly folded on the end of his bed. Then he caressed the place in the wall where, only a few months before, Officer Bowles had written the date when Peter had decided to confess.

"There is but a short time left," Captain Allen said. "Perhaps no more than an hour. How would you like to spend your final moments?"

Peter reached for the basket and lifted the corner of the cloth. He laid the contents out on the bed, cut himself a large piece of cake and poured a large tumbler of tea. He then proceeded to eat heartily.

After his last meal, he walked to the small desk, sat down, and thumbed through the papers strewn about. "I'm going to write a letter to Tilly Comeau, if you can please deliver it to her afterwards. I want all of my possessions to go to her. Additionally, any money that is made from the printing of my final confession is to go to her."

Officer Bowles nodded.

Peter lowered his head and began writing furiously.

When Sheriff VanBlarcom left the cell, Benjamin ducked behind the corner to gain himself some more time to explore. He snuck further down the hallway to examine the room across the hall from Peter's cell.

The room measured no more than ten by eight feet and was constructed under the jailhouse porch. The walls were built of stone. It was probably one of the dreariest places Benjamin had ever been in his life. It was to now serve as the housing for the gallows.

In the ceiling were two holes, six feet apart, through which the rope passed into the porch above, where it was carried over two pulleys. When one end of the rope was tied, lump lead on the other end weighing around three hundred pounds was held suspended six feet from the floor by another rope fastened to the ceiling. When the word was given, this rope would be cut and the weight would fall, the other end of the rope would lift Wheeler by his neck two feet or more clear of the cellar floor. Probably with an awful jerk.

To ensure sufficiently quick action, and death by dislocation of the neck rather than slow strangulation, Benjamin noticed that there was a four-foot length of slack in the rope. This meant that the weight had to drop these four feet before tightening the rope and meeting the resistance of Wheeler's weight. Peter Wheeler wasn't for the drop; the drop was for him.

Benjamin stepped back, looking at the death trap before him. In a few moments, they would discover if this contraption, constructed to carry out the justice of the law, would indeed function successfully, or whether it would end in a sickening vision of a man kicking out his life at the end of a rope for those present to witness.

Benjamin closed his eyes and slowed his breathing.

His reverie was broken by a thumping noise from the ceiling above.

"Peter, that is our signal that it is time," Officer Bowles said.

Peter looked up from his writing desk, "I'm not quite finished this last letter. Can I please have ten more minutes?"

Benjamin could see the officer nod, and Peter returned to his writing. After a few minutes, he put down his pen, straightened his papers, and slowly slid his chair back. He stood and faced the officials in the room.

Officer Bowles pulled out a chisel and mallet from his satchel, and in one blow, broke the chains that had tethered Peter to his cell for the past several months.

"Let us have a few moments of prayer," Captain Allen suggested.

The officials encircled Peter and laid their hands on him.

Captain Allen's voice echoed in the room. "Heavenly and Almighty God, Peter Wheeler comes before you humbled and sorrowful, aware of his sin, and ready to repent. Lord, forgive him. Wash away his sin, purify him, and help him to turn from this sin. Let him find a new life in you and launch his soul into eternity."

At the *amen*, Peter announced, "I have taken one life for the devil, and now I am offering up my own to Jesus. I am now willing to pay the penalty."

While this was happening, it was still possible to hear the thinned crowds shouting outside. Benjamin compared their hoarse voices to that of human vultures who awaited the rising of the sun.

He turned to hear the sound of men descending the stairs, then stepped back in the corner and joined the tail end of the line of jury members, as if he had been with them all along.

Rows of chairs were arranged along the wall of the room housing the death contraption. The dreary room was lit by a lantern and a lamp that cast a weird, yellowish gleam over everything. Silently, the men took their seats.

An instant later, the squeaking of hinges caused the men to turn their heads. The door to the cell had swung open and in walked Peter Wheeler, stepping strongly and boldly.

Peter stood in the centre of the room; his gaze fixed above the assembled witnesses.

Officer Bowles pinioned his arms to his side, then knelt and secured his feet with a leather strap.

Standing again, he asked "Do you have any last words?"

Peter addressed the group. "I leave the chamber of death and I am going to my doom. I have given the *Digby Courier* the only true confession about the time that I killed her. What I have told in my confession, it is true, and also what I said about the Morine girl and Tilly Comeau. Friends, forgive me. I know that I have done wrong. If I am lying now, I am not lying unto man, but unto God."

Officer Bowles then put the noose around Peter's neck and drew it tight, placing the knot behind Peter's left ear. As he did so, Peter leaned forward and kissed the man on his forehead.

Captain Allen approached Peter, and Peter kissed him on both cheeks. Benjamin could see tears welling in the captain's eyes.

Benjamin realized his breathing was suddenly tight, his heart pounding in his chest. He fancied, looking at the other witnesses around him, that they were experiencing the same nervous anticipation.

He drew his attention back to the centre of the room. In the circle of light stood a man in the prime of his life, full of vigour, only lacking freedom. The expression set on Peter's face was not of the earth.

Benjamin wondered if Peter was looking back over his life. *Or is he thinking about the future and what was about to happen to him?*

Then, Officer Bowles placed the black hood over Peter's head, closing his view of the world forever.

Thickly, from beneath the awful hood, came Peter's final words, "Lord,

I am coming."

The death process was put in motion.

Benjamin's body clenched, and he felt as if he would vomit. What must the wretched man be feeling and thinking? His thoughts were probably busy with things beyond what other mere mortals could ever comprehend. Benjamin's body reacted so strongly, he felt as if he may have been the one in the noose.

Sheriff VanBlarcom struck the ceiling with a pole, signalling to the officer above to cut the supporting rope, which released the weight, causing it to come crashing down. Peter shot upwards.

The weight reached the ground, but the movement carried Peter still further up before he dropped back down until his feet were 12 inches above the floor with a sickening thud that tested every fibre of the rope. There was an unmistakable snapping sound. It was so loud that Benjamin was sure the people outside the prison walls could have heard it.

The knot slipped to the back of his neck, the head fell forward on his breast, the body spun around a few times. As it turned, it swayed from side to side, quickly at first, then more slowly.

The diabolical machine had done its work well.

The lamplight streaming over Peter's body cast a shadow on the floor and traced his movements as he swayed. The shadow appeared to move in some mysterious dance of death.

Then Sheriff VanBlarcom held the legs to steady them. Peter's body shivered three times as his spirit left it, and then all went still.

The room was filled with the silence of the tomb.

It took the doctors fully twenty-eight minutes and several investigations with their stethoscopes to declare Peter's life to have ended. Benjamin thought it an eternity. He was paralyzed and traumatized from what he had just witnessed. The scene had been gruesome to the extreme, far worse than he had imagined it would be, in that close, dank, cellar.

Although the full process had taken half an hour, the doctors who examined Peter indicated that death had been almost instantaneous. The neck had been dislocated by the drop and Peter would have felt very little, if any, pain.

Officer Bowles reached up and, with a large knife, cut the rope, and the medical men gently carried Peter's now-lifeless body, back into the cell he had left only thirty minutes before in full strength and health. They laid him out on the bed, and the doctors made the official declaration of the time of death.

Twelve sworn men signed their names to the court document indicating that Peter Wheeler was dead.

While the administration of death continued across the hall, Benjamin stayed in his seat with the gallows before him. He was paralyzed and unable to move.

His eyes remained fixed on the cut end of the rope. Despite the sharpness of the sheriff's blade, the rope was frayed and swayed slowly in the wafts of air in that awful room. The movement reminded Benjamin of what had just happened, the image of which would be forever burned into his mind.

One thought pushed at him, insistently and very uncomfortably. *Has the death of Annie Kempton really been avenged?*

18: Lord, forgive me for it

By the time Benjamin finally willed himself to move, daylight was breaking. The pinks of the morning dawn reflected off the water in the harbour. God's creation still went on.

As he stepped outside, he noticed carriage upon carriage arriving at the jailhouse. These would-be witnesses, who had been told the execution was happening later that morning, were just arriving now.

Benjamin felt like telling them two things. First, that the execution had indeed already happened, and second, that witnessing one was not what people imagined. There was no thrill or excitement. There was little sense of justice being served. It was a morbid, gruesome, sordid affair he hoped he never had to experience again.

As he was willing his feet to take him back to the inn, Officer Bowles came up from behind.

"Not an easy night, was it?" asked the officer.

"You handled yourself most gracefully, sir. I can tell that Peter had a strong affection for you and appreciated your kindness. I'm not sure how you do it."

"I have the strength of the Lord behind me."

"Do you believe that Peter was really as repentant as he seemed?" Benjamin asked.

"I do. I believe that his confession, which should come out in print later today, is also true. I know that people seem to think it is impossible for such a fellow to sincerely repent, but from what I have seen of him, I believe he has."

Benjamin nodded. Then it struck him. *What if the confession is merely words Peter thought people wanted to hear?*

Officer Bowles continued, "I have spent a great deal of time with him and have studied him carefully. I have taken him on every tack and have been severe as well as kind with him. Some people have gone to him, spent five or ten minutes and formed their opinion of him accordingly. In most cases, they have formed it before coming at all."

"That is certainly true."

Right from the very first day, or even first hours, people had cast the blame upon Peter. As an outsider who didn't look like everyone else, he became an easy target of hate, Benjamin thought.

"I have watched him closely, have tried to show him his true position, and to give him what guidance I could," Bowles said. "He always received my efforts attentively and, while I do not know if he ever fully realized the awfulness of his position, I sincerely believe he was repentant and received a measure of comfort in his penitence."

Benjamin felt the bile rising in his stomach. What if Peter had made his confession to appease not only this man—this good man, Benjamin reminded himself—and not only the crowds, but God? He had been so concerned about his mortal soul, and perhaps had concluded that a confession was the only way to enter heaven.

"There was always something nagging at me about the true nature of the crime, I have to admit," he said.

Officer Bowles smiled slightly. "His crime was a terrible one and he has come to see it himself. His confession is a reasonable one and, again, I believe it is true. My opinion comes from a close observation of the man, without prejudice."

"I can see how you believe that," Benjamin said.

But he was growing uneasy. Peter's final moments were replaying in his mind.

Sheriff VanBlarcom's arrival interrupted the conversation.

"Gentlemen, I am about to make an announcement to the crowd awaiting out front. You may wish to come here, or vacate the premises, as it is about to become very congested."

"What's happening?" Benjamin asked.

"We have laid Wheeler's body out in a rough coffin in the place of execution. We are about to announce that anyone who desires to view it, will be given the opportunity to do so between eight and ten o'clock this morning. We suspect that hundreds will come through to see that justice has been done."

The Sheriff sighed. "But more likely they will want to satisfy their morbid curiosity."

"I suppose you have to appease them this way, since they will feel robbed of their opportunity to witness the hanging," Benjamin said.

"Exactly. Then we are going to inter the remains at about noon in the grave that was dug last night, up behind the jail. Captain Allen will lead a small service of prayer and commitment, as he was so diligent at looking after Wheeler's spiritual welfare."

Benjamin nodded.

Not wanting to be anywhere near the morbid scene, he decided to walk back to his inn to see if he could get some sleep. He feared it would be a long time before he could sleep again; the image of the night's hanging swam before his eyes.

By the time he rounded the corner, the crowd had multiplied and what he estimated to be a thousand people were milling about. The anger and tension were obvious.

Benjamin walked amongst them like a fish swimming upstream, heading in the opposite direction, away from the jailhouse. Their shouts and angry cries hurt his ears and gave him a pounding headache.

"How dare he change the time of the execution?"

"It was our God-given right to see that man swing!"

"That sheriff ought to be sued for what he did!"

"I drove over 30 miles to get here, only to learn that the execution has already happened. I consider this a personal offence. I do not appreciate being taken for a fool!"

"Inexcusable!"

"That old man is no longer fit to be sheriff!"

Benjamin heard the same grievances over and over again. The crowd's anger seemed to be greatly out of proportion to the event.

When he finally reached the door, the innkeeper, who had been watching the crowds through the window, greeted him. He was flustered, worked up. Benjamin's arrival allowed him to vent his anger.

"Can you believe they changed the time of the hanging? It's unthinkable that that would happen here, of all places!"

Benjamin just stared at the man.

"I wonder which doctor came and got his bones. I know quite a few who were vying for them, to display them in their office. Would be quite the thing to have bones of a murderer on display! Such a crime that justice was not properly served."

The innkeeper kept talking, utterly unaware the Benjamin had just witnessed Peter's execution and would not wish the opportunity on anyone, especially an angry mob.

"I heard they gave the man opium before his execution, to dull the pain and make it easier for him. I'm going to write and demand they do an autopsy to make sure they did not. That man needed to feel every second of pain to punish him for what he inflicted on that poor young girl."

Benjamin could take no more. He was tired and his stress was at an all-time high. "He was not given any drugs, sir, rest assured."

"How can you be so certain? They say one thing and do another!"

"Because I was there."

The innkeeper gasped, but Benjamin kept going.

"The idea of an opiate having been administered is laughable. We all saw Wheeler walk unassisted to the gallows and heard him speak in his natural voice and with his usual fluency. If such had been the case, it would not have escaped the notice of the two doctors present, nor would Wheeler have appeared as he did in his last moments. The jury were all satisfied as to the regularity of all the proceeding and their verdict is in the coroner's hands. So, when someone who wasn't actually there makes these comments and accusations, it is not appreciated."

The innkeeper looked offended. "Well, they shouldn't have changed the time. People were depending on a certain schedule."

"Although I wasn't around then, many people talked last night about the Thibault hanging that happened almost twenty years ago, up the way in Annapolis Royal. You look old enough to remember that."

The innkeeper stared open-mouthed, shocked by the Benjamin's offensive tone.

"In that case, the mob tore down the fence that had been erected, and when the unfortunate man dropped, there was no screen whatsoever, making the hanging a public one. On top of that, a great deal of damage was done to the town and people who were there at the time speak even now about the savage yells that went up from the crowd. Well, the sheriff received warnings that something similar was going to happen in Digby. He decided to have the execution happen indoors and at a different time."

The innkeeper kept staring at Benjamin, afraid to interrupt his outburst.

The innkeeper tried to hold his own. "Well, I still think people are planning on serving him with legal notice for his unlawful behaviour."

"Sheriff VanBlarcom is being unjustly criticized." Benjamin rubbed his eyes, suddenly aware of the bone-deep fatigue afflicting him. "My friend, it is, or rather it is not, surprising how readily an excited or disappointed man can arrive at false accusations. The attack on the sheriff can be traced, I would wager a guess, directly to his political opponents and to those who were intent on seeing Wheeler hanged in public. It would appear that, in the last few days, many men who were credited with average intelligence have, without cause, declared war against their sober judgment and the powers of reason."

The innkeeper had had enough of the discussion and silently handed Benjamin his room key. Benjamin snatched it from him and climbed up to his room to try to get some sleep before leaving. He hoped he would not have to return for a long time.

~

Benjamin would have left the day after the execution, but the crowds were so thick and the train so busy, he thought he had better give it some time before trying to make his way back to the city. He needed to put some distance between himself and what he had witnessed and experienced in Digby and Bear River during the past eight months, but he forced himself to wait two days.

He purposely avoided reading the special edition of the *Digby Courier*, although he had picked up his copy before he left town. Part of him was jealous of Simon for scoring such an incredible story, and part of him just didn't want to hear all the details again.

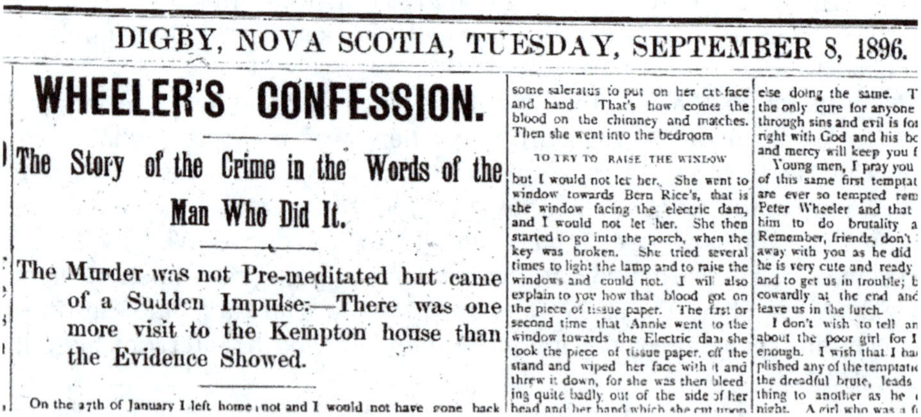

DIGBY, NOVA SCOTIA, TUESDAY, SEPTEMBER 8, 1896.

WHEELER'S CONFESSION.

The Story of the Crime in the Words of the Man Who Did It.

The Murder was not Pre-meditated but came of a Sudden Impulse:—There was one more visit to the Kempton house than the Evidence Showed.

On the 27th of January I left home not and I would not have gone back

some saleratus to put on her cut face and hand. That's how comes the blood on the chimney and matches. Then she went into the bedroom

TO TRY TO RAISE THE WINDOW

but I would not let her. She went to window towards Bern Rice's, that is the window facing the electric dam, and I would not let her. She then started to go into the porch, when the key was broken. She tried several times to light the lamp and to raise the windows and could not. I will also explain to you how that blood got on the piece of tissue paper. The first or second time that Annie went to the window towards the Electric dam she took the piece of tissue paper off the stand and wiped her face with it and threw it down, for she was then bleeding quite badly out of the side of her head and her hand which she cut upon

else doing the same. T
the only cure for anyone
through sins and evil is fo
right with God and his b
and mercy will keep you f

Young men, I pray you
of this same first temptat
are ever so tempted rem
Peter Wheeler and that
him to do brutality a
Remember, friends, don't
away with you as he did
he is very cute and ready
and to get us in trouble; b
cowardly at the end and
leave us in the lurch.

I don't wish to tell an
about the poor girl for I
enough. I wish that I ha
plished any of the temptati
the dreadful brute, leads
thing to another as he
night. A girl who was a f

Figure 6: The final confession

But now, sitting quietly on the train, with the Valley fields full of their late-season crops flying by, Benjamin spread the newspaper out on his table. He would force himself to read it twice: the first time to absorb it, and the second time so he could summarize its contents for the next day's edition of his own paper. His readers would be desperate to read it after so much interest and concern.

He closed his eyes for a moment, took a deep breath, and willed himself to read as a professional would, disinterested, distant from the events.

The first part of the new confession read like the last. It included Peter visiting Annie at noon, followed by him going around the fields at five o'clock, and hiding under the floorboards of the barn while Annie milked the cow.

He recounted heading to town, meeting up with Hardy, and then the younger boy suggesting they go up to check on Annie. The two went up to the house, but only Peter went in. Hardy said he did not want to wait for Annie to come out, so they returned to Tilly's house. Hardy left after eight o'clock that night.

It was at this point in the story that the new material in Wheeler's final confession began:

> After I was sure everyone was asleep, I changed into my day clothes. Then, I got a big block of wood and put it against the door so it wouldn't blow back and forth. Then, I went to the curtains and rolled them up and raised the window up a little at a time. This took quite some time, as I didn't want to make too much noise since Tilly was not a sound sleeper. Once I raised the window, I put a stick under it and went out and started running.
>
> Lord, forgive me for it. I saw no one and no one saw me but the Almighty. God is the only witness that saw me or knows anything about it.
>
> When I arrived at the house, I knocked on the door, and Annie answered when she saw it was me. I told her there was a crowd of drunkards around, so I had come up to make sure she was alright. After showing me the flowers she had made, she started to head back to bed.
>
> There had been no harm said between Annie and me during that time until that monster Satan got to go in her room. There's where the first of the fracas took place. I tried to keep her in the room, but she was too quick and strong for me. I tried to hold her from going into the dining room and she caught hold of the table and upset it and everything on it. Among the things that were on the table was a milk pan which was filled with the night's milk. That was broken on the floor and Annie and I both fell with her face on the broken milk pan. She cut her hand and the side of her head and also her forehead. Then, she tried to light the lamp and I pulled her away from it and she dropped the chimney. She tried

257

also to get matches off the mantelpiece and she wanted to get matches in the pantry to find something to put on her cut face and hand. That's how come the there is blood on the chimney and matches.

Then, she went into the bedroom and tried to raise the window, but I would not let her. She went to the East window, facing down towards my house, but I would not let her raise that either. She tried several times to light the lamp and to raise the windows and could not.

I will also explain how the blood got on the tissue paper. One of the times Annie went to the window she took a piece of the tissue paper off the stand and used it to wipe her face with it and she threw it down, for she was then bleeding quite badly out of the side of her head and her hand which she had cut upon the broken milk pan.

I did not accomplish lust, nor she had not been struck by me then. She then turned to me and said, 'Peter, I will never tell on you if you will let me alone,' and I felt then like stopping. Something says, 'Don't you stop.' So then, we got into another tussle.

That's when she said, 'Peter, kill me.' It was a very hard blow when I heard that word. I said, 'Why Annie, do you want to die?' 'Yes, kill me.' And it was still harder for me when I took that stick and hit her and the knife to finish the deed the way I did.

I only struck her with the stick once, I think, and that was on the side near the back of the head. She then laid on the floor just where she was found, and I was on the opposite side of her when her throat was cut. It was almost like driving a knife into my own heart. But it wasn't me alone or I would have never got up out of bed and done what I did. It was that dreadful Satan. He is the cause of a good many men's and women's ruin, if not in one way, in another.

I washed my hands in the Kempton porch before leaving. This was just half past one o'clock on the morning of January 28. I started then running for home. I expect I was five minutes going from their home. I crawled back into the window the same way I crawled out and went into the kitchen where my bed was and lit the lamp. It was about twenty minutes to two o'clock. I put the window down and unrolled the curtains and took the block of wood from the door. I examined my clothes for blood and washed off what little I could find.

No one saw me going or coming and I saw no one. The Lord is the only witness and detective who knows anything about it and is a true witness. I am also writing a true confession before him.

I never realized what I had done until after I came from Kemptons' after the milk the next morning. When I went for the milk and went into the house and saw the state of the room, it appeared strange to me. I still did not believe that she was dead until I put my hand on the side of her forehead.

Then, it came back to me. 'See Peter, what you have done.' I tell you friends you might think that I am just talking, but if it had been my own mother or sister, I would not have felt any worse than I did when I saw poor Annie lying on the floor and knew that I could not speak to her nor she to me. I could have stood there and had twice the same thing done to me.

I understand that the people won't believe that this accident took place in the middle of the night. What good would it be to me to sit down and write a lot of lies? It would be a queer way to seek repentance.

Benjamin looked up from his reading, staring out the train window as it passed apple orchards heavy with their ripe, ruby treasure. Something did not sit well with him, and he agreed with Peter that it was indeed a queer way to make a confession.

He drew his finger down the densely-packed text. It was as if every piece of evidence was accounted for and carefully slotted into the confession, as if he had been heavily coached. What about this? What about that? Had Peter altered his story each time to satisfy these questions?

In any case, this confession still did not align with the prosecution's case. There was no mention of a broken ceramic milk bowl on the floor. The doctors had clearly stated under oath that the cuts on Annie's head were from the stick, not from falling on broken pottery.

Had a notoriously strong young woman in the prime of her life begged her assailant to kill her, after suffering only minor and certainly survivable injuries? Even by this, Peter's last confession, it seemed clear that Annie's honour had remained intact. What, then, would she have feared that would lead to her wish to die?

Benjamin knew too many stories where the devil's temptation was strong in man, but could he really possess someone like Peter in this way? Was he being sacrilegious in doubting this?

Was the garnering of this confession aimed at proving that the officials hadn't made a mistake?

His head was spinning, and there was still more to read. At the end of the confession was Peter's analysis of the evidence.

> You can see that Detective Power was wrong as to the hour of the deed. He said the murder happened around five o'clock, but it actually happened much later. I suppose you remember that Tilly Comeau said she thought I was laying on the quilts with my clothes on when she went to bed. Well, that was when I was just getting home from the Kemptons'.
>
> Detective Power was also wrong about the night's milk. It was there and it was upset, and the earthenware bowl broke on the floor.

Benjamin could easily see, based around each piece of evidence that was found, that Peter had woven a story around it to explain its existence. He paused to reflect on that.

Again, the confession was almost too perfect. It was as if a list of facts had been read off, and Peter responded to each of them, spinning them into his story. Benjamin wondered with more than simple curiosity: what had gone on in Peter's mind as the confession was drafted?

What struck him the most was the part about the footprints in the snow around Tilly's house. Numerous witnesses said no footprints were found there. If this were the case, how could Peter's story of windows and running and coming and going be plausible? Besides, Herbert Comeau had already stated that on the afternoon of Annie's death he had climbed in through the window to retrieve his axe. It just wasn't adding up.

Benjamin, ever the newspaperman, suddenly realized something: what he wouldn't give for one last chance to ask Peter what he meant by his confession. He shook his head to rid it of the thought: Peter was beyond the reach of any journalist. Of any mortal man. Perhaps this is why he requested that his confession only be printed after his death.

Below his confession, Peter had written his own sermon as a warning to others who might be tempted by the devil.

> Friends and strangers, I will now ask you to take warning. The best and only cure for anyone in darkness through sins and evil is for them to get right with God and his boundless love and mercy will keep you from trouble.

Young men, I pray you take warning of this same first temptation. If you are ever so tempted, remember poor Peter Wheeler
and that lust caused him to do brutality and murder. Remember,
friends, don't let Satan run away with you as he did with me, for
he is very cute and ready to tempt us and to get us in trouble, but
he is very cowardly at the end and is sure to leave us in the lurch.

Remember, the longer you are in sin, the blinder you become.
Don't refuse to give up your sinful ways. Be wise when God
knocks at your heart's door and offers you his light, which is salvation. Freely accept it. It is free to all, without money or price.

As he read further in the full-page spread, Benjamin saw there was an interview with Peter about some of these points. He chuckled, thinking
about how well Simon had kept this a secret for so long.

He read the interview with great interest, hoping it would make some
sense of the confession and quell his sense of unease.

Simon

Simon pulled his stool closer to the cell door and balanced a large notepad on his knees. He took a pack of cigarettes out of his breast pocket
and tried passing them through the bars to Peter.

"No, thank you. I've quit! Addiction like that is a sin, and I need to do
everything I can to get into heaven."

Simon nodded and returned the pack to his pocket. He looked around
at the ten-by-twelve-foot cell. It was a good thing that Peter was such a
small man, for the ceiling was no more than six feet high. He was thankful he wasn't the one confined to such a small space. He felt he would last
only a week before going mad.

Over the past few months, Simon had noticed Peter's room become
more decorated, though, and felt more like his space. There were hand-
printed signs on the walls:

"Touch not, taste not, handle not which all are to perish with the using
and after the commandments and doctrines of men."—followed by a few
versus from Colossians.

Biblical reminders were everywhere and inescapable. Simon supposed that Peter had little else to do or think about than his mortality.

"I cannot thank you enough, Peter, for allowing me this opportunity to
print your final confession."

"Just remember all the proceeds are to go to Tilly Comeau."

"Yes, we will make sure she is looked after."

"She has been so kind to me."

"I do know that, too. So," he said, changing the subject to the reason for him being there, "let me ask you about some of the details in your confession."

"This is true confession this time. I know people were not satisfied that I had fully told the truth in the last confession, so this time, I am doing my best to give my one true confession."

"Burning question," Simon said, "was the crime premeditated?"

"No."

Simon raised an eyebrow. "Then what was your purpose in going under the Kempton barn that afternoon? People think you were there to spy."

"Well, that's a queer place to spy," Peter said with a laugh. "I was there for eggs."

"Had you ever been there for eggs before?"

"No."

"Then how was it you happened to be there that day?"

"Because while I had been talking with Annie at noon, she said the hens were laying there. I wanted to get some eggs to take with me to the woods the next day. But then, all of a sudden, the devil put it into my head that there was the place to get my eggs. Late in the afternoon, I heard the hens cackling and I started on the steal and went up around and under the barn."

Simon nodded. That was plausible.

"Then you say Annie came in to milk the cow. How could you see her?"

"No, but I heard her, and I was where she would have seen the light if I had struck a match."

"Well then, if you did not have it all planned through the day, when did you decide to assault her? Didn't you think about Annie being alone and that Tilly wasn't going up? And why did you go to bed undressed if you didn't plan to get up in the night?"

Simon felt his brain was on rapid mode, and he tried to spit out the questions as fast as he could write the answers.

"I didn't undress because Tilly was around. It never came into my head to go up there until I woke up at twelve. Then the devil seemed to say it was a good time for me to carry out the threats I had made."

"You didn't plan on killing her, then?"

"No, I certainly did not. I never thought of it."

262

"Wasn't it risky in your leaving the window up while you were gone? Suppose Tilly had woken and found you had left?"

"It was risky, but I never stopped to think about that, and the devil seemed to help me."

"Annie believed your story about the crowd of drunks, did she?"

"Yes, of course! She had put a wrapper on before she came to the door. I had worked with her father and knew the family well, and she had full confidence in me. I lied to her about the crowd as an excuse for disturbing her, and so I could get in."

"How many blows did you strike her?"

"That is the one thing I don't remember exactly. I can't say. The devil had such a hold on me that I was beside myself."

"Do you expect that the people will believe that Annie asked you to kill her just as if were a pleasure?"

"I don't know what the people will believe. I only know I am telling the truth and God knows it is true. Annie said, 'Peter, please kill me.'"

Simon harrumphed. He still thought Peter was lying about this point, but his story was unshakable.

"Didn't she say it as if she meant she would rather be killed than submit to your abuse? Wasn't she frantic with pain?"

"She was crying terribly. Of course, she was suffering for the pain from the blows. It must have been awful."

Simon gritted his teeth. Peter couldn't seem to connect the fact that he was the one making her cry out in great pain. "Suppose that Tilly had not sent you for milk the next morning. Would you have gone up to the house or left it for someone else to find the body?"

"I would have left it for someone else, I think."

"Peter, are you really sorry for your crime or only because you have to die for it?"

"I am sorry from my heart. If I had been myself, I would never have done the deed. I didn't realize what I had done for a long time. I know my sentence is right. I deserve to die, and hanging is too good for me."

Simon nodded. It was the first statement he truly agreed with. "Would you rather be kept in prison for life?"

"No, I feel that I ought to die, as I have caused Annie Kempton to die."

"Are you afraid of your coming punishment?"

Peter paused a moment. He rubbed his hands over his buzz-cropped hair and through his thick moustache. He took a deep breath before he answered.

"No, I do not feel a fear of death. It's right that it should come."

Simon looked upon the man and, for the first time in the past few months, he felt pity. Yes, this man was a criminal, a murderer, a wretch of the deepest dye; but he was still a man, a human, created with the same powers, in measure at least, as everyone else.

Before he could turn too soft, Simon reminded himself that this man's wretched career was a sorry illustration of the depth to which human nature can fall.

He looked up from his notepad and stared into Peter's eyes for the first time. "Peter, if you were a boy again, would you have a different life?"

Peter stood and looked at himself in the looking glass, as if he could see the small boy on an island in Mauritius.

"I guess I would," he said. "It's too late now, though."

The reporter

Benjamin looked up from the newspaper. He silently congratulated Simon for asking some very poignant questions. But it wasn't enough. There were still many points that were unexplained, pieces of evidence that didn't line up.

He was happy to see Simon's *Digby Courier* had included another section in which it compared Peter's confessions to the Crown's theory of what happened.

The prosecution's case had been received with wide credence and seemed so clearly worked out, with every bit of evidence seeming to connect itself undeniably with the complete story. It drew together all the circumstantial evidence and was the only explanation that appeared plausible.

However, now that Wheeler had confessed, Simon urged his readers to consider that it wasn't necessary for people to hang on to preconceived ideas, provided the confession was consistent with the facts proved by the evidence.

In his column, Simon outlined a few of these points, starting with the time of the murder. He reminded readers that the doctors had initially thought the murder was conducted around midnight, until the evidence showed that Wheeler was in the area earlier in the day.

Would a man be ever so villainous to lose regard for his own safety as to commit a deed of such brutality at a time when he knew people to be not far away and when he knew someone might happen in at any moment? If he struck the girl insensible, then planned to return in two hour's time, might she not recover in the meantime and make his brutality known? If at eight o'clock he took Hardy Benson up to the house with him, expecting that the girl was then lying insensible, would he want Benson to find her so? Then, when Benson would not enter the house, would he really complete the fiendish deed when he knew Benson was only a few steps away and might come in after all? Midnight was a vastly more probable hour for the murder.

Benjamin agreed with all the questions that Simon raised. The bigger question missing from this list, however, was why the defence team did not ask these questions at the trial.

Benjamin kept reading.

It looked as if Wheeler's plan was to keep Tilly Comeau from the Kempton house that night, but it may not have been. He didn't know until eight o'clock in the evening that Annie was alone. She had obviously changed her mind about getting one of the Morine girls to go stay with her.

Benjamin nodded. Another good point that should have been considered much earlier. He wondered which theory people would use to explain the tragedy—that of the Crown or that of Peter Wheeler. He knew that after the first confession came out, many in Bear River refused to believe his version of events, remaining steadfast to the Crown's theory. Would that be the case now?

All we can know is that this is Peter Wheeler's truth. Further than this, we cannot know. These facts are reasonable and plausible. But how the public will receive this confession is now the public's own concern.

This was the crux of the problem. *Were we*—and Benjamin considered himself part of this—*so intent on avenging justice for poor Annie that we lost sight that a man's life was at the other end?* Benjamin knew Peter was an outsider from a foreign land, alone in the world, making him an easy target. It was easier to cast blame to the outside rather than look deep inside.

There was no way to truly know what happened on that fateful night in January in Bear River. God was the only witness and is the only one who knows everything about it.

It was a sad drama, a sorrowful chapter.

The world is wide, and in its vastness there are many diversities. There are many enigmas in life, and many things we mourn but cannot understand, Benjamin contemplated. *The story of Peter Wheeler and Annie Kempton will forever be one of those.*

With that, Benjamin folded the newspaper up, leaned back in his train seat and watched the world fly by.

Epilogue

One year later

The sun shone brightly on the town of Digby, burning off the early-morning fog that had rolled in from the Bay of Fundy.

Sheriff VanBlarcom rose with the birds, got dressed and went out to enjoy his early-morning walk. He slowly patrolled the perimeter. He checked the condition of the jailhouse and yard, ensuring everything was secure and in place.

As he rounded the corner to the back of the jailhouse, something caught his eye. Something seemed out of place.

The sheriff quickened his pace and walked towards the area where those who had been hanged on site were buried. At the back of the area, marked only by a small wooden sign, was the grave of Peter Wheeler.

As he stepped closer, VanBlarcom noticed that earth in the vicinity of the grave had been turned up. He knelt and found a series of footprints in the freshly-turned soil.

Upon further examination, he discovered the entire grave was dug up. He could see the top of the wooden coffin he had put there only a year before.

"What in tarnation?" he cried out as he bent to brush away some of the dirt.

Peering into the hole, he saw signs a tool had been used to pry the coffin lid open.

Were they would-be medics trying to steal Wheeler's body in the name of science? Were they part of a vengeful group trying to get their own justice around the anniversary of the hanging?

Whoever they were, the deed seemed to have taken longer than they had expected, and the approaching daylight had probably frightened them off before they could finish.

VanBlarcom looked around and found a shovel leaning against the fence, left behind by the would-be body snatcher. He used it to pry open the lid, to ensure himself that no damage had been done to Wheeler's body.

As the lid popped open, VanBlarcom jumped back in surprise. Staring up at him was Peter Wheeler, looking not much different than he had the day he died.

"Oh, my heavenly day!" a voice called from the road above the jailhouse.

A group that happened to be walking by peered down at the sheriff and the convicted murderer.

So much for keeping this news quiet, VanBlarcom thought. He stood back as the group came rushing over the fence to have a closer look.

"As fresh as when he first went in!" said one.

"Quick! Let's go tell the others!"

Knowing crowds would be flocking to the spot all morning, the sheriff sat on a bench in the corner of the garden plot and waited.

After they have satisfied their curiosity, maybe, Peter Wheeler can finally be left alone.

ERECTED TO THE MEMORY OF

ANNIE KEMPTON,

AGED 15 YEARS

WHO LOST HER LIFE JAN. 27, 1896,

IN HER FATHERS HOUSE, IN A DESPERATE

STRUGGLE TO PRESERVE HER HONOR.

THE SUBSCRIBERS HEREBY EXPRESS

THEIR PROFOUND RESPECT FOR THE DEPARTED

ONE AS A HEROINE IN HER MAINTENANCE

UNTO DEATH OF THE HIGHEST VIRTUE OF

A CHRISTIAN CIVILIZATION — THE SACRED

HONOR OF WOMANHOOD.

Figure 7: Annie Kempton's memorial in the Bear River cemetery.

Laura Churchill Duke

About the book

Footprints in the Snow is a historical, creative, non-fiction novel. This means that I have woven historical facts together in a creative way. I have imagined many of the conversations, although a great deal are based on trial transcripts and newspaper articles. I have also embellished or altered some of the facts to fit the theme of the novel.

I tried to structure this novel differently than my other two books, to give readers a different perspective. This time, I chose Benjamin, the Halifax journalist, to be the narrator of the story. A lot of Benjamin's questioning does come from his newspaper articles, but he also reflects me and what I am thinking and feeling about what is happening as the story evolves.

The idea to have one central character telling the story was based on a suggestion author and mentor Christy Ann Conlin made to me. She had suggested this as a format for *Two Crows Sorrow*. Although I did not use the idea for that novel, the idea stuck with me.

The idea of flashbacks as a way to unveil the story is not new, but after having read *Anxious People* by Fredrik Backman, who is one of my favourite authors, I fell in love with the idea of how each character revealed what they knew through flashbacks in the main scene. That format was one of my inspirations.

The following are examples of information that I changed for the purposes of the novel.

In 1896, newspaper stories did not have bylines. This lent a certain anonymity, allowing reporters to write as they wished without being personally responsible. Anonymity happens today with social media, where people feel freer to write or say anything, as they may be using a false name or fake profile.

Because of the lack of bylines, I am not entirely sure who the journalists were. I have researched prominent reporters at the time and have based the characters upon these historical figures, but we cannot be certain of their names. Therefore, the characters of Benjamin and Simon are representative of all reporters of the time.

The names of people who appear in the book are the actual names as were recorded in the newspaper articles and trial transcripts. The only change I made was calling Herbert Parker, Charlie Parker so there wouldn't be two Herberts, and not too many names that started with 'H' in the story.

There really was a fireworks display in the community of Bear River, put on by wealthy residents who had been living in the United States. Unfortunately, these fireworks occurred in 1897, and not 1896, so poor Annie Kempton would not have been alive when they took place.

I took some liberty with the character Charles Dunn, who helps out at the initial inquest as a detective. Some newspapers report him as Charles Bunn, while other say Dunn. Some say he is from the American Detective Agency and the others say the Amherst Detective Agency. I can find no record under either name. However, I did find a Dunn as a jury member, so made the creative leap to make this character the aiding detective. I just don't see how someone from Amherst, let alone anywhere closer in the United States, could have arrived so quickly to the scene.

It is easy to see how modern forensics would have been useful in analyzing this crime scene. This is subject of the novel *The Lynching of Peter Wheeler*, by Canadian forensic anthropologist Debra Komar, published in 2014. Although I have read this book in the past, long before I ever thought about writing this book, I did not consult it again, wanting to draw my own conclusions. I do highly recommend reading this non-fiction account of the story if you are interested in learning more about the case, especially from such an expert.

Fingerprint analysis would have been helpful in this case. Unfortunately, scientists only really began to understand the significance and unique nature of fingerprints in the 1880s and 1890s. It wasn't until approximately 1911 that fingerprints were used as evidence in a court of law in Canada. This was much too late to help Peter Wheeler!

Again, from a modern perspective, it is interesting to read about medical experts' ideas of blood spatter, blood types, and rigor mortis. As Nova Scotia Medical Examiner and Forensic Pathologist Jake Yorke said to me, they were "just winging it" in forensics back then. What will we look back at and say about what we are doing today? It's also important to remember that science in the courtroom was just really beginning at this time, and people did not put a lot of trust in the findings. This may also account for why much of the logic, especially concerning the crime timeline, was discounted.

There is a wonderful connection between *Footprints in the Snow* and

Two Crows Sorrow. Some of the newspaper interviews with William Robinson, the convicted murderer in *Two Crows Sorrow*, mention the story of Peter Wheeler. Wanting to know more, I began delving deeper into Peter Wheeler's story. Having happened only eight years prior to his own murder trial, the story must have been well-known for William Robinson to have heard of it, especially as he was living outside the area during that time.

What was the connection?

During William Robinson's trial in the Kentville courthouse, there was a massive rain and windstorm. Suddenly, the cupola was ripped from the newly-constructed building, and went flying through the air. Fortunately, no one was hurt. Robinson draws a reference to Peter Wheeler's trial which also took place in Kentville. In the midst of the trial, the stove pipe comes crashing to the floor, hitting Peter Wheeler in the arm. Robinson claims that since Peter Wheeler was hit with the stove pipe, and was subsequently found guilty, and because no one was hurt when the cupola went hurtling through the air, it was a sure sign of his innocence.

There are a lot of rumours as to what happened to Peter Wheeler's body following his burial behind the Digby courthouse. One such rumour is that, later that same month, September 1897, grave robbers dug up the body, while others claim it became a skeleton on display for classes at Acadia University in nearby Wolfville.

Sadly, what happened to Peter Wheeler in 1896, is still happening today. Recently, I watched the Netflix documentary *Murder by the Coast*, about a woman, Dolores Vazquez, who was condemned for murdering a young woman, predominantly because she was a lesbian. The media tried her as guilty from the start, so it was no surprise that she was convicted of the crime. That is, until two years later, when DNA evidence revealed the real killer was a man who had been stalking women in the area. Dolores was condemned before the trial. She was an outsider, and therefore easy to blame. Times have not changed.

The issues in *Footprints in the Snow* are just as important today. As a member of the media myself, the issues of journalistic integrity and not spreading unfounded speculation as facts are particularly relevant to my work. We are sadly losing our ability to critically analyze information without appropriate facts and have developed a fear of the "other."

We will never know what actually happened in the case of the murder of Annie Kempton. Was Peter a convenient scapegoat? Were his confessions born out of a fear of going to hell? Was he guilty of the heinous crime?

Laura Churchill Duke

I leave it to you, dear reader, to decide.

LCD

Book club discussion questions

1. Do you believe Peter Wheeler was innocent or guilty? Like Benjamin the reporter, did your feelings change as you read this novel? What changed your mind, or what kept your opinion constant?

2. What role, if any, did the media play in the conviction of Peter Wheeler?

3. Does the media (print and online) influence people's behaviour today? What about in terms of finding someone innocent or guilty? What are the repercussions?

4. Peter Wheeler was a C.F.A., a "Come from Away" as we say in Nova Scotia. Did the fact he was an outsider play a role in his conviction? Does this happen in today's world?

5. Discuss the themes of racism and sexism in the book. In the trial, taken verbatim from the transcript, Justice Townshend says: *There were a few witnesses who gave evidence as to motive. I do not put any trust into the words of the little Black girl, Myrtle Godfrey, but that decision is entirely in your hands. Then, there is Stanley Rice and Charlie Parker. You must remember that many young men are in the habit of engaging in filthy talk about girls, and they don't have any actual intent. Then there is the testimony of that boy from the Reserve who saw the light in the window. I think this is important; however, we shouldn't pay much attention to his idea of time. We all know that these people are rather indifferent to such matters of time.*

6. Tilly is maligned by the community for being an unwed mother. How much did prejudice against her affect the outcome of this story?

7. The use of the flashback scenes and change of perspectives is a literary technique the author decided to use for the first time. Did you find these flashbacks helpful and added context, or were they distracting? How would you have incorporated the information

they provided into the novel?

8. Do you think that Peter Wheeler had a fair trial?

9. What practices or theories in the medical examinations of the time do you find surprising? What practices today do you think we will look back on and wonder "why did we do or think that?"

10. The question of salvation plays a big role in the story. Peter is told, and believes, that without a confession, he will go to hell. How much did religious faith play a part in Wheeler's conviction? Are there signs of this happening today, or is the threat of hell less of a concern as North America becomes more secular?

Acknowledgements

No man is an island, and that is certainly the case when it comes to writing a novel—especially one that requires so much research and background work.

As the story happens in Bear River, Nova Scotia, I was so fortunate to literally have my own personal tour guide there. Michelle Reid-Milbury, the owner of Myrtle & Rosie's Café, is a regular participant in the Burger Wars for Campaign for Kids promotion that I have organized every year for almost a decade. Michelle makes award-winning burgers and has also twice won the award for the best burger. Please check out her restaurant when you next visit Bear River.

In getting to know Michelle over the years, I would talk to her about the new book. Michelle has been a great support and has connected me with several people, including her father-in-law, Glen Milbury. Having grown up in Bear River, Glen was well familiar with its history and answered many of my questions.

Michelle's husband, Blake Milbury, is an experienced wilderness guide who took my husband, David, and me on a walk to the old Kempton foundations where the murder took place. He pointed out many key areas which helped me in my descriptions of the area.

Ken Flett, chair of the Bear River Historical Society specially opened the Oakdene Centre for me to browse through the museum's collections in the off season.

Much research was conducted in the Digby Admiral Museum archives, with lots of help from Sue Beard. Jeff White, Greg Turner and Helen Ackerman (who happened to be my elementary school music teacher) all helped me with further understanding Digby's history and the location of the various buildings, including the former jail.

When it came to researching the newspapers of the time, Phil Vogler sent me countless clippings from his collection of newspapers across North America. I spent hours on the microfiche machine at Acadia University and was often aided there by Jean Kelly. I was able to read important documents from New Brunswick newspapers and archives with thanks to Roger Drummond of the NB Provincial Archives, and Leah Grandy of the UNB Archives. My dear friend Juanita Rossiter helped me in terms of anything else archival.

I had lots of other random questions when writing, which were helpfully answered by many. Kentville historian Louis Comeau provided me photographs and floor plans of the first Kentville courthouse, while lawyer Kyle Williams provided legal information of how the court system works.

I am blessed that Jake Yorke is not only often on my monthly trivia team, but also happens to be a medical examiner in Nova Scotia. I provided Jake with gruesome snippets of the trial transcripts for him to explain to me how medical knowledge has changed since 1896. It was so exciting to chat with someone who was equally interested in blood pooling, cooling of deceased bodies, and rigor mortis.

Brian Smit is always open to me asking questions about anything farming related—and this time about milking cows. The late train enthusiast Roger Prentice helped me understand the railway system through the Annapolis Valley during the late 1800s.

Knowing that I was going to title the book, *Footprints in the Snow*, I had been taking and collecting a variety of photographs that might be used on the front cover. I gave the folder of images to my friend Emily Ellis, a creative genius and film maker, who did a phenomenal job designing the front cover. To create the design, Emily chose a photo taken by my internationally-renowned artist cousin on PEI, Haley Lewis. As an artist, Haley has an incredible eye for beauty, and I fell in love with a picture she posted on Facebook of footprints in the snow in her backyard. Thank you to Haley for allowing me to use this photograph.

What makes this extra special is that Haley's sister, Lori Lewis, took the image that was featured on the cover of *Two Crows Sorrow*. My grandfather, George Lewis, who was Lori and Haley's uncle, took the image of the potatoes used on the cover of *Rooted in Deception*. These covers are truly an example of the incredible creativity of my Lewis family. I only wish my uncle, their father, had lived long enough to see this third novel and the extension of the family connection!

I am thankful to Brenda Thompson and Andrew Wetmore of Moose House Publications for agreeing to take me on once again as one of their publishing projects. Andrew's ability at helping me tighten the manuscript is second to none, and Brenda's sleuthing was able to track down a copy of the script for the production about the Annie Kempton murder.

This book would not have been possible without the constant support of my friends. Jennifer Vardy Little is not only my newspaper editor, but also helps me with editing and grammar-related questions. Christianne Rushton and Ann Greener (with her purple editing pen) have read many drafts of the manuscripts and offered advice and suggestions to strengthen the story line. Elizabeth Jackson, Ann, and my husband, David, all helped with the final edits—the remaining mistakes are all mine.

Jennifer Williams Saklofske is a constant support and champion advocate who lets me drone on endlessly about the writing process and everything related.

My sister, Sharon Churchill Roe, also deserves much thanks. I began writing this book when Acadia University was on strike. As we spent hours each day walking the picket line together, I would tell her every minute detail of the story, and she had no choice but to listen—or I would have told Mom and Dad that she wasn't listening to me. Sharon is quick to agree to perform at my book launches, this time singing a folk song about the Annie Kempton murder, as was collected in the 1940s by Helen Creighton. She also provided feedback on early drafts of the manuscript.

A huge thank you to the rest of my family for their support and understanding during the whole process. My father regaled me with stories of growing up in Digby and helped me understand what was where. Thanks also go to my mother, my brother, my husband, David, and my two amazing sons, Daniel and Thomas—who have finally listened to the audiobook version of *Two Crows Sorrow*!

Thank you to all my readers and supporters who keep asking when the next book is coming out. None of this is possible without you!

Laura Churchill Duke

About the author

Laura Churchill Duke is the author of the award-winning novel *Two Crows Sorrow,* and *Rooted in Deception*.

When she is not writing novels, you can find Laura teaching communication in the School of Kinesiology at Acadia University, working as a free-lance journalist for newspapers in Atlantic Canada, or presenting community news on CBC Radio's Information Morning. She is also co-owns the home organization business, Your Last Resort.

Laura lives in Kentville, Nova Scotia with her husband and two sons. Find her at

LauraChurchillDuke.ca.